Still Seeing Things

Books *by* JOHN MASON BROWN

STILL SEEING THINGS

MORNING FACES

SEEING MORE THINGS

SEEING THINGS

MANY A WATCHFUL NIGHT

TO ALL HANDS——AN AMPHIBIOUS ADVENTURE

INSIDES OUT

ACCUSTOMED AS I AM

BROADWAY IN REVIEW

TWO ON THE AISLE

THE ART OF PLAYGOING

THE MODERN THEATRE IN REVOLT

UPSTAGE

LETTERS FROM GREENROOM GHOSTS

THE AMERICAN THEATRE (1752–1934)
AS SEEN BY ITS CRITICS
(edited with Montrose J. Moses)

JOHN MASON BROWN

Still Seeing Things

McGraw-Hill Book Company, Inc.
New York   *London*   *Toronto*

STILL SEEING THINGS

PUBLISHED BY THE McGRAW-HILL BOOK COMPANY, INC.

Printed in the United States of America

TO

DONALD MITCHELL OENSLAGER

AS VALUED AS A FRIEND

AS HE IS ADMIRED AS A

SCENIC ARTIST

Thanks are due, and once more gladly given, to *The Saturday Review of Litterature* for permission to reprint these selections from SEEING THINGS, a department appearing weekly in its pages.

Contents

Contents

· ix ·

The Proper Study

*WINSTON CHURCHILL as a
painter with words and brushes, or a
man of action as an artist, and a consideration of the multiple endowments of one
of history's most exceptional figures.*

꒜꒜꒜꒜꒜꒜꒜꒜꒜꒜꒜꒜꒜꒜꒜꒜꒜꒜꒜꒜꒜꒜꒜꒜꒜꒜꒜

Academician Extraordinary

THE STYLE is the man. Of writers we know this to be
true, and certainly of no writer is it truer than of Winston
Churchill. But is it equally true of painters? Of most painters
yes, though not of Mr. Churchill. In this, as in nearly everything else, he is exceptional. If his personality and activity
were known to us only by the eighteen colored reproductions
of his brushwork included in *Painting as a Pastime,** we
would, to put it mildly, be misled.

These Churchill paintings are not the products of an amateur who mistakes a filled canvas for a good one. Their touch is
professional. Their colors are pleasant and bright, even if in
some of the landscapes they are almost too pretty-pretty in a
postcard manner. Most of these pictures have a certain charm,
and a few can claim more than this, possessed as they are of real
delicacy and grace.

Nevertheless, were all we know of Mr. Churchill to be de-
duced from these paintings, we would indeed be misled. Our
first, our inevitable guess would be that the man who had done

---

* *Painting as a Pastime.* By Winston S. Churchill. New York: Whittlesey
House (McGraw-Hill Book Co., Inc.). 1950. 32 pp. 18 color plates. $2.50.

them must be a Royal Academician. The paintings are sufficiently conventional to persuade us of this. So far, of course, we would be right because Mr. Churchill is a member of the Royal Academy; in fact, the only part-time painter on its roster. On it he is listed, with accuracy, as Honorary Academician Extraordinary.

From then on, however, our surmises would be wrong. For we would swear the man responsible for these paintings must be a soft-spoken fellow, calm and mousy, and very much at peace in a peaceful world. We would assume that his schedule was uncrowded, his life unrushed. We would suspect him of avoiding action and of having been protected from violence of any sort. We would know that he had traveled, but we would imagine him as creeping quietly into one sleepy resort after another, seeking the sun's warmth and finding inner tranquillity.

Dedicated as his thinking would seem to be to flower arrangements, aristocratic interiors, quaint fishing vessels securely beached or moored, waveless lakes, dreamy mountains, and trees unblown by any breezes, we would feel safe from contradiction were we to state that his mind was tightly shut against every kind of storm and bolted against upheavals, naval, military, and political. We might be tempted to go even further and maintain, since all his chairs, little boats, beaches, groves, and rooms are without occupants (except in two canvases where it is difficult to tell whether the people are male or female, mortals or penguins), that he had no interest in men and no knowledge of their tempestuous ways. In short, we would be persuaded that here was an artist, lacking in gusto but appreciative of nature, whose unruffled temperament was forever in a vacation mood.

Such deductions would, of course, be almost wholly false. Few painters have put as little of themselves into their paintings as Mr. Churchill has done. There is a reason for this. He has turned to oils not only to take a vacation but to take a vacation from himself. Even if this had not been his reason, how could Mr. Churchill or anyone else be expected to do full justice on canvas to the many lives he has lived, his multitude of talents, the countless adventures he has survived, or the dimensions of his spirit?

No known colors are sufficiently strong to suggest his colorful personality. No wall nor ceiling is large enough to contain the tumultuous mural of his careers. Paintings by Mr. Churchill are one thing; paintings which would be truly Churchillian, quite another. To achieve Churchillian stature, they would have to possess something of the muscularity of Michelangelo, the vitality without the fleshiness of Rubens, the historical sweep of Le Brun, David's interest in court pageantry, the energy of Gericault, the romanticism of Delacroix, the drama of Goya, Meissonier's eye for military details, the dash of Sargent, Winslow Homer's and Tom Lea's feeling for ships and the sea, and the informed accuracy of the combat artists in all the services who, during wartime, recorded the trials of men in uniform.

Mr. Churchill is one of this planet's most flamboyant figures. He is an anachronism not because his politics are so conservative but because his endowments are so varied. The past, however, has never made a richer, livelier, or more vital contribution to the present than in his case. In many respects Mr. Churchill is the greatest of the Edwardians; in others, the last of the greater Elizabethans. The smoke screen created by his cigars cannot hide the fact that he has faced our world and enriched it as a reincarnation of the Renaissance Man. Certainly, for sheer virtuosity we have not seen his equal in our time, nor are parallels in other epochs easy to find.

Had the Duke of Marlborough been the Elder Pitt and the Elder Pitt, Gibbon, the result might have been named Winston Churchill. Mr. Churchill is a writing man who is a man of action. He is a soldier who turned war correspondent; a war correspondent who entered politics; a politician who emerged as a statesman; a statesman who excels as a strategist; and an orator whose words have been worth divisions. He is an historian who has made even more history than he has written. His energies are furious, his courage without limits, and his appetite for living so enormous that once someone rightly said life has melted in his mouth like butter.

Considering everything else that he has managed to get done, it is not surprising that he should have also found time to paint. Nor is it surprising that the two delectable essays "Hobbies" and "Painting as a Pastime," now joined together under the title of the latter, should have first appeared in a book by Mr. Churchill called *Amid These Storms* (1932). There they concluded, with the sudden hush of an armistice, a volume all turbulence and battle. Since it was chiefly devoted to such matters as murderous anarchists, political clashes, meetings with the Kaiser at two maneuvers before World War I, memories of trench warfare in 1916, the U-boat menace, and an account of Mr. Churchill's experiences in the air in 1912 when aviation was in its hazardous infancy, no wonder Mr. Churchill named the book as he did. Storms have been incessant in the climate of his life. If sometimes he has provoked them, at most times he has dominated them. Thunder and lightning have never frightened him. He can himself release lightning bolts and answer thunder with a thunder of his own.

Had it not been for the storms of both war and politics, Mr. Churchill might never have lifted a paintbrush. If I use this expression instead of saying he might never have turned painter, it is because, as a writer and orator, Mr. Churchill has long been one of the most masterful of painters. He has executed his finest brush strokes with his pen. Great events have sat for him as his favorite model. Language has served him as his palette. His writing may at times be marred by oratory; his prose may be aimed at the ear instead of the eye. His cadences for their fullest effect may need the orchestration of his voice and his sibilants. Even so, his narratives are stirringly visual. They are hung with pictures. With words Mr. Churchill has proved himself a supreme colorist, fond of vermilion, khaki, and navy blue, though occasionally surrendering to purple. He is as boldly skillful at seascapes and battle scenes as he is at portraiture and exposition. Indeed the canvases by which he will always live and by which all of us have been moved are to be found in his books, not in galleries.

He was forty when first he turned to painting with paints. His fortunes were not at their happiest. Reverses at Gallipoli had brought about his departure from the Admiralty at the end of May, 1915. He remained a member of the Cabinet and of the War Council. He was left in a position where he "knew everything and could do nothing." His unbearable inactivity after his immense and exciting activities left him gasping. As he put it, he was like a sea-beast fished up from the depths or a diver too suddenly hoisted, and his veins threatened to burst from the fall in pressure.

His first attempt was made one Sunday in the country with his children's paintbox. He liked the experiment so well that the following morning he bought a complete outfit for painting in oils. The next step was to *begin*. But how? Where? And with what color? His hand "seemed arrested by a silent veto." For once in his life Mr. Churchill was timid. With a tiny brush and with tremendous caution he at last made, in the area where he knew the sky ought to be, a blue mark "about as big as a bean." Then he stopped. His career as a painter might have stopped, too, had not Sir John Lavery's wife arrived at that moment, asked for a big brush, and with large, fierce strokes proved to him that the canvas could not hit back. If Mr. Churchill has never felt any "awe" of canvases since, he has found infinite pleasure in attacking them.

That delight, the delight of carrying in your pocket a key to "a wonderful new world of thought and craft, a sunlit garden gleaming with light and color," he communicates in every wise and witty line of *Painting as a Pastime*. Mr. Churchill's is a remarkable essay. It is personal, warm, and perceptive. It is basted in the rich juices of experience; written with unashamed enthusiasm; written from the heart, yet written with a smile. To find its match in felicity and charm, one must turn back to Hazlitt's "On the Pleasure of Painting."

No two men could be less alike than William Hazlitt and Winston Churchill. A gulf divides their minds and temperaments and endowments. Yet in two of their passionate absorptions—the English language and painting—they are blood brothers. Although Hazlitt turned to writing after having attempted to be a painter and Mr. Churchill did not paint until after his fame in both public affairs and literature had been securely established, both men express sentiments almost interchangeable on the joys of painting.

"From the moment you take up the pencil, and look Nature in the face, you are at peace with your own heart. . . . The mind is calm, and full at the same time. The hand and eye are equally employed. . . . The hours pass away untold, without chagrin, and without weariness; nor would you ever wish to pass them otherwise." That is Hazlitt, but it could be Mr. Churchill, because it is he who says, "Go out into the sunlight and be happy with what you see. Painting is a complete distraction. I know of nothing which, without exhausting the body, more entirely absorbs the mind. Whatever the worries of the hour or the threats of the future, once the picture has begun to flow along, there is no room for them in the mental screen. . . . Time stands respectfully aside, and it is only after many hesitations that luncheon knocks gruffly at the door."

There are differences, however. Where Hazlitt, whose life was tempest-tossed, writes about painting as a sedentary man, Mr. Churchill writes about it with equal skill as a man who has seen and relished combat in the field. Only he, with his fondness for military metaphor, would seize upon such a Churchillian word as "audacity" as a painter's first requirement. Only he would liken a painter to a commander in chief and a canvas to a battleground. Only he would compare "proportion" and "relation" in painting to the reserves upon which a general must depend, or insist that, if a canvas is not to represent a defeat, it, in the manner of a victory, must be the result of a good plan.

Although, in passing, Mr. Churchill pays delightful tribute to books, libraries, a change of interest as a means to rest, the heightened powers of observation brought about by surveying any object with a painter's eye, and to such impressionists as Manet, Monet, Cézanne, and Matisse, perhaps the most exciting aspect of his essay is the reverent affection which he, the man of action, feels for art and the artist. He condescends to neither; he has only admiration for both. A great painting is to him "an intellectual manifestation the equal in quality and intensity of the finest achievements of warlike action, of forensic argument, or of scientific or philosophical adjudication."

The world by some, in moments of oversimplification, is held to be divided into Greeks and Romans. The first are supposed to symbolize the lovers and creators of beauty; the second, the givers of laws and the doers of deeds. But it is one of the distinctions of British history that it abounds in fusions of the two temperaments which prove the fallacy of such an easy division.

When, on the night before he was to face Montcalm on the Plains of Abraham, General Wolfe said he would prefer being the author of Gray's "Elegy" to the glory of beating the French on the morrow, he demonstrated that double endowment Englishmen can possess for being, so to speak, both Greek and Roman. Sir Philip Sidney, as a warrior-statesman who had written *Astrophel and Stella*, *An Apology for Poetry*, and *Arcadia*, had proved this long ago. So had the Viscount of St. Albans, that Lord Chancellor better re-

membered as Francis Bacon. Indeed, from the distant days
when a king named Alfred translated Gregory the Great and
St. Augustine and a hard-working man, variously employed
as a soldier, a commercial agent, an M.P., a Clerk of the
King's Works, and a Deputy Forester for the Crown, found
time to write *The Canterbury Tales*, the tradition had per-
sisted. Macaulay, Disraeli, and Bulwer-Lytton were among
its torchbearers. Fortunately, it has not perished. The Lord
Tweedsmuir who was John Buchan continued it. So has
General Wavell, who in the midst of the last war compiled
an anthology of poetry known as *Other Men's Flowers*.

The list, though far longer than hinted here, has never
possessed a more spectacular entry than Winston Churchill.
From his days in India his energies and curiosities have
been superhuman. Even in his thirties when Mr. Churchill
was new to the Cabinet, Sir Edward Grey was complaining,
"Winston, very soon, will become incapable from sheer activity of mind of being anything in a Cabinet but Prime
Minister." Most people never really live the one life at their
disposal. Mr. Churchill would have found one life grossly
insufficient, had he not discovered a simple solution to the
problem. He has lived many lives, and lived all of them to
the full.

"What do you do?" was a question asked occasionally of
Annapolis graduates by officers of the Royal Navy during
the last war. By this they did not mean "What is your specific
assignment?" They took that for granted. They meant "What
do you do in addition to your job? What is your outside interest, hobby, or diversion?"

Mr. Churchill has held almost every important position
in His Majesty's Government. But, hard pressed by arduous

duties though he has been, he has a gusto of mind, spirit, and body which has demanded releases beyond his official tasks. He has written more books, and certainly more important books, than most authors whose whole careers are devoted to book-writing. Even getting these done has not robbed him of leisure and the need of filling his free hours. Hence his painting and the joy he has found in it.

To live, most men fortunately must work. How civilized they are is better measured by how they employ their leisure than by what is the employment which has earned it for them. Mr. Churchill's is a mind which cannot tolerate inactivity. He rests it by recharging it. Instead of emptying it of all thought, he refreshes it by a change of interest. He is as impatient with the idle rich as he is with the idle poor. He divides rational, industrious, and useful human beings into two classes: (1) those whose work is work and whose pleasure is pleasure and (2) those whose work and pleasure are one. The life of those belonging to the second category is, as he sees it, "a natural harmony. For them the working hours are never long enough. Each day is a holiday. . . ." No wonder Mr. Churchill describes such persons as "Fortune's favored children." In or out of office, he has always been one of these himself.

March 4, 1950

PLAYWRIGHT-into-biographer, or
the exciting growth of Robert E. Sher-
wood, a dramatist who has become as
at home with the intricacies of world
history as he has long been with the
mysteries of the stage and screen.

On a Larger Stage

ALTHOUGH Al Jolson used to sing it in his full-
throated, spring-happy way, it is with Robert E. Sherwood, not Mr. Jolson, that I shall always associate "When
the Red, Red Robin Comes Bob, Bob Bobbin' Along." Those
who know him well assure me that, late in a good evening
and almost as a proof of that evening's goodness, Mr. Sherwood is inclined (when sufficiently urged) to cock a derby
on his head, grab a cane, and hoof his way, grim-faced as
death, through "the Red, Red Robin." The point—indeed,
the pay-off—of Mr. Sherwood's act is that he is of course the
last person in the world anyone would expect to erupt into
such a routine.

He is a very solemn-seeming fellow; lantern-jawed, Lin-
colnian in his gauntness, and so slow of speech that often his
words appear to be railway stations apart. Moreover, he is
tall, skyscraper tall. Being such a flagpole of a man, his legs
have a long way to go to reach the floor. When lifted off it,
they move swiftly, if not gracefully, and are endangering.
They demand as much clearance horizontally as is required

vertically to keep Mr. Sherwood's head from bringing down the roof.

Seeing Mr. Sherwood turn hoofer (I regret to say I have only seen him in action twice) is quite an experience. I know it was for me, particularly the first time. That was on a special evening at a special moment. It was at a small party in London just about a week before the Normandy invasion. Needless to say, none of us, unless it was Mr. Sherwood, knew precisely when the invasion would come. But it was very much in the air, in our minds, and in our hearts, too. There was no escaping the sense of its nearness, or the sense of uncertainty that went with it. I was to return to the *Augusta* at Plymouth the next morning, and had gathered this was to be my last sight of London before D-Day. "Last" was a word which just then contained meanings it does not now hold.

The party was given by C.B.S.'s Charles Collingwood at his picture-strewn apartment (no doubt, I should say "flat"). Edward R. Murrow (of "This Is London" fame) and his wife were there. So were Alfred Lunt and Lynn Fontanne. In spite of constant air raids, they had been playing for triumphant months in *There Shall Be No Night*. Mr. Lunt, as a matter of fact, was helping with the cooking this evening, which is one guarantee of how good the dinner was. Ernie Pyle was present, too. Although we were all congratulating him on having won the Pulitzer Prize, he was far prouder of having just been chosen the "Year's Outstanding Hoosier." Mr. Sherwood was also there. The war and the coming invasion were the other guests. Though mainly unmentioned, they were the guests of honor.

What we talked about I do not now recall. Everything, I suspect, except what was uppermost in our thoughts. I remember only that, starved as I was for theatre and book talk, the evening stood out for me as a blissful oasis. Like all good times, it seemed short. Before I knew it, it was after midnight. Before I knew it, too, Mr. Sherwood, at someone's request, was "obliging" with "the Red, Red Robin." A hat was slanted on his head, a cane was in his hand, his voice, though not quite so good as Jolson's, was filling the room, and he was imperiling us all by bob, bob, bobbin' along.

As I say, I have seen Mr. Sherwood do his number once since then—undertaker-faced and just for fun. But that night it was more than for fun that he did it. It was in agony. He was not merely dead-panning his way through an absurd routine. Like his own hoofer in *Idiot's Delight* (a part Mr. Lunt had played), he was dancing in a world where bombs were falling and mass annihilation would soon begin.

I have never seen a face more filled with sorrow or tortured with compassion than was Mr. Sherwood's as he went grimly, fearfully, through his number this spring evening when England was in glorious bloom and the youth of Britain and America and their allies was also gathered in full bloom on the south coast and at ports all around that bristling island. Mr. Sherwood, you see, knew as the rest of us did not, and had long known, the backstage secrets of the highest echelons of what was then history-in-the-making. For a sensitive and imaginative man such knowledge must have been an oppressive load to carry. Yet how much he knew, I never suspected until recently when, on trains and off, early by day

· 15 ·

and far into the night, I read with breathless absorption his *Roosevelt and Hopkins: An Intimate History.**

This is an amazing book. It is intimate, wonderfully intimate, and yet it is history, full-scaled and far-flung. Immediately it takes its place—a high honor—on the same slim shelf with Winston Churchill's *The Gathering Storm.* The rolling periods are deliberately missing. So are the antitheses so dear to Macaulay. So is the majestic drum-roll of a modern Gibbon. The orator's music at its mightiest, ringing directly in the reader's ears in spite of the interference of the eyes, is also absent.

The glorious seascapes; the magnificent panoramas; the tapestries executed with unforgettable words; the grand manner of the historian writing formal history and his own place in it, too; and the doer's sense of the direct control of events —all of these Churchillian qualities are likewise lacking. They are missing by design as surely as because of temperament. Even so, there are compensating virtues.

A different kind of eloquence replaces Mr. Churchill's. It is the eloquence of extreme simplicity. It is as unlike Mr. Churchill's as was Mr. Roosevelt's—a fact which is not surprising since in the preparation of his speeches Mr. Roosevelt depended so often on Mr. Sherwood's aid. The sentences are for the most part short and seemingly unstudied. There are no purple passages. The prose is unembellished and swift-moving. Instead of cascading magnificently in the great tradition, it speaks the democratic idiom, movingly, effectively, sometimes humorously. The result, which is as American as *The Gathering Storm* is British, is of equal

* *Roosevelt and Hopkins: An Intimate History.* By Robert E. Sherwood. New York: Harper & Bros. 1948. 962 pages. $6.

significance. As a behind-the-scenes chronicle of the appalling
global happenings of our times, and of the men who have had
to make those terrible and great decisions which have charted
our individual lives and shaped the world's present and future, Mr. Sherwood's book is as invaluable as Mr. Churchill's.

Here, in one long but endlessly exciting volume, is at once
the vast sweep of major events and the day-to-day trivia
which lie behind, and color, them. Here is Clio with her
hair up and her hair down. Here are the eye-witnesses and
the principals saying off and on the record what has not
hitherto been revealed. Here is the whole bulging cast of
recent history—of the nation in the first days of the New Deal
and the W.P.A. years when Harry Hopkins was more spend-
thrift with other people's millions than any Brewster has
ever been with his own. Here, too, and in far greater detail,
are the nation and the world when this same Harry Hopkins, lion-brave, desperately ill, and by then selfless in his
ambitions, had risen to the test of tremendous times and
soared to dimensions which even his enemies have had to admit were heroic. Here are the records of two ill men who
were determined to make a sick world well. Here are the
cheers and smears of high office. Here are the crowds, and
here is the loneliness of leadership. Here are Roosevelt,
Churchill, Stalin, and the rest of the stars at their most
stellar as well as at their most human.

Here, in short, is the palace *with* the alcove, the glorious
with the tawdry, the laughable with the tragic, the epic with
the personal, and the good with the bad. Moreover, it is all
set forth so unpretentiously, in sentences so unadorned, that
the uncommon skill of its telling and the herculean labor
represented by its tireless and honest research pass all but

unnoticed. Make no mistake about it, however; the skill is
still there. It is present on every modest page, anxious as
it may be not to call attention to itself. It is there, and so is
something else. I mean the spirit lying behind and inform-
ing Mr. Sherwood's book. This proves as big as were the
days with which Mr. Sherwood deals.

I do not propose to discuss Mr. Sherwood's volume in detail. I have no excuse for doing so. It speaks for itself. I only
wish to touch upon it, because my suspicion is that too many
of the reviewers who have written about it have succumbed
to an understandable temptation. They have given too much
credit to Mr. Sherwood's being a playwright when explaining the vividness of his characterizations and the sweep of
his narrative.

Undoubtedly, the fact that Mr. Sherwood is a dramatist,
and an able one, has helped him. It guarantees that he has
a sense of scene and that crises are his affair. It means that
he has an eye for those unintended revelations which people are not aware they are making about themselves. It
means that he sees the significant details of a setting and that
human speech loses none of its pungency in his reproduction
of it. Undoubtedly, too, Mr. Sherwood's *Roosevelt and
Hopkins* is his finest drama and the most titanic in scale he
has so far written. Yet, though the instincts and training of
a playwright may be definite aids to the work of a colorful
historian, the mere fact that Mr. Sherwood is a dramatist
does not explain his success as a negotiator of either prose or
history.

The majority of contemporary playwrights, including those
who excel at the theatre's elliptical form, produce only the
thinnest porridge when they turn to undramatic prose. Shaw

is, of course, the glorious and blinding exception. He is un-
usual in this as in all things. Nonetheless, a strange and stub-
born truth remains. It is especially true of our present-day
American dramatists. In spite of the number of them that
have conquered the telegraphy which is dialogue, Thornton
Wilder, Maxwell Anderson, Irwin Shaw, Philip Barry, William Saroyan, Elmer Rice, S. N. Behrman, Paul Green, and
Mr. Sherwood are among the few who have also been able
to sustain straight prose.

Most of our dramatists, even the outstanding ones, when
they turn to nondramatic prose are apt to be as awkward and
skill-less as is Eugene O'Neill or as Tennessee Williams
showed himself to be in an article he contributed recently to
the Sunday *Times*. Perhaps this is why so few of them ever
venture to have their say in prefaces.

Mr. Sherwood is different. Otherwise Mr. Roosevelt
would not have relied upon him as one of the men called in
to help him write some of his most pivotal speeches. Anyone who, in the old pre-Lucean days of *Life*, read Mr. Sherwood when he opened up the continent for motion-picture
criticism in this country, must remember the ease, sparkle,
and force of his reviews. Certainly, anyone who has read the
prefaces with which Mr. Sherwood has seen fit from time to
time to accompany his printed plays must be gratefully aware
of the vitality, integrity, and charm of his prose. Whatever
one may have thought of this or that of his plays (although
I have admired some of them immensely, I cannot pretend
to have admired them all, and certainly not equally), Mr.
Sherwood's prefaces have stood in a class by themselves. No
other American dramatist has approached him in this field.

Remembering how fine and personal these prefaces were,

I reread them on finishing Mr. Sherwood's book. My hope was, of course, that they would supply me with some clues as to Mr. Sherwood's subsequent evolution and prepare me for the man who has grown so grandly with the measuring years. I was not disappointed. The prefaces did offer some explanation. But interesting and unveiling as they are, they did not go the whole way. How could they? The advance is too great that Mr. Sherwood has made in now being as completely at home with the most intricate of world events as he has long been in his writing for the stage and screen.

Assuredly, it is a giant's march from such a farce comedy as *The Road to Rome* (some meanie at the time dubbed Mr. Sherwood "Shaw in short pants") to the Homeric scale of *Roosevelt and Hopkins*. I doubt if in the theatre's long history any playwright has ever been so close to great events as Mr. Sherwood was or has turned with his success from make-believe to the most colossal of realities. You may name Machiavelli, Sheridan, or that Bacon some die-hards are willing to contend was Shakespeare's stand-in as dramatists who also figured on a scene larger than the stage. But the affairs they dealt with were, you must admit, sissy stuff compared to the Rand-McNally scale of history at which Mr. Sherwood occupied a ringside seat.

I find that Mr. Sherwood in his preface to *The Road to Rome* introduced his "dramatization of a guess" about the purely fictitious wife of Fabius Maximus with a serious and able historical sketch of Hannibal's life and times. In the course of this essay, he confessed—and this can now be taken as prophetic—that he saw "no earthly reason why history should continue to be chastely academic and formidably dull."

For *Waterloo Bridge,* a worthy failure, Mr. Sherwood

wrote a preface containing an unforgettable description of London during World War I. This is a description which must have come as often to his mind in London during World War II as I know it came to mine. In his preface to so gay, yet nostalgic, a comedy as *Reunion in Vienna,* Mr. Sherwood indicated what was happening within him. At what was for him a supposedly comfortable moment (1931), he was writing from a deep inner despair. Even then he was alert to what was going on outside the petty, though fascinating, duchy of the stage. As long ago as *Acropolis* (1933), he saw the menacing parallel between the Periclean Age, threatened by Sparta's totalitarianism, and what was occurring in Hitler's Europe.

In *The Petrified Forest* (1934) his hero spoke sadly for the vanishing race of intellectuals. "Brains without purpose," said he of them. "Noise without sound. Shape without substance." The international gangsters were by then taking over. Mr. Sherwood, however, was an intellectual who found himself early—very early. He was never fooled by what Hitler and Mussolini would ultimately mean. *Idiot's Delight* made this clear. "It was completely American," says Mr. Sherwood, "in that it represented a compound of black pessimism and desperate optimism, of chaos and jazz." Although written at a time (1936) when all of us hoped for peace, it was as "violently anti-Fascist" as it was "definitely antiwar."

Thereafter, further events and realizations intruded on Mr. Sherwood's thinking, and he wrote *There Shall Be No Night* (1940). His preface in this instance was a frank autobiographical reconsideration of his career and shifting attitudes. It was the statement of a man who had ceased to be antiwar and had come to realize sorrowfully that the time for action was at hand. The onetime debunker was prepared to turn doer. His negative beliefs had become flamingly positive. The whole early development of Mr. Sherwood is set forth in that preface. It is the wavering record of so many of us in the in-between years. With this difference. As a seismograph Mr. Sherwood is far more sensitive than most.

Mr. Sherwood had come back, international-minded and a war-hater, from the first war in which he had served in the Canadian Black Watch and had been gassed. He was pro-League in those days, or at least for some kind of English-speaking union. This lasted briefly. Until 1919, as a matter of fact, when he was persuaded by George Harvey's writings that the League was futile. In 1920, Mr. Sherwood confesses "with deep shame," he cast his first vote as an American citizen for Warren Harding, thus doing his "bit in the great betrayal." In 1926 he wrote his first play, *The Road to Rome,* because he had heard it said that, if a man does not write his first play by thirty, he will never write it. Mr. Sherwood was nearly thirty.

Since then, and until the second war, though the theatre was the center of his life, Mr. Sherwood's interests have never been limited to it. This is why, particularly in the light of his subsequent activities on the William Allen White Committee; with Mr. Roosevelt; as overseas director of the OWI; and on dangerous wartime missions the world over, it seems at once inadequate and inaccurate to ascribe the excellences of his *Roosevelt and Hopkins* merely to the fact that Mr. Sherwood is a dramatist. He is the dramatist he is because of the man he is, and the historian he has become because of the man he has grown into.

It would be encouraging to believe that many other Americans, during these same desperate years, have developed under their testing as Mr. Sherwood has developed under his. I can think of no one in his profession, and few outside of it, who has been more selfless and courageous in his service to his country than Mr. Sherwood, or who has achieved a more enlightened understanding of what is finest and most beckoning in the democratic credo. It is not Mr. Sherwood's distinguished dramatic talents which have made him so capable an historian. Nor is it merely his writing gifts. It is the largeness of his mind and spirit. If Mr. Sherwood resembles Lincoln in his towering gauntness, the real resemblance comes from within. Some of the precious Lincoln stuff is in him.

November 13, 1948

*HELEN HOKINSON, the hilarious
world she discovered that will always
bear her name, and some discussion of
those well-bred, well-fed, culture-
hungry, and beminked matrons she
described as her "Best Girls."*

Helen Hokinson

WHEN HIS old friend William Archer died, Shaw, writing for once completely from the heart, confessed the impoverishment he felt at the idea of returning to an "Archerless London." "I still feel," he added, "that when he went he took a piece of me with him."

All of us, if only we have lived long enough, have been wounded beyond healing by similar losses. All of us, as the years slip by, face increasingly the problem of living with the abiding subtractions of death. These create gaps which cannot be filled and leave us suddenly lonely in the midst of crowds.

A few weeks back, when Helen Hokinson was among the fifty-five needlessly snuffed out in that air crash over Washington, thousands of us experienced once again this dreaded sense of deprivation even though ours had not been the privilege of knowing her personally. There is a difference, however, between the London without Archer to which Shaw returned and the America without Helen Hokinson in which

we find ourselves. She is gone; abruptly, wastefully, tragically
gone. Yet ours is by no means a Hokinsonless world. Her
dying did not put an end to what we had all come to identify
with her. That part of the American scene which she had
staked off as her own can still be found everywhere, and its
inhabitants will continue to bear her name so long as they
present milliners with dilemmas and girdles with problems.

My Best Girls she called them, those denizens of women's
clubs, beauty parlors, art galleries, summer resorts, and Lane
Bryant, when she gave a title to one of her collections of
New Yorker drawings. This is what they were. Precisely
that. Miss Hokinson's affection for her ample dowagers was
so clear every time she caught their lines in hers that they
were never offended by the fun she made of them. Symptomatic of the pleasure they took in her work was the letter she
once received from a lady, a Hokinson lady of course, in
Needham, Mass., who wrote, "More power to you and the
girls. The more I grow to look like them, the more I love
them."

What doubtless had equipped Miss Hokinson for dealing
with American matrons in a manner not only unequaled
but unexcelled is that in her art school days, when she had
left Chicago for New York, she studied dynamic symmetry.
Her women were never to be confused with Clare Boothe's.
They were stouts seeking in all matters to be stylish rather
than worldlings straining to be smart. Their sins of the flesh
were dietary, not temperamental. They were—every mother's
daughter of them—benevolent creatures waging a breathy,
though losing, battle against the most innocent of appetites.
If they carried more weight physically than they did intellec-

tually, it was not because they failed to include culture among their pursuits.

Wherever their minds may have remained parked, those tiny feet of theirs, which terminated their plump legs, were forever carrying their bodies into bookstores and museums or leading them to lectures, matinees, or concerts. That is, of course, when Miss Hokinson's well-fed, well-bred, and thoroughly minked ladies were not molesting flowers, cajoling maids, tangling traffic, indulging in very private college reunions, massacring good liquor with unforgivable feminine additions, breaking down global problems into Westchester terms, or attempting to become sylphs again by submitting themselves to the costly Spartanism of Elizabeth Arden.

If they were resistant to the higher things, at least they were not dishonest in their reactions to them. Pretense was never one of their follies. At the Metropolitan's exhibition of French tapestries they were not embarrassed to ask an astonished guard, "Does it matter which end we do them from?" Confronted with abstract paintings in the Museum of Modern Art, one of them said, "I never know how far away to stand to make them look good." Picking up a volume in a bookstore, another inquired of the saleswoman, "Would this be all right for a friend who isn't interested in much of anything?" Turning to some companions, all of them as much alike as sister ships, still another summoned the honesty to complain during the intermission of a play, "It overwhelmed Brooks Atkinson, but it isn't overwhelming *me*." Or, listening to the Philharmonic, one of them, instead of parroting the program notes, offered as her sole comment: "I often wish I had kept up my mandolin lessons."

I have my reasons for citing these examples of that delectable offbeat in sense we associate with Miss Hokinson's world and work. All of these examples happen to be culled from her last book, *When Were* You *Built?* And that volume, significantly enough, was dedicated to James Reid Parker, whose captions, as she put it, "have inspired most of these drawings." In other words, as we are apt to forget, Miss Hokinson did not work alone. Mr. Parker was her silent partner. He was her idea man, and theirs one of the happiest of collaborations. Without any of the frictions of the lords of the Savoy, they found themselves as perfectly matched as Gilbert and Sullivan.

If Miss Hokinson's was the seeing eye, Mr. Parker's was the hearing ear. And what an ear it was—wonderful in its genius for seizing upon the absurd, wonderful in holding its nonsense close to truth, and also wonderful for the incredible accuracy with which it pounced upon *the* word among all other words to make its satiric point without letting any blood. Take, for instance, the dowager saluting a street cleaner on Christmas Day with "*Joyeux Noël*, my good man!" Or asking the captain of an ocean liner when it passes a cruiser, "Aren't we going to toot?" Or rising at a business meeting of a woman's club to announce, "I'm sorry, Madam President, there won't be any treasurer's report this month because we have a deficit." Or remarking to the instructor at a skating rink before taking to the ice, "I warn you, my right foot is a rebel."

The impact of such captions is instantaneous. They tell their own story and raise their own laughs. At least they seem to. But, as Mr. Parker would no doubt be the first to admit, they depend for their full relish upon the women—the Helen Hokinson women—we visualize as we read them.

Miss Hokinson's delineation of these women grew in cer-

· 27 ·

tainty with the years. To realize this, one has only to follow her career from the first collection of her *New Yorker* drawings, *So You're Going to Buy a Book!* (1931), through *My Best Girls* (1941), to *When Were You Built?* (1948). During that richly productive period a type she had stumbled upon emerged as a species branded with her name. In no time this modest and retiring woman from Mendota, Ill., who had once done an unsuccessful comic strip for the *Mirror* called "Sylvia in the Great City," created a comic pattern cherished and admired by all Americans, including those from whom it was derived.

They were quite a group, these Hokinson dowagers. Funny, they certainly were. Yet they were also human, very human, and poignant, too. Their feelings belied their contours. They could not bring themselves to realize that their youth had left them. Regardless of the shadows they cast, they were girls at heart; girls who, though they had grown big, had never grown up. The calendar was unable to tarnish or remove their naïveté. They were innocents both abroad and at home. One of the most ridiculous and touching of their characteristics was that their idea of mischief remained juvenile. They were worldlings whom neither time nor exposure could make worldly. A reliable contributor to the hilarity they unfailingly provided was the contrast between their ingenuousness and the sophistication of their surroundings.

Economics was beyond them. The only figures with which they concerned themselves were their own, and even these they could not master. Their chief problem was idleness. Time hung heavy on their dimpled hands. Like all women who are unemployed, they had to seek employment in order to fill their empty days. Theirs was the usual solution. They were incessant shoppers. They were more intrigued with what covered their heads than with what filled them. Hats were their joy, and the search for them was a release from inactivity.

Gregarious as they were, Miss Hokinson's matrons were lonely, a fact which they confessed by squandering their affections on diminutive dogs. Even Philip Wylie could not have disliked these women since they were entirely innocent of momism. They were too busy babying themselves to mother anyone else. Foolish and self-indulgent as they were, they were never guilty of meanness. They were a friendly breed. This explains why they made so many friends. Miss Hokinson's fondness for them was transparent and contagious. Hers was the rarest of satiric gifts. She had no contempt for human failings. She approached foibles with affection. She could ridicule without wounding. She could give fun by making fun, and in the process make no enemies.

The New Yorker's loss is ours. It is saddening to realize Miss Hokinson will not draw her dowagers again. We, however, can derive some solace from the fact that the special world she discovered is still very much with us. Every time we see or chance to overhear pampered ladies of a certain size and vintage, Helen Hokinson will be with us, too. She will be in our minds and also on our lips. The truth is she has become a living part of our vocabulary.

December 10, 1949

*THE TWO Philip Barrys, the sophis-
ticated worldling who wrote charming
and successful comedies, and the questing experimentalist who knew the torments of the larger agonies.*

≈≈≈≈≈≈≈≈≈≈≈≈≈≈≈≈≈≈≈≈≈≈≈≈≈≈≈≈≈

The American Barry

FRIENDSHIP should be a private pleasure, not a public
boast. I loathe those braggarts who are forever trying
to invest themselves with importance by calling important
people by their first names in or out of print. Whether they
know or only pretend to know the persons they would have
us believe are their intimates, such first-naming for effect
makes me cringe. I find it vulgar beyond comfort or forgiveness. Yet I have no other choice in the paragraphs which
follow than to refer to Philip Barry as Phil. In my thoughts
and feelings he was "Phil" to me ever since those distant days
at Harvard when in 1921 I first came to know him in Professor Baker's Workshop.

We were close friends then and for the next few years, and
though I seldom saw him thereafter (indeed, not on the old
and treasured basis until last summer and this fall), I never
ceased to consider him a friend. Our friendship was bound to
have its dormant interludes if for no other reason than that
professionally we were, as he saw it, Montagues and Capulets.
Like many another creative writer, Phil had no fondness for

· 30 ·

critics. He was human enough to be pleased when he was praised. Even then, however, the audacity of those who could not write a play daring to pass a snap judgment on those who could, and who had labored long to do so, always struck him, quite understandably, as an impertinence. It was an impertinence which he found hard to endure.

I well remember, for example, how neatly he got back at me for an unfavorable notice I had written about a play of his, which one I now forget. Phil was presiding at a dinner given for Professor Baker at the Yale Club. Both of us, being housebroken, had taken pains not to mention either the play or the notice. When the time came for him to introduce me, he did so by telling the story of an enormous police dog who was running as fast as his long legs could carry him away from a tiny Pekingese in full pursuit. Another police dog, as large as the first, witnessed this odd chase and managed to catch up with his friend. "Why, in heaven's name," he asked, "should a big brute like you be running away from that miserable little Pekingese?" "Don't you know," panted the first police dog, "that that little Pekingese has the coldest nose in town?" Although he flattered my nose, I got the point. So did everyone else.

There are any number of good reasons for resenting critics. But Phil's resentment always seemed to me to possess a special validity. He was a meticulous craftsman, a stylist in his dialogue who used the language lovingly, precisely, and with originality. More accurately, he was an artist in the proudest, hence least fancy, sense of the word. He had scant respect, therefore, for the serviceable clichés of journalism. His impatience was instinctive with its quick, often clumsy writing. He at once distrusted and disliked the precipitous ease, the thundering finality, and the occasional exhibitionism of its judgments.

If critics were not exactly Phil's dish, neither was Broadway. He was a person who scored his successes there without ever surrendering to its limitations. He stood apart from—and above—the brassy competence and spiritual emptiness of the commercial theatre. "Show biz" was never his business. He was a dramatist whose pride in his craft was genuine. Playwriting is so special a form that most dramatists get along nicely without writing, at least in the literary sense that writing ordinarily implies. Phil was different. He was both a man of the theatre and a man of letters. One of the unique and beckoning characteristics of his plays was that they were written no less than playwritten.

Phil's thoroughness as a craftsman I came to recognize even at Harvard. I was a stage-struck sophomore when first we met, and he a graduate student from Yale. I was then nourishing the misconception that I could act and was to appear in Professor Baker's production of a fledgling effort of Phil's known, somewhat regrettably, as *A Punch for Judy*. Phil had already had one year in Cambridge with Baker. When *A Punch for Judy* went into rehearsal, he was working in New York in order to be able to come back to Harvard for a second year.

Long before Phil appeared in person for the final run-through, all of us in the cast had come to feel his personality. The bulletin board in Massachusetts Hall was studded with his detailed instructions about the habits, tastes, and personal lives of the characters we were supposed to be playing. The postman was kept busy bringing us letters from New York filled with no less minute background information. We were told whether the people we were impersonating would use

Colgate or Pebeco toothpaste. We learned about their apti-
tude for bridge and their attitude toward Robert W. Service
and Edna St. Vincent Millay. We were given their golf scores,
briefed on their politics and finances, and in general supplied
with the kind of dossier we now associate with the F.B.I. Obviously, Phil's characters lived for him before the first curtain
rose and continued to live after the final one had fallen.

Then one night there was Phil himself; Phil on hand to
judge the effect of his letters and the effectiveness of his efforts
and ours. He sat next to Professor Baker and, although shy,
was nonetheless assured. He was sandy-haired then; the
smile into which his tight, thin lips would spread was charming; his blue eyes, though capable of coldness, were, as they always remained, exceptionally bright. If we found the evening
an ordeal, so did he. No one, however, could have asked for a
more appreciative audience. In his nervousness he laughed so
uproariously at his own jokes that it was only when the run-
through was over and he began consulting his copious notes
that we realized what a perfectionist he was and that none of
our ineptitudes had escaped his attention.

A Punch for Judy, unlisted in *Who's Who in America,* was,
as I have indicated, the work of a novice. Even so, it was a
script which was brightened here and there by those felicities
which were to become the trademark of Phil's work. During
his next year at Cambridge he proved that he had ceased to be
an amateur by writing *You and I,* which won for him the
Herndon Prize, his first professional production in New York,
and immediate recognition.

Phil could easily have gone on (most dramatists would have
done so) writing such spirited comedies about privileged
worldlings as *Paris Bound, Holiday,* or *The Philadelphia*

Story. These were perhaps Phil's most successful plays. They are certainly the ones popularly associated with his name. They had sparkle, finish, bounce. Although glib and sometimes mannered in their phrasing, their charm was real, their originality unmistakable, and their tenderness a quality which neither their laughter nor their sophistication could obscure. Plainly they were what a wide and properly admiring public wanted. If their characters had a grand time playing games, they gave most spectators the same grand time by doing so.

With equal ease Phil could, no doubt, have continued to write affectionate or probing studies, such as *In a Garden, Tomorrow and Tomorrow,* or *The Animal Kingdom.* These dealt wittily and compassionately with threatened marriages among the well-subsidized. They, too, were scripts which won their large and enthusiastic audiences. They were blessed with that whimsical individuality in both expression and feeling which were as special to Barry, Philip, as they were to Barrie, J. M.

But Phil, pleased as he was by his successes, was always proudest of his failures. He was a highly complicated person, not one man but many men who, because of their very differences, were constantly at war with one another. Phil was as serious at heart as he was gay on the surface. He was at once a conformist and a noncomformist, a sophisticate and a romantic. He was a good American from Rochester who never ceased to be Irish. The accent of his spirit, regardless of the accent of his speech, remained Gaelic. The fey quality was there, the ability to see the moon at midday. He had the Irish gift for both anger and sweetness, and the Irish ferment in his soul. He was a Catholic whose thinking was unorthodox and restless. Even in his comedies, when apparently he was being audacious, he

· 34 ·

employed the means of Congreve to preach sermons against divorce which would have won a Cardinal's approval.

In the manner of his most typical characters Phil chose to live as a worldling. Like them, he was to be found on Park Avenue, in Paris, London, Antibes, Cannes, Easthampton, Hobe Sound, or Watch Hill. Yet the world of fashion in which he moved, in spite of offering him comforts and amenities that he prized, never satisfied his interests or nourished what was forever questing and perturbed in his nature. If he enjoyed the luxuries of that world, he despised its stuffiness. His dwelling in it did not prevent him from seeing through it. At home as he was in its plush apartments, its villas, and its *cabañas,* he never accepted its values. Though pursued by Society, he was also pursued by the Furies. The contentment he found in opulent surroundings only bred discontent within him. This discontent kept him from ever growing stodgy and was responsible for some of his most interesting experiments.

When he started to write, life was far simpler than it now is. How much simpler it was is made clear by the problems which agitated the characters in his earlier plays. They were concerned with what was then referred to as "expressing themselves." Aside from the question of divorce, the most agonizing decision some of them had to make was whether they would go into business or follow Art (with a capital "A," naturally). Even these characters, however, in plays correctly welcomed as comedies, confessed their unhappiness in a revealing manner. Again and again they were able to face life only by retreating into the past. Almost always their escape from the realities was to flee to an attic studio, a nursery left untouched, or a room redecorated for a particular reunion so as to summon memories.

One of Phil's many fine traits was that he refused to be atrophied by success. As early as 1925, when he wrote *In a Garden*, it was clear that in his own quiet-voiced and courageous way he was as much of an experimentalist as those noisier and more sensational figures whose breaks from convention consist largely of surrenders to stunts. Innovation is usually supposed to be the contribution of the wild-eyed and the long-haired who are only happy at aesthetic barricades. Phil, as I once tried to point out, was one of the few Americans who could write a comedy of manners without having to rent a tuxedo. But a black tie never kept him from being unconventional.

Though it was a box-office failure, one of the most delectable fantasies written in our time on the subject of the eternal cleavage between progress and reaction was *White Wings* (1926). In it Phil elected to state his theme in terms of a proud family of street cleaners who for years had followed the horses—with a broom, of course. The archenemy of these street cleaners, the people whose activities inescapably denied them their employment, was a family of early motorists. Phil followed *White Wings* with *John*, a Biblical play about John the Baptist, which in spite of being another failure was another indication of his bravery.

Ultimately, Phil the metaphysical seeker after first causes, who seemed to have so little in common with Phil the writer of society comedies, produced *Hotel Universe* (1930) and *Here Come the Clowns* (1938). It never seemed to me that in either of these more ambitious plays he quite succeeded in doing what he had set out to do. He may not have lost his way after a promising first act in *Hotel Universe*, but I must confess I lost mine. Even so, I was conscious—as who could help being—of the growth which this attempt showed in him. When Phil sought to state the dilemmas of the modern world in terms of a vaudeville theatre in *Here Come the Clowns,* I found myself confused though interested. All of us who are reviewers are condemned to living with our regrets. One of mine has always been that I failed to recognize in *Here Come the Clowns* the virtues which, I have come to see, far outweigh its faults.

The biggest things for which Phil reached may have eluded his grasp. He has always had my complete respect, however, because of having risked the perils of overreaching himself. All too few are blessed with this daring; all too few are ignited by the torments of the larger agonies. The fact that Phil was sensitive to these anguishes and had the hardihood to try to give them dramatic statement must be counted among the many reasons why his going represents a genuine loss even as his living represented a distinguished and irreplaceable gain.

December 24, 1949

THE INFORMATIVE and fascinating letters of a man who, because he was a great editor, played father confessor, cheer leader, baby-sitter, and Dutch uncle to some of the outstanding authors of our time.

Counselor-at-Large

MEMORY is nothing if not unpredictable. Why, for example, should I still remember from my undergraduate days (having forgotten so much else) a sentence of William De Witt Hyde's? "One creative line," it insisted, "is worth all the creative editing in this ably edited world."

Mr. Hyde, I now discover, had tossed that one out in 1911, when the world unquestionably was better edited than it is at present. No doubt what he said stands even now as an evaluation of such writing as is truly creative. But, having recently read *Editor to Author*,* a collection of Maxwell E. Perkins's letters, Mr. Hyde's pronunciamento no longer seems to me as safe from challenge as it once did. Letter after letter by Mr. Perkins has forced me to realize not only how dependent creative writing can be upon creative editing but how rare such editing is.

This collection of Mr. Perkins's letters, which his co-worker

* *Editor to Author:* The Letters of Maxwell E. Perkins. Selected and edited, with commentary and an introduction, by John Hall Wheelock. New York: Charles Scribner's Sons. 1950. 315 pp. $3.75.

at Scribner's, John Hall Wheelock, has affectionately introduced and assembled, is a delightful volume. It has more to
say about writing than can be learned in most classrooms or
garnered from a whole shelf of textbooks on the subject. It has
the virtue of informality and the intimacy of conversation. It
leads us into the world of manuscripts emerging rather than of
completed books. It takes us out of the library or bookstore
straight into the publisher's inner office and the author's study.

By allowing us to share the problems and agonies of writers
as varied as James Huneker, Edward Bok, John Galsworthy,
F. Scott Fitzgerald, Ring Lardner, Struthers Burt, Stark
Young, Sherwood Anderson, Marjorie Kinnan Rawlings,
James Boyd, Ernest Hemingway, Marcia Davenport, and
Thomas Wolfe, it sheds a great, great deal of light and is constant in its fascination. It has about it something of the same
interest and revelation which distinguish such volumes as
From Ibsen's Workshop, Chekhov's *Personal Papers* or
letters, Somerset Maugham's *The Summing Up* and *A
Writer's Notebook*, or André Gide's *Journals*. The difference
is, of course, that *Editor to Author* speaks *to* writers, not *for*
them. Yet in the process it somehow succeeds in doing both.

If it does this, and does this admirably, it is because Max
Perkins (as he was known to everyone in the trade including
those who like myself were unfortunate enough never to have
met him) was possessed of all the uncommon gifts which combine to make a great editor. And a great editor, as Mr. Wheelock quotes Taine as having said, is an artist whose medium is
the work of other men.

This was singularly true of Perkins. Although he may have
begun by wanting to be a writer himself, he spent his most
fruitful years in seeing to it that others should write their best.

His being blessed with selflessness did not mean, however, that Perkins was unendowed with positive qualities. Without these he would have been neither the man nor the editor he was.

He had a Yankee's integrity and a Cavalier's appreciation of the arts. In a world where many read but few care about writing or the writer's problems, Perkins's understanding of both was intuitive and profound. When he said to an author, "You are a writer," he was paying the highest compliment at his command. Good writing was the passion of his life. He could sense it at once. He respected it and fought for it. His talent for discovering it was no less exceptional than his ability to encourage it. But, though he played father confessor, cheer leader, baby-sitter, Dutch uncle, hand-holder, and family solicitor to many of the outstanding authors of our times, his opinions were never dogmatic and his suggestions always tentative.

"Do not ever defer to my judgment," he wrote to F. Scott Fitzgerald early in their relationship. What is more, Perkins meant it. He did not wish to intrude upon the work of others. He wanted his authors to do their own writing. He wanted their books to speak for them and to belong to them. This was his invariable attitude, even when he was laboring to persuade Thomas Wolfe not "to feel a certain shame at the idea of turning out a book of reasonable dimensions."

According to Mr. Wheelock, Max Perkins was "not by any means always amiable." His scorn, however, was directed at the windy bores, the hopeless incompetents, or the blind zealots who were convinced that only such books should be published as agreed with their prejudices. With writers, no matter how difficult, who had won his trust his patience was unending. He served them not only as a friend but as the most en-

lightening of teachers. His teaching was wonderfully camou-
flaged. It was gentle, indirect, and human. It stemmed from
his loving knowledge of books no less than his superior critical
faculties.

An editor of Perkins's stature is bound to be one of the best
critics. He is not a critic in the sense of the reviewer who is in
at the kill. Like a director in the theatre, he is a critic who is in
at the birth. His work is done in advance, not afterward. His
task is to build up rather than to tear down, to encourage instead of dismiss. He does not write mere appraisals of what
has been done. He throws out hints as to what should or could
or might be done. His judgments are constructive. They are
based on an ability to understand an author's intentions often
more clearly than the author himself does in the early stages of
writing. They spring from a deep sympathy with the writer
and an alertness to what is best in him and his materials.

All of these perceptive and nurturing attributes Max Perkins possessed to an exceptional degree. His was a high and
proud code for publishing itself. A publisher's first allegiance,
as he saw it, was to talent. He felt strongly that only that
which is false is killed by discussion. To his way of thinking,
a publisher had a public responsibility. Hence he could not be
a partisan. His job was to keep readers impartially informed
about vital issues. Scribner's policy, as he phrased it, was "to
publish for an author rather than to publish individual
works."

Perkins had his definite theories about writing. With F.
Scott Fitzgerald, he believed that many authors have been
aided by being brought up in a *métier* utterly unrelated to literature, which gave them something to write from. He was
leery of courses in composition. "As to perhaps a couple of

years of college," he once wrote a young man, "I should think that that might be of great advantage, in a general sense, but don't try to learn about writing there. Learn something else. Learn about writing from reading. That is the right way to do it. . . . The way they teach literature and writing in college is harmful. It results in one getting into a habit of seeing everything through a kind of film of past literature, and not seeing it directly with one's own senses." Perkins felt newspaper training was preferable to the academic approach. "What really makes writing," he pointed out to James Boyd, Jr., "is done in the head, where impressions are stored up, and it is done with the eye and the ear. The agony comes later, when it has to be done with the hand, and that part of it can gain greatly from seeing how others do it, by reading."

Perkins's greatest hope was always invested in his young discoveries. He had a good reason for this. "We know," said he, "what the old authors can do and, although some of them do admirably, they seldom surprise us. But the young writers may do anything."

Young and old, he knew his authors well and to them he gave himself unstintingly. Through his knowing eyes we have many revealing glimpses of their writing habits and personal characteristics, and their mental and physical quirks. To him Gertrude Stein "looked like a grand old Indian squaw—as if she were very wise, too, and had lived, as they say." Ernest Hemingway, for whom his admiration was as great as his affection, was a man who had a habit of going through town "like a hurricane." Galsworthy "never overrated himself as a writer" and in his last years had no real sympathy with the times in which he found himself. F. Scott Fitzgerald, in a moment of despair, once confessed to Perkins that he was not a *natural* writer. And Sherwood Anderson was markedly susceptible to hurt feelings.

The recurrent despondency of authors, the despair with which they live because of measuring what they are able to do with what they would like to have done, is little guessed by readers. Nor is it, after all, the public's concern. Yet it was with writing friends, subject intermittently to such attacks, that Perkins was accustomed to work.

Certainly none of the authors with and for whom he labored was the victim of greater despair than Thomas Wolfe. The story of their relationship has long since become part of the mythology of modern letters and publishing, but never until *Editor to Author* have the true and absorbing details been available. That Wolfe was a writer of phenomenal power, few would deny. Yet in most fine writers an editorial sense is an adjunct to their creative talents. This was not true of Wolfe. His was a torrential genius which stood desperately in need of channeling. Although he could write superbly, apparently he could not function as his own editor. Perkins served him as this other self. His patience, his tact, his insight, his perceptions, his bigness of spirit and mind, and his own genius for friendship no less than for editing are at their shining best in his letters to Wolfe.

The manner of their working together is perhaps most clearly revealed in a letter Perkins wrote to Ernest Hemingway in 1934 when *Of Time and the River* was being put into publishable form. "We have got a good system now. We work every evening from 8:30 (or as near as Tom can come to it) until 10:30 or 11:00, and Tom does actual writing at times, and does it well, where pieces have to be joined up. We are organizing the book. That is the best part of the work we are doing. It will be pretty well integrated in the end, and vastly more effectively arranged. The fact is, Tom could do the work, but his impulse is all away from the hard detailed revision. He is mighty ingenious at times, when it comes to the organization of material. The scheme is pretty clear in his own head, but he shrinks from the sacrifices, which are really cruel often. A couple of nights ago, I told Tom that a whole lot of fine stuff he had in simply ought to come out because it resulted in blurring a very important effect. Literally, we sat here for an hour thereafter without saying a word, while Tom glowered and pondered and fidgeted in his chair. Then he said, 'Well, then will you take the responsibility?' And I said, 'I have simply got to take the responsibility. And what's more,' I said, 'I will be blamed, either way.' But he did it, and in the end he knew he was right."

As everyone knows, Wolfe ultimately left Scribner's and went to Harper's. Perhaps, as Mr. Wheelock suggests, he was irked by the current rumor that he was unable to get his books into final form without Perkins's aid. Even so, the friendship of the two men proved enduring. No doubt the perfect tribute to Perkins, and the best indication of what he could mean to those with whom he worked, is to be found in a very moving letter he received from Wolfe. It was the last he ever wrote. It was written shortly before his death, against doctor's orders, from the hospital where Wolfe had been struggling with pneumonia. It reads:

"I'm sneaking this against orders—but 'I've got a hunch'—and I wanted to write these words to you.

"I've made a long voyage and been to a strange country, and I've seen the dark man very close; and I don't think I was too much afraid of him, but so much of mortality still clings to me—I wanted most desperately to live and still do, and I thought about you all a 1,000 times, and wanted to see you all again, and there was the impossible anguish and regret of all the work I had not done, of all the work I had to do—and I know now I'm just a grain of dust, and I feel as if a great window has been opened on life I did not know about before—and if I come through this, I hope to God I am a better man, and in some strange way I can't explain I know I am a deeper and a wiser one—If I get on my feet and out of here, it will be months before I head back, but if I get on my feet, I'll come back.

"—Whatever happens—I had this 'hunch' and wanted to write you and tell you, no matter what happens or has happened, I shall always think of you and feel about you the way it was that 4th of July day 3 yrs. ago when you met me at the boat, and we went out on the café on the river and had a drink and later went on top of the tall building and all the strangeness and the glory and the power of life and of the city was below—Yours always, Tom."

April 8, 1950

INTRODUCTION *to* The Viking
Portable Charles Lamb *in which Elia,
the man, the critic, and the writer, is
placed against the tragic story of his life
with his sister Mary.*

꙼꙼꙼꙼꙼꙼꙼꙼꙼꙼꙼꙼꙼꙼꙼꙼꙼꙼꙼꙼꙼꙼꙼꙼꙼꙼꙼꙼꙼

The Shorn Lambs

I. *Charles and Mary*

AMONG the tantalizing "ifs" of literature is what Charles
Lamb might have been like as man and writer if, in a fit
of madness, his sister Mary had not slain their mother when he
was only twenty-one. The "gentle Elia" the world loves was
the product of ungentle and terrible events. He was the step-
child of a calamity as bloody as any to be found in the most
bloodstained Elizabethan dramas of which Lamb was later to
become a champion. To a tragic extent Lamb's life, hence
Elia's character, was carved out for him by the case knife
which poor, deluded Mary drove straight and deep into their
mother's heart.

Surely never in the strange annals of authorship has the
world gained so much in pleasure or an innocent man lost more
in freedom than in the instance of the catastrophe which resulted in Lamb's becoming the most beloved bachelor of
letters literature has produced.

When he quit his desk at the East India House on the afternoon of September 22, 1796, and started to walk home through the London he loved, Lamb was not without his worries. His sister Mary, ten years his senior, had already shown symptoms of insanity. Not for the first time, either. As a person who had himself been confined the previous year for six weeks in a madhouse at Hoxton, these symptoms may have had a special meaning for him. In any case, Mary's condition was sufficiently disturbing to have sent Lamb, on his way to work that very morning, in search of a doctor who was not to be found. Aware though he was of the gathering clouds, Lamb could not have been prepared for the violence of the storm which had broken out in the house where he lived with his old father, his invalid mother, his sister, and his Aunt Hetty.

The sight he beheld when he opened the door was of tabloid gruesomeness. Above the bustle of Little Queen Street he may have heard the cries of his father and the shrieks of Mary and her assistant as he approached his home. If he had not, the landlord's presence was in itself a warning. Certainly his eyes must have disbelieved the nightmare of reality which confronted them. The room, in which the table was laid for dinner, was in a turmoil. Charles's aged aunt was unconscious on the floor, "to all appearance like one dying." His senile father was bleeding from a wound in his forehead. His mother was dead in a chair, stabbed to the heart by Mary who was standing over her with the case knife still in her hand. Lamb arrived only in time to snatch the knife from her grasp.

What had provoked this scene no one knows. Perhaps, as a professional seamstress, Mary had been overworking, and the stress of a dependent household had become too great for her. Perhaps the final straw had been the additional cares which had come her way because of the leg injury recently suffered by her brother John, her elder by a year and a half. Perhaps, as moderns have hinted, an ugly, long-suppressed animosity between her and her mother had at last erupted. In any event, Mary had had an altercation with the young woman who, in her mantua-making, was her helper. Mary had reached for the knives and forks on the table, throwing them at this frightened girl in the hope of driving her from the house. It was one of the forks thus thrown which had struck her father. Her mother might have been spared had she not attempted to intercede in the apprentice's behalf.

"I date from the day of horrors," wrote Lamb to Coleridge soon after the disaster. Although by this he meant merely to place in time events described in his letter, he unwittingly summarized the rest of his adult life. To these sensational occurrences which cost him dearly, we owe, in part at least, the writer we cherish as one of the least sensational of authors. For the next thirty-eight years Lamb lived a gallant and, on the whole, a cheerful prisoner to the happenings of that fatal afternoon. In no sense of the word a tragic hero, he emerged as the hero of a tragedy. We pity him the more because he was without self-pity.

There are people, luckless mortals, who by the injustice of circumstances or because of a certain granite in their characters are doomed to be caryatids for the suffering of others. Charles Lamb was one of these. He could have fallen back on the law and allowed his sister to be committed to a public insane asylum. He could have walked out on Mary. In other words, he could have done what his older brother John did and wanted him to do.

Yet even when John washed his hands of the whole problem, Lamb was able to rise, "not without tenderness," to his brother's defense. He knew John to be "little disposed . . . at any time to take care of old age and infirmities." Charles went so far as to persuade himself that John, "with his bad leg, had an exemption from such duties." He was well aware that John would make speeches about the money needed to maintain Mary in a private institution. But Charles and John, though brothers, were made of very different stuff. Young and poor as he was, Charles faced the fact without complaining that "the whole weight of the family" had been thrown upon him. From the outset he was determined, regardless of the sacrifices, that Mary should not go into a public asylum.

Nor did she. Instead, he assumed full responsibility for her. More than that, he devoted his life to her. Because of this utter devotion his own life was altered inescapably. Had it not been for Mary, age would not have fallen so suddenly and engulfingly upon him. Without her, we might be able to imagine Lamb as a young man rather than always picturing him as a smoky and eccentric oldish fellow, settled in both his habits and his singleness, whose youth had come to an abrupt end with his childhood. Without Mary, Charles's dream children might have been real. The "fair Alice W—n," she of the light yellow hair and the pale blue eyes for whom he claimed to have pined away seven of his "goldenest years," might have been the "passionate . . . love-adventure" he once described her as being instead of a reference, true or fanciful, which biographers have been unable to track down. He might not have waited so many years to propose to Fanny Kelly, the actress with the "divine plain face," and Fanny might even have accepted him.

Without his "poor dear dearest" Mary, Charles might have continued longer to try his hand at poetry and not so soon, as he put it (with wonderful inaccuracy, in his case), have "dwindled into prose and criticism." His spirit would have been gayer, his laughs less like sighs. He might not have been so "shy of novelties; new books, new faces, new years." The present, not the past, might have been his delight. He would not have been driven, as driven he was by the events of that appalling afternoon, to find happiness by thinking back to happier days. Retrospection would not have become his refuge. The "boy-man" that he felt himself to be would not have clung with such tenacious affection to his own boyhood. The texture, the range, the very tone and temper of his work would have been different.

From the moment of his mother's murder and the time that he stepped forward to become Mary's legal guardian, Lamb knew that he and Mary were "in a manner *marked*." This was bound to be a portion of their fate. There was no hushing their story. It not only pursued them; it ran ahead of them. Sometimes it even forced them to change their lodgings. No shelter could be found from the nudgings, the whisperings, the stares, and the embarrassments it provoked. Charles's determination to care for Mary involved more than living with her. It also meant his living with the knowledge that everyone around them knew her case and their history. If this increased his shyness, it also brought him and Mary closer together. It was only one more of the many bonds, tender and tragic, which united them.

Fortunately, theirs was a relationship based upon more than the perilous stuffs of gratitude or an embittering sense of obligation. Positive as each of them was as a personality, they were united not only by misfortune but by shared tastes and minds which, in spite of dissimilarities, were complementary. When dedicating a volume of his verse, Charles called Mary his best friend. From the dedication of his life she knew she had no better friend than he. Their devotion to each other was genuine and abiding. It shines through their letters. It is unmistakable in every reference to Mary as Bridget in Charles's essays. They were collaborators in life no less than in literature. No brother and sister in history are more inseparably linked. To Lamb their life as old bachelor and maid was "a sort of double singleness."

The glimpses we have of them together are at once heart-warming and heartbreaking. "You would like to see us," wrote Mary to Sarah Stoddart, "as we often sit, writing on one table (but not on one cushion sitting), like Hermia and Helena in the *Midsummer's Night's Dream;* or, rather, like an old literary Darby and Joan: I taking snuff, and he groaning all the while and saying he can make nothing of it, which he always says till he has finished, and then he finds out he has made something of it."

That is a picture of them at their happiest. It belongs with those other pictures we conjure when we imagine them together. Playing cards. Seeing a play. Going to exhibitions. Reading books, she doting on narratives—any narratives; he delighting in the reflective passages of the older authors. Visiting friends. Enjoying the adventure of one of their short summer journeys. Presiding over one of their delectable "evenings" at home (held first on Wednesdays, later on Thursdays), which Hazlitt immortalized with his "How often did we cut into the haunch of letters, while we discussed the haunch of mutton on the table!" Or discussing, in the financial

· 51 ·

comfort of their later years, the greater pleasures they had known when, in their youth, they had been forced to skimp, save, and plan in order to make a purchase or crowd their way into the pit.

Against these brighter moments must be set the darker ones. These are black indeed. By common agreement Mary, in her right mind, was one of the most amiable and admirable of women. But Mary was not always in her right mind. She was "perpetually on the brink of madness." If this was Mary's tragedy, it was also Lamb's. Their sunniest days together were never cloudless. The threat under which they lived was fearful and incessant. At all times the Furies stalked them. Small wonder this brother and this sister have been likened to a cockney Orestes and Electra.

Mary's was a recurrent illness. There was no telling when it would return. There was only the certainty that return it would, with ever-increasing frequency, with ever-mounting seriousness. Some hints, such as a sudden moroseness or irritability on Mary's part, preceded its coming. For these dreaded signs Charles watched anxiously. Apparently Mary did, too.

"You would laugh, or you would cry, perhaps both," Mary wrote in another letter to Miss Stoddart, "to see us sit together, looking at each other with long and rueful faces, and saying, 'How do you do?' and ' How do *you* do?' and then we fall a-crying and say we will be better on the morrow. Charles says we are like Tooth Ache and his friend Gum Boil, which though a kind of ease is an uneasy kind of ease."

Their ease at its best was the epitome of uneasiness. Surely few scenes could be more touching than the one several of their friends had witnessed. It was the common sequel to each reappearance of Mary's symptoms. When these had shown themselves, Charles would get ready to take her to the private asylum at Hoxton. She would gather together a few clothes, replace with a bonnet the mobcap she wore indoors, and prepare for the street. He would lead her, unresisting, to the door. Then they would start out hand in hand, two figures as somberly dressed as Quakers, walking the whole way, weeping as they walked, and carrying Mary's strait jacket with them.

Even so, Mary, between interruptions, brought Charles a happiness almost as complete as was the unhappiness her madness had brought upon them both. The debt we owe her is at once incalculable and unpayable. If, as readers, we delight in Lamb as he is, we do so because his writing is the product of his life as it was. He never objected to his lot. He faced it squarely, gaily, without whining, and with inexhaustible courage.

The world that knows him as the "gentle Elia" does Lamb an injustice. Gentle he always was with Mary and in most of his writings. It was, however, his strength which enabled him to be gentle and not any softness which forced him into being so. He hated the phrase "gentle-hearted" when applied to him as much as Sir James Barrie abhorred the word "whimsical." "For God's sake (I never was more serious)," wrote Charles to Coleridge; "don't make me ridiculous any more by terming me gentle-hearted in print, or do it in better verses. . . . The meaning of gentle is equivocal at best, and almost always means poor-spirited."

Certainly Lamb was anything but poor-spirited. He had a resilience unknown to noisier men and a toughness unsuspected by those who have read him sparingly, and then only in his fanciful or sentimental moods. Did he look like a clerk? He did not act like one. He was no Timid Soul. He was fiercely independent. His father may have been a servant, but in a snobbish age Lamb was subservient to no one. He was at all times ready to stammer out his opinions without fear. Everyone who described him noted the sadness of his brown eyes, the thoughtfulness of his expansive brow, the sweetness of his expression, and the smallness of his body. Lamb knew that physically he was "less than the least of the Apostles." A friend thought he looked so fragile that "a breath would overthrow him." But there was iron in his "immaterial legs." His slight body contradicted the largeness of his spirit.

Although Charles knew great sorrow, he was not discontented. If he could refer to Mary and himself, playfully though correctly, as "shorn Lambs," his belief in the tempering wind was nonetheless strong. Living with sorrow was as much a habit with him as climbing up on his high stool each morning to work as a clerk at the East India House. The prospect of any change so staggered him that he convinced himself he would no more reverse the untoward accidents and events of his life than he would alter the incidents of some well-contrived novel. Such was his love of life that he even loved his own. He meant what he said when he confessed, "I am in love with this green earth; the face of town and country; the unspeakable rural solitudes, and the sweet security of streets."

II. *The Man Who Was Lamb*

THE PORTION of the earth that Charles Lamb loved best was not green. He preferred cobblestones to grass any day. He was a city man if ever there was one; a cockney in every inch of his small person. The nightingale never released a song so sweet to his ears as the sound of Bow Bells. Had he been compelled to choose between Skiddaw and Soho, Wordsworth's mountain would have had no chance. The pleasure William found in a daffodil, Charles derived from a chimney sweep.

He did not object to nature—for others. But human nature and the hum of city streets were his delight. Although, with Mary, he liked to venture into the countryside, for a while and as a break, even in the country he was a cockney on vacation. He dared to write to Wordsworth, of all people, "Separate from the pleasure of your company, I don't much care if I never see a mountain in my life." Nature to him was "dead"; London, living. The sun and the moon of the Lake District did not shine for him as brightly as the lamps of London. It was not the beauties of the outdoors which he found "ever fresh and green and warm," but all the inventions and assemblies of men in the congested boroughs by the Thames.

Few writers have described a city more affectionately than Charles his London. Few have outdone him in making strangers, both by the calendar and geography, feel like citizens of vanished times and places. There were scarcely any aspects of the metropolis he did not cherish. He, to whom much of life was denied, often shed tears of joy on his night walks about London at encountering so much life.

He never tired of the lighted shops of the Strand and Fleet Street; of the innumerable trades, tradesmen, customers, coaches, crowds, wagons, and playhouses; of "all the bustle and wickedness round about Covent Garden, the very women of the Town, the Watchmen, drunken scenes, rattles"; of the city's pungent smells and the very dirt and mud; of the sun shining upon houses and pavements; or of the print shops, the old bookstalls, and the coffeehouses. He rejoiced in the sense they gave him of London being a pantomime and a masquerade where life itself was at last awake. The city for him was at once a stimulant and an escape. Urbanwise, he lived on it no less than in it. He measured his fortune, good or ill, by his distance from the Strand. He was jubilant when, after one of their frequent changes of address, he found that the house in which he and Mary were then stopping was "forty-two inches nearer town."

The city he lived in, though a metropolis, was not for him a capital. Its government was an irrelevance; its politics nonexistent. An historian, hoping to find in Lamb's essays or letters some reflection of the great events of turbulent years, would be hard put to determine whether history had by-passed Lamb or he history. He lived through England's wars as if Europe were at peace. So far as he was concerned, they were undeclared and unwaged. He came to admire Nelson, admitted Wellington's existence, had no love for the early Hanovers, in a mild way championed Queen Caroline's cause, and was curious about Napoleon's height. But the French Revolution left no visible mark upon him, and, though he must have heard of Trafalgar, Austerlitz, and Waterloo, we never hear of them through him.

Did the younger Pitt die in 1806? For Lamb he never seems to have lived. Did "Boney" threaten England with invasion? Did the Peterloo Massacre spill blood in Manchester? Were trade unions allowed for the first time? Did the Prince Regent's marriage to Mrs. Fitzherbert rock society? Were both the Roman Catholic Emancipation and the First Reform Bill passed? Contemporaneous as he was with all of these occurrences, Lamb was apparently the contemporary of none of them.

Unlike such of his intimates as Coleridge, Hazlitt, Leigh Hunt, and Wordsworth, he had no interest in public affairs. Society for him was always a circle of friends and never the collective well-being of a community. "Public affairs—except as they touch upon me, and so turn into private," Lamb wrote to Thomas Manning, "I cannot whip up my mind to feel any interest in." By his own admission, he was deaf to the noises which kept Europe awake, and could not make present times present to him.

He was as insulated against political events as he was susceptible to human, literary, and gastronomic values. In his scheme of things "important people" were unimportant, and for him the "Great World" possessed no fascination. The bearers of titles, more than leaving him unimpressed, left him unamused no less surely than official leaders left him unled. A benevolent eccentric himself, he delighted in the benevolent eccentricities of others. The heads he prized were not those highly placed but those "with some diverting twist in them"; heads lightened by "out of the way humors and opinions."

His absorptions were personal, not public, and small-scaled rather than outsized. Covent Garden was his Buckingham Palace; the art galleries were his House of Commons; the bookstall, his House of Lords. Londoner, utter and complete, though he was, Lamb never felt, thought, or wrote as a citizen but always as an individual. He took the same pleasure in the "delicious juices of meats and fishes, and society, and the cheerful glass, and candle-light and fireside conversations, and innocent vanities and jests, and irony itself" that he did in the passages, sublime or melancholy, of his favorite old authors. If the oddities of authorship were dear to him, so were the oddities of people and places, and it was these which enchanted him in London.

The London through which Lamb trudged was apt to be two cities—the one he saw as a man, and the other he remembered from his youth. Accordingly, even when solitary, he seldom walked the streets alone. For the author whose attachment to the past was so great that he could exclaim, "Hang the age; I'll write for Antiquity!" London's past was superimposed upon its present. On his strolls he was attended by the shades of the boys and teachers he had known as a student at Christ's Hospital; by the ghosts of departed players or of journalists with whom he had worked; or by the figures of Old Benchers, long since dead, whom he had watched in his boyhood in the Inner Temple. These rose constantly before his eyes. So double was Lamb's sense of time, so eager his search for reminders of his "joyful" days, that, in spite of his best known poem, the "old familiar faces" were for him never "all, all . . . gone."

London offered Lamb a source of vicarious life. The city which touched and diverted him by doing so provided him with a release from both his "cold bed of celibacy" and his long years of confinement at the East India House. During most of his writing life, Lamb was a full-time clerk, a part-time author. He contended that his real "works"—"more MSS. in folio than ever Aquinas left, and full as useful"—were the great ledgers he had filled day after day for the thirty-three years of his clerkdom, and not the printed volumes to be found at booksellers. There was little of the free-lancer in his nature. There could not be. His being married, as he put it, to Mary's fortunes meant that he was unable to run risks with his own. Instead of writing to live, he clerked in order to be free to write. Generous as he was in his gifts and loans to others, he could not afford to be without steady employment himself.

He was horrified when Bernard Barton confided he was thinking of giving up his job in a Quaker bank to live by his pen. "Keep to your Bank," he urged Barton, "and the Bank will keep you. . . . What, is there not from six to eleven P.M. 6 days in the week, and is there not all Sunday?" For Lamb this was writing time enough. It spared him the insecurities of being a "slave to Booksellers" and "the miseries of subsisting by authorship." It meant that, when at last he was at liberty to write, his pen felt its "promotion." His writing was thus kept an escape from drudgery, and so avoided being drudgery itself.

He was, of course, fond of seeing himself as a prisoner at the India House; of claiming that he sat there like Philomel all day (but not singing) with his "heart against this thorn of a desk." But he liked his job better than he guessed, and was lost when he retired from it. The routine of working at India House from ten to four at once supported and soothed him. It comforted him in his loneliness and appealed to what was essentially gregarious in his nature. He missed the friendly eminence of the high stool upon which he had sat for so many years. He missed not hanging his hat each day on the same peg. He missed the amiable ease of an office where, though he labored faithfully, he could still find time to write some of his best letters. He missed the companionship of his "old desk fellows"—his "co-brethren of the quill." He missed "the hot huddle of rational creatures." He missed, too, being able to excuse his habitual tardiness by such an explanation as "I m-make up for that by g-going away early."

The truth is he missed his chains. Like many another, he came to realize they had become a necessary part of his apparel. Nothing in his story is more poignant than the sadness which inundated him when, at fifty, his dream of liberty became a reality and he was freed from what he had thought was bondage. During the next nine years, until his death in 1834, he sensed that freedom in itself could be a bondage. He had lived so long "*to* other people" that he could not happily fill his own emancipated hours. Time stood still for him and was empty in its idleness. He lost the "Wednesday feelings" and the "Saturday night sensations" he had once known. To his despair he discovered he walked about, not to and from. Having all holidays, it was as though he had none. No Babbitt and no Dodsworth could have been more rudderless upon retirement than was this man, part Yorick, part Jaques, when he was at last freed by a generous pension.

His Yorick side is known to every reader whose knowledge of him does not stop with the *Tales from Shakespeare*, "The

Dissertation on Roast Pig," or "Dream Children." Lamb turning suddenly to Martin Burney at cards to comment, "Martin, if dirt were t-trumps, what a hand you would hold!"; Lamb crying out, "Wordsworth says he could have written *H-Hamlet* if he'd had the m-mind!"; or Lamb answering Coleridge's question as to whether or not Charles had ever heard him preach in the days of his Unitarian ministry with, "I never heard you do anything else"—all these are instances of his "punch-light" humor which, though familiar, have not become tired.

As a conversationalist, his stammer was part of his comic equipment. He relied upon it the way acrobats rely upon a net. He was a fellow whose jests were infinite, instantaneous, impudent, and deflating. He had the virtues, and the wisdom, of not being a continuous conversationalist. His stutter, like his discretion, made that impossible. His hatred for the "long and much talkers" was as lusty as theirs for him. He knew the value of silences, broken suddenly and unexpectedly, and, one gathers, of dead-panning his way to a joke. Pomposity he despised, dullness he abhorred, and seers he loathed when they were "seering."

To be at his best he had to be among people he knew and liked. To strangers and incompatibles he was an enigma, if not an irritant. Carlyle, with his genius for fermentation, was never sourer than on the subject of Lamb. "A more pitiful, ricketty, gasping, staggering, stammering Tomfool I do not know," fumed he. "He is witty by denying truisms and abjuring good manners." Yet to Hazlitt, as to many another, this same Lamb was "the most delightful, the most provoking, the most witty and sensible of men. . . . No one ever stammered out such fine, piquant, deep, eloquent things in half a dozen half-sentences as he does. His jests scald like tears: and he probes a question with a play upon words."

Among his friends, on the kind of drinking, talking, smoking evening which he cherished, his relaxation was to enliven the passing moment as certainly as, when alone, his consolation was to dream of the moments that had been. He had a reply—and an unanswerable one—for those who complained he was always aiming at wit. He said that to do so was at least as good as aiming at dullness.

Macready was shocked to hear Lamb confess at Talfourd's one night that "the last breath he drew in he wished might be through a pipe and exhaled in a pun." Lamb's fondness for puns was notorious. He loved them as much as all people dislike them who cannot make them. There is no such thing as stooping to a pun. There is only the challenge of being able to rise to a good one. Few cadavers could be deader or more emaciated than those occasional puns which, in his letters, Lamb quotes approvingly, pointer in hand, with the subtlety of a window demonstrator. Lamb, however, knew a pun must be heard, not read, and heard at the moment of its birth if it were to live completely or to be fully enjoyed. "A pun," wrote he, "hath a hearty kind of present ear-kissing smack in it; you can no more transmit it in its pristine flavor than you can send a kiss."

That Lamb laughed and could make others laugh, everyone knows. But the nature of his laughter, the keen and enjoying manner in which he detected frailty, the amused details which underwrite his fantasy and are the basis of his reveries, along with the man who could be as realistic in his observation of men as he was in facing the unpleasant realities of his own life—these are what the sentimentalists forget who have made him as sentimental as themselves.

Many authors suffer at the hands of their detractors; just as many (and no less cruelly) at the hands of their admirers. Lamb belongs to this well-nigh smothered brotherhood. He has almost been killed, not so much by his own kindness, which was true and very human, as by the bogus, treacly kindness which others have palmed off as being his. Thornton Wilder once described a modern playwright, addicted to cute and elfin phrases and marshmallow thoughts, as writing in the manner associated with Lamb by people who have not read him. This false notion of Lamb, with its attendant misunderstandings and proper revulsions, is a ghost which, worse than haunting the real Lamb, has all too often obscured him.

In his eagerness to canonize Lamb's palpable and radiant virtues, Thackeray may have dubbed him "Saint Charles." Charles, however, was the more of a saint because he was so much of a man. Although there are those who choose to bury him in lavender, to cushion him on sachets, and to confuse him with old lace, they do Lamb a genuine injustice.

Lamb could be sweet beyond comfortable endurance. He could be whimsical to a disquieting extent. He could dip his pen far too deep in sirup and produce copy, on occasions, which to modern eyes reads like literate valentines from yesteryear. These, however, were the excesses into which his tenderness led him. They were the expressions of his frustration, his regrets, his loneliness, and, in a way, of his period. Though full of sentiment, Lamb was no sentimentalist as a man, and only as an author when he nodded, which he was mortal enough to do at moments. That he was kind and that he was witty, everyone knows. But that he was both kind and witty at one and the same time has so surprised his admirers that some of them have overlooked entirely the sharpness of his mind and tongue.

In his letters, as in his talk, a spade was a spade. It was only in his essays that it became a shovel, a gardener's utensil, or something like Triptolemus's tool. When he informed Manning that Coleridge's wife was expecting a baby, did he do so by referring to "a little one" or "an addition to the family"? He did not. As directly as if he were a GI in the Army, he wrote, "Coleridge is settled with his wife (with a child in her guts)."

No one has written about childhood more tenderly than he. Even so, his was not the bachelor's idealization of all children. He knew that the young, like their elders, were either amiable or unamiable. He saw no reason "to love a whole family, perhaps eight, nine, or ten, indiscriminately—to love all the pretty dears because children are so engaging." His phrase, when a sick child had at last been removed from his home, after robbing Lamb of his rest, was, quite simply, "The little bastard is gone."

He pulled no punches with his friends, and was much too good a friend to do so. His candor was as great as his charm. "Cultivate simplicity, Coleridge," wrote he, "or rather, I should say, banish elaborateness. . . . I allow no hotbeds in the gardens of Parnassus." No one ever derived more amusement from a friend's faults than Lamb did from those of poor, foolish, bumbling George Dyer. His letters about Dyer, like his references to him in his essays, are as full of mocking laughter as they are of love. Few people have played more knowledgeably, or with greater relish, upon human frailty than Lamb did when, by "beslabbering" a book Joseph Cottle had written, he so appealed to its author's vanity that Cottle forgot all about his dead brother in the next room.

Although by his own confession he could not hate anyone he knew, Lamb was terrifyingly aware of people's defects. Shelley's voice was to him "the most obnoxious squeak I ever was tormented with, ten thousand times worse than the Laureat's, whose voice is the worst part about him except his Laureatcy." Lamb's aversion to Byron's character was "thorough" and his admiration for his genius "very moderate." "He is great in so little a way" was Lamb's summary of his Lordship.

Once at Godwin's, Holcroft and Coleridge were fiercely disputing which was better, *man as he was* or *man as he is to be*. "Give me," said Lamb, "man as he is *not* to be." If, in general, he was willing to take all people as they were, he was taken in by no one. His eye for human absurdity was as keen as his enjoyment of human oddity. Was it a poor relation remembering a birthday so as to drop in just in time for dinner? Was it a liar spinning fabulous yarns on a boat to Margate, or a fact-loving bore on the top of a stagecoach? Lamb saw their failings plain. His gentleness did not prevent his feelings from being strong. "Now, of all God's creatures," wrote he, "I detest letters-affecting, authors-hunting ladies." His loathing for booksellers was equally strong. So was his disrelish for the Scots. Lamb was as "essentially anti-Caledonian" as ever Dr. Johnson was.

The fact—the fine, the beckoning, the all-conquering fact—about Lamb is that he could look "with no indifferent eye upon things or persons." "Whatever is" was to him "a matter of taste or distaste." He knew, as some of his admirers have forgotten, that he was "a bundle of prejudices—made up of likings and dislikings—the veriest thrall to sympathies, apathies, and antipathies." Without these prejudices Lamb would not be Lamb. Nor would he be Lamb had he not felt and phrased them in a way so unmistakably and beguilingly his own that, though it has won him countless friends, it has removed him from the reach of imitators.

III. *Elia* versus *Lamb*

AN AFFECTIONATE rather than a passionate man, Charles Lamb's prejudices were his substitutes for passion. It was in them that he lived, and because of them, in part, that he lives for us. They were the proofs of his awareness, his sensibility, his discernment, his humanity. Characteristically enough, he chose to refer to these prejudices as "imperfect sympathies" no less than as prejudices.

One of the major paradoxes of his paradoxical mind was that, as a rule, he could be sympathetic even when he was being witty. His wit was the expression of his love, not his contempt, for men. People who would have irritated others amused him. His knowledge of life was too complete for him to be surprised by human frailty. If he never failed to observe it, he seldom failed to enjoy it. Since he expected it, he was tolerant of it.

His was the laughter of acceptance not protest, of recognition instead of revulsion. His gaiety was as divorced from scorn or cynicism as it was wedded to melancholy. It smiles without being insulting. Unchilled by the arrogance which is the curse of professional wits, it is as warm and human as the "rather smoky, and sometimes rather drinky" little man from whom it emanated. It sprang from a superior mind, unconscious of its superiority; a mind which is the more endearing because its modesty remains unlost in the midst of its most dazzling exhibitions of prowess.

Lamb's mind was the antithesis of neat and officelike. It resembled an antique shop or an old bookstore where, in spite of the clutter, the dust, and the overlay of accumulation, the proprietor can at a moment's notice bring to light whatever treasure is desired. It never judged "systemwise" but always by "fastening on particulars." It was proudly unmethodized, desultory, tangential. If it worked obliquely in ways beyond prediction, it was because it fed upon the tantalizing obliquities of life no less than of literature. Its knowledge was a matter of informed tastes rather than of pursued facts.

Lamb had no desire to keep up with the Joneses. He had a hard enough time keeping up with the whims of his own interest. The topical left him uncoerced; the popular unpersuaded. When a new book came out, he read an old one. He would have been both amused and amazed by the manuals, digests, and sugar-coated textbooks in which those who mistake facts for learning nowadays stalk culture as if it were a butterfly to be pinioned in a net. Although the most bookish of bookish men, he was no chaser after information for information's sake. Instead, he was a savorer, content to taste and retaste what was best or most flavorsome in the volumes he cherished. If his devotion to what was special, limited, and wayward in his preoccupations was one of his limitations, this did not bother him. Lamb was comfortable in his ignorance of what he did not choose to know.

The Proper Study

On all matters relating to science, Elia could boast he was "a whole Encyclopaedia behind the rest of the world." He was equally, and just as proudly, unknowledgeable about geography, modern languages, the shapes and textures of the commonest trees, herbs, or flowers, and tools, engines, or mechanical processes. In spite of his attachment to the past, history as a mere sequence of events had so little interest for him that he could brag he had never deliberately sat down to read a chronicle even of his own country. As for astronomy, it did not exist in the orbit of his shining concerns. "If the sun," wrote he, "on some portentous morn were to make his first appearance in the west, I verily believe that, while all the world were gasping in apprehension about me, I alone should stand unterrified, from sheer incuriosity and want of observation."

One of the reasons for Elia's dislike of the Scots was that no excursions could be taken with them, since they always insisted upon keeping to the path. Lamb's thinking, though it could lead to the summits, was nothing if not excursive. The straight highroads dear to historians were not the routes he either elected or was equipped to travel. When he did not spurn the obvious views and inevitable sights, he preferred to reach them by a back door or secret passage. He gave both his mind and heart (the combination, in his case, meaning his attention) to the ignored vistas and overlooked curiosities. Even these he approached by those unblazed trails which, to the personal essayist, are the royal road.

If these footpaths were roads which led to himself, the reason was his modesty, not his egotism. Lamb was one of the most autobiographical of authors. To read him on virtually any subject is to read about him. It is to know him with a sense of daily intimacy with which few writers are known. In his copy Lamb could no more escape from himself than in his living he could leave Mary. Yet self-centered in the ordinary sense, he was not. The world, for the conceited man, starts and ends with himself. For Elia, Charles Lamb was merely the point of departure to the world around him. Although with him the first person singular was a favorite pronoun, as he used it, it somehow managed to seem printed with a small "i."

Lamb was too unpretentious to pretend to be omniscient. He was poignantly aware that few people are able to speak for themselves, much less for others. Speaking of and through himself was his way of speaking for all. He knew his own voice contained the echoes of other voices. In this way he chose to write, intertwining with his identity griefs and affections which were not his own, "making himself many, or reducing many unto himself."

Since truth to Lamb was as personal as everything else, facts enjoyed no immunity from his prankishness. It diverted him to distort them when, as Elia, he wrote of his friends, his family, or himself. His love of mystification was one of the abidingly boyish aspects of his character. It pleased him in his essays to mislead his readers by false scents; to write Oxford when he meant Cambridge; to make Bridget his cousin, not his sister; to merge Coleridge's boyhood with his own; or to paint himself as a hopeless drunkard when, as a matter of fact, he was a man who, though he loved to down a drink, was seldom downed by drinking. By deliberate, sometimes mischievous, design his familiar essays were but the "shadows of fact." They were "verisimilitudes, not verities." Yet Lamb was present, quintessentially if not factually, in their every phrase and sentence. At least an important part of him was present, though not by any means the whole man.

Closely related as Elia is to Charles Lamb, they were not —they are not—in any sense of the word identical. When it came to authorship, there were two Charles Lambs. If not that, there was, at any rate, one Lamb who wrote in two styles so different that he could be suspected of employing his left hand for the one, his right hand for the other. As in the case of countless others, ink-stained or ink-free, Lamb had a public and a private manner. He did not write to his friends as he wrote for the magazines. Although in either case a natural-born essayist, and a matchless critic of books and men, his style, which was always intimate, altered according to whether his pen or a printer was to be the transmitter of his words.

Hazlitt's portrait of him as a nobleman of another day caught the spirit, not of Lamb the private letter writer, but of Lamb the public essayist. Certainly, the Lamb who contributed to periodicals was not the Renaissance figure Hazlitt envisaged. Yet Hazlitt was right beyond dispute in dressing this Lamb in the clothes of an age other than his own. When he wrote for publication, Lamb did go into costume as surely as, when he dashed off notes to his friends, he donned a dress so modern that after the passage of more than a century it seems as contemporary to us as it did to them.

The highly, at moments even dangerously, self-conscious artist we cherish as Elia emerged late in Lamb's life as the flowering of his varied career as a professional writer. By that time Lamb had long since mislaid, except for album purposes, the poet of slight endowment he had started out by being. Years before, too, he had discarded the novelist whose all but nonexistent talent for narrative stamped *Rosamund*

Gray and his contributions to *Mrs. Leicester's School* as no more than apprentice work. He had also buried the dramatist with "no head for playwriting" whose blank verse tragedy *John Woodvil* was but the feeblest of Elizabethan echoes, and whose little farce *Mr. H . . .* was so disastrous a failure that its author had joined in the hissing.

In the same way Lamb had outgrown those un-Lamblike *Tales from Shakespeare* upon which he had collaborated with Mary. Although he had predicted such a potboiler would be popular "among the little people," he had never guessed how enduring its popularity would prove among those grownups of little courage who, apparently, are grateful for anything which spares them Shakespeare in the original.

The first volume of the *Elia* essays was published when Lamb was forty-eight; the second, and last, ten years later. In print, and in such memorable papers as his "On the Genius and Character of Hogarth" and "On the Tragedies of Shakespeare," Lamb had already established not only his brilliance as a critic but his unique public manner as an essayist. Yet during all these formative years, in fact from his first preserved letters to Coleridge before and after Mary's murder of her mother, right down to the last note scribbled off to Mrs. Dyer (about a book, appropriately enough) five days before his death thirty-eight years later, Lamb was the possessor of an epistolary style quite at odds with the style we know as Elia's.

More than being the best introduction to Lamb, Lamb's are among the world's best letters. In them we almost hear him talk. To be sure, his stutter is gone, and an incredible fluency has replaced it. But, as in all good letters, the illusion of direct communication is maintained. Both the moment and the mood are captured in all the heat of their passing sorrow or amusement. The small details, the great agonies, the first impressions, the play of mind and the play on words, the reflections by means of which a particular instance is lifted into a generality, the tastes of food, the smells of London, the look of friends, the résumé of last night's party, the book just read, the anecdote just heard, this day's sadness, the next day's gaiety—they are all there, caught hot, caught frankly, and transferred without effort by a pen scratching swiftly against stolen time at the office.

Perhaps the speed of their composition was the guarantee of their simplicity. In any case, again and again Charles's letters deny their datelines by remaining undated. They are not so much the products of an age as they are models for all time. Whether they are "thank-you" notes for a visit paid or a roast pig sent; apologies for having to be carried home from an overconvivial evening; his proposal of marriage to Fanny Kelly; the gossip of London dispatched across the oceans to Manning in China; religious musings; discussions of death; the account to Coleridge, magnificent in its dignity, of his mother's murder; appraisals of Defoe, Cervantes, Godwin's *Chaucer*, or the second edition of the *Lyrical Ballads*, they are perfect of their kind.

They show the warmth, the originality, the humor, or the grandeur of the astonishing little man who wrote them. They are the spontaneous distillations of a writer, instinctive and superior. They make us companions not only in Lamb's daily living but in his adult life. Their every episodic entry fits into a sequence. Without meaning to do so, they form an autobiography from which Lamb's biographers must quote and to which everyone who would know him must turn. They give us Lamb unadorned; Lamb, the writer, without self-consciousness, hence often at his finest; Lamb, so to speak, at his slippered ease, relaxed, using short sentences, hitting directly; Lamb employing the most vivid and abrupt of colloquialisms, thus avoiding the calculated, beautiful, and antique cadences so dear to Elia.

The difference between the letter writer who signed himself C.L. and the essayist known as Elia is the difference between a candid camera close-up and a full-length portrait in oil, appareled for effect and so posed that its very casualness is studied. It is the difference between jewels unset and a necklace painstakingly matched. It is, in short, the everlasting difference between the impromptu and the planned.

When Thackeray's "Saint Charles" wrote for the public prints, he heard voices, Joan-wise. The sonorities of such favorite prose writers as Sir Thomas Browne, Burton, Marvell, and Fuller haunted his ears. "I gather myself up into the old things," wrote Lamb. More accurately, he gathered the old authors up into himself. Their outmoded language was an expression of what was backward-glancing in his spirit. It pleased him by being out of date. It orchestrated his melancholy. Not only that. When appropriated for his casual personal essays, its very gravity served as a foil to his humor.

Lamb loved the stately rhythms and obsolete words of these older writers. While playing chameleon to their style, he could achieve a style of his own. He imitated in order to create what is inimitable. The borrowed pencil Hazlitt accused him of employing as an essayist was put by Lamb to his own uses. He was aware that, as Elia, his writings were "villainously pranked in an affected arrangement of antique modes and phrases." But he knew these writings would not have been his, had this not been so. "Better it is," said he, "that a writer should be natural in a self-pleasing quaintness, than to affect a naturalness (so called) that should be strange to him."

Quaint Elia was, and is, and in a manner pleasing not only to himself but to readers everywhere once they have become Elians. This is no hard thing to do, if only in a more hurried age, when prose is thinner and the language employed more often than it is enjoyed, readers are willing to give Elia and themselves a chance. His essays never were *in date*, except for what is dateless in their insight. Stylistically, they were intentional anachronisms when they were published. Their antique flavor was, and remains, a source of their charm.

To modern eyes, accustomed as they are to sentences being the shortest distance between a subject and a predicate (if, indeed, they extend that far), the long, leisurely, and intricate constructions of Lamb the essayist may at first glance appear forbidding. Yet forbidding is the very last word anyone in his right senses, and with the slightest acquaintance with Lamb, would dream of using for those gloriously warm and intimate essays which Lamb wrote as a critic of life, or of art, the theatre, and books. If, at the outset, their subtle and sustained sentences seem difficult, with their "methink's," their "thee's" and "thou's," their "art's," "wert's," "reader's," and other pressed flowers from another day, or their addiction to such words as "agnise," "additaments," and "dulcifying," these difficulties soon turn into delights. However truffled, archaic, or self-conscious was Lamb's formal style, it is rich in its rewards. Costume prose it may be, but costume jewelry it never was because its gems are genuine.

More than taking knowing, Elia survives it. His better

essays belong in that class of literature he described as being "perpetually self-reproductive." They bear reading and rereading, and then can be read and reread again. They are habit-forming rather than time-passing. If the style in their case is not the whole man, it is at any rate the essayist. Elia cannot be separated from it. Nor would anyone who has once cultivated a taste for that style be denied its enjoyment. Although, as a word man, Lamb was deaf to music and could complain about its "measured malice," Elia was able with words to release an incomparable music of his own.

He was the opposite of those writers he dismissed as being "economists only in delight." His prodigality with the pleasures he provides is limitless. The joy he creates from small things is large. The conceits in his phrasing are redeemed by the sincerity of his feeling. If he seldom wrote a bromide, it was because he seldom thought one. The commonest reaction became uncommon in his statement of it. His vocabulary was as much his own as his mind, and both were unpredictable.

As is true of all good essayists, not too much of Elia is to be read at one sitting. He fatigues, not by the ardor of his emotions, but by the incessant probing of his perceptions, by the sudden quiet dartings of his mind and the abundance of his allusions. To be enjoyed fully, he must be lingered over, read with the same disregard for the present that he showed, savored, as he savored the subjects of his choice. He is a writer who does not raise his voice. He avoids emphasis. His finest phrases spill from his pen without warning. They are tucked away, not paraded. They come jostling, one so close upon the other that they are apt to be overlooked. To miss them is to miss the true satisfactions of Elia, because in his phrases he gives the pleasures other authors give in their paragraphs.

His mood is ruminative, his mind associational. For all the amusement to be had from the felicities of his observations, his was an essentially tragic nature. He was a tragedian who smiled instead of crying. This not only deepens his humor. It insures its humanity.

On the subject of his family, his youth, his London, the places he had visited, or the "characters" he had known, his vision was as detailed and unblinking as it was in his criticism. Yet, uncanny as was his accuracy as a reporter, Lamb was never a journalist. What he wrote as journalism somehow managed to be literature. "In eternity," pointed out Sir Thomas Browne, "there is no distinction of Tenses." This line in the *Religio Medici* was one which, as both a familiar essayist and a magazine critic, Lamb must have hugged to his heart. For him datelines did not exist. He had no interest in news and less sense of it. News, as he saw it, was whatever happened to interest him, however personal or remote. The measure of his ability is that he made it interesting to his contemporaries, and even now makes us feel contemporaneous with it.

As a critic no less than as a man, Lamb lived in a world where watches had stopped. Yet he creates the illusion that they are still ticking. What he was fond of reviewing was not last night's or last week's play but his memories of twenty or thirty years ago. Although this was all a part of his being unable to make present times present to him, it has never prevented him from making times past present to us.

IV. *Lamb as a Critic*

IF Charles Lamb does not belong in the company of the greatest critics, neither do they belong in his. It is not so much that they stride ahead of him as that he elects to amble to one side of them, well off the main thoroughfares. Even in criticism, he is a lonely figure who goes his own way. That the paths of his choice happen to be bypaths is part of the enticement and originality of his approach. He is one of the most satisfying and least pretentious of critics; major in a minor way, though major nonetheless.

Greatness, among other things, is bound to involve scale. Size, spiritual or actual, is part of it. Breadth, width, depth are among its common dimensional attributes. These qualities, in the ordinary heroic sense, were not Lamb's. Perfection, however, is not a matter of size. Although a Borglum may reach the peaks by mutilating them, because he produces bigger works than a Cellini does not mean he is the better artist. It was on the Cellini scale that Lamb worked. In criticism, as in his essays, he was a jeweler, a goblet-fashioner, an unrivaled craftsman in gold and silver. The fact that he was not a titan does not condemn him to being a midget. As a critic, he was an extraordinary artist. His genius as an artist is the reason for his greatness as a critic.

Dryden, Dr. Johnson, Coleridge, Hazlitt, or Shaw, for example, rejoice in a muscularity, a lunge, an intensity, a bigness, or a purpose Lamb does not possess. Yet he possesses charms they cannot claim, perceptions they do not have, and merits which are not theirs. They delve into fundamentals which for him have no interest. They risk complete estimates of a man, a work, or a period which he avoids. They come to their subjects head-on, excelling at large-scale frontal attacks where he excels at minor skirmishes and sudden, fruitful forays at the flanks or behind the lines. Or, convinced that the truth as they have seen it is the whole truth, they can fight lusty battles for causes which leave him unmobilized.

Critically, they and their kind are warriors; male, aggressive, and so magnificent in their energies that they are forces. Lamb is no force. He is only a phenomenon, and a joy. To the embattled realm of opinions he brings his vagaries rather than his convictions, his paradoxes instead of principles. He does not destroy; he re-creates. His critical weapon is a gold miner's sieve, not a battle-ax. He rises to appreciation with the same happy subtle discernment most critics muster for depreciation. He writes less to persuade others than to state for himself what, for the moment, he has been persuaded of. Even his deliberate half-truths are so engagingly advanced by him that, in the reading, they seem preferable to the full truths advanced by others. If Lamb proves little, he almost always proves delightful. In his case, that is enough. Having sought pleasure, he gives it. "It is not in my method," said he, "to inflict pain. I leave that to heaven."

"Criticism," noted Dr. Johnson, "is a study by which men grow important and formidable at very small expense." Lamb had no desire to be either. He disliked "being treated like a grave or respectable character." His sympathy with professional critics was nonexistent. He abhorred all the airs they take on, without the graces, and the way they pride themselves upon being unable to share in the joys of others.

Lamb's attitude toward the theatre was typical of his attitude toward books and paintings. Theatrically he remained in spirit, as in his fondest recollections, a gallery god long after financial ease and his own prominence assured him the best of seats. He could neither understand nor tolerate the "frigid indifference" and "impenetrability" of those who sat in the boxes. Even in the pit he deplored the beginnings of "that accursed critical faculty, which, making a man the judge of his own pleasures, too often constitutes him the executioner of his own and others!"

To Lamb such standoffishness, worse than being incompatible, was downright "vile." Professional critics and reviewers, in his eyes, were "animals." Fastidious, special, and searching as were his tastes, he preferred to identify himself with the *genuine spectators*. By these he had in mind such simple people as a "shopkeeper and his family, whose honest titillations of mirth" could not wait "to take the cue from the sour judging faces about them." In spite of his own inquiring and scholarly spirit, Lamb gave his love to the "uninquiring gratitude" of such spectators. Although with them he mistakenly identified himself, he wrote delectably from an unmistakable capacity for enjoyment which they might well have envied.

Lamb's shortcomings as a critic are self-evident. He does not soar as one of the eagles in a profession more often than not wingless. He hovers like a bee, avid for the taste of honey. Moreover, beelike, he is quick to find it, to linger over it, and to transfer it. He neither intends to be reliable nor pretends to be impartial. He must be read with a caution which comes from understanding him, and from being both able and willing to enter into the game he can play. Since he is truer to his whims than his subject, he is not to be taken literally. He must have foreseen that modern dictionaries would define an opinion as a "judgment based on grounds short of proof." At any rate, he does not bother about being infallible. He writes quite frankly and disarmingly from his prejudices.

He is apt to be fanciful when he seems most dogmatic, or only half in earnest when he appears to be most serious. This aspect of Lamb not only eluded Macaulay but exasperated him. Yet it is the point and pleasure of Elia's defense of that "Utopia of Gallantry" which, as he saw it, was the true setting of Restoration comedy and hence lifted it beyond moral judgment "out of Christendom into the land of cuckoldry." It is no less clear in the famous contention of Lamb, the most ardent of theatre-lovers, that Shakespeare is the playwright whose works are "less calculated for performance on a stage than those of almost any other dramatist whatever."

George Saintsbury, a devoted and discerning "Agnist" if ever there was one, had to admit that, notwithstanding his excellence as a critic, Lamb could be guilty of *capriccio* (a word which Elia, no doubt, would have praised every bit as much as did the professor). This is why Saintsbury insisted Lamb, rather than Leigh Hunt, deserves to be known as the "Ariel of Criticism." Beyond dispute, that is better than being the Caliban.

When he described such critics as belong to the "Occult School," Hazlitt had Lamb in mind. "They discern no beauties but what are concealed from superficial eyes," wrote he, "and overlook all that are obvious to the vulgar part of mankind. . . . If an author is utterly unreadable, they can read him for ever; his intricacies are their delight, his mysteries are their study. . . . They will no more share a book than a mistress with a friend." The charge of occultism, in Lamb's case, is not unfair. It is just in spite of Lamb's affection for the gallery gods. It is part and parcel of his addiction to oddity. Yet, like the affectations of his public style, it is the natural expression of himself.

Lamb's blind spots were many; his tastes more eccentric than catholic. If he rejoiced in his lack of orthodoxy, so should his readers. Any mediocrity can be orthodox. (Most of them are.) Lamb, however, was nothing if not exceptional. Even the historical persons whom he once startled a company of by naming as the people he would most like to meet were unaverage choices. Heading his lists were Pontius Pilate, Sir Thomas Browne, and Dr. Faustus.

In matters literary or artistic he was no less individual. He could discover no merit in *Candide* or *Gil Blas*. As an ardent admirer of Smollett, he was persuaded by Hazlitt, and then only with difficulty, to concede Fielding's superiority. When current authors were being discussed, he talked endlessly of John Donne and Sir Philip Sidney; when others were devouring the Waverley Novels, like as not he was poring over George Wither. If he was allergic to Scott, Byron, and Shelley, he was among the first to recognize Coleridge, Burns, and Wordsworth. His pioneering did not end there. As a critic of painting, his major concern may have been, unfashionably enough by our contemporary standards, the story told. Even so, he was the first to show a proper appreciation for Hogarth and Blake. Moreover, when he writes of their paintings, he so succeeds in using his pen as a brush that he turns painter himself.

Coleridge did not lecture on the early English dramatists,

except for Shakespeare, until 1818. Hazlitt's courses were not given until three years later. Yet it was in 1808 that Lamb published his *Specimens of English Dramatic Poets Who Lived about the Time of Shakespeare*. In them, in spite of the spade-work already done by specialists, Lamb can be said to have made well-read, though unscholarly, Britishers feel for the first time that Marston, Heywood, Webster, Beaumont and Fletcher, Massinger and Ford were writers they *ought* to know. His notes, fragmentary and informal as they are, are among the most personal and revealing of his critical writings. Shaw, being Shaw, could lament Lamb's fondness for these figures as a "literary aberration." He could say he forgave this addiction of Lamb's "as we forgive him his addiction to gin." But most people, including Shavians, would not deny their debt to Lamb because of the way in which he salvaged the beauties of a body of literature which had come to be almost ignored.

No one has written about the theatre with greater warmth or perception than did Lamb about vanished players or the play-houses of his youth. By common consent, owing to common experience, few things are apt to be deader than the review of a forgotten play or a tribute to an actor the reader has neither heard about nor seen. Writing about the stage is usually doomed to be as evanescent as the pleasure or pain which prompted it. Those of us who attempt it professionally know, to our sorrow and chagrin, that what we devote ourselves to doing amounts to tattooing soap bubbles. In spite of its discouragements, this is a process not beyond achievement as is proved by those uncommon, blessed instances when journalism takes on the stature of criticism and criticism that of literature. This happens when the copy read, having lost its immediate or practical usefulness to the reader, somehow survives in time without relying upon news interest, not as a guide to pleasure but as itself a pleasure, self-sustaining and self-contained. It happens when yesterday endures as today and tomorrow.

Lamb joins the proud company of the elect who have been able to pass this test, and to pass it triumphantly. He could put reviewing to his own uses as when, for example, he proposed to Fanny Kelly (with negative results) in a notice of *Rachel*. "What a lass that were to go a gypseying through the world with!" sighed he in the public prints, pretending to quote a mythical neighbor. But, more than putting criticism to his own uses, he could put it to ours.

Bensley, Powel, Munden, Liston, Dodd, and Elliston are truly forgotten men. Except to a stage archivist, their names could not mean less had they been stumbled upon on broken tombstones in an abandoned graveyard. Yet Lamb's writing about them is so lively that not only do they live for us as if we had seen them but we know we are the luckier for having seen them through his eyes. To choose where choice is difficult, Bensley who seizes upon the moment of passion with greatest truth "like a faithful clock never striking before the time— never anticipating, or leading you to anticipate"; Bensley looking, speaking, and moving through the part of Malvolio as an old Castilian nobleman; Bensley keeping back "his intellect as some have had the power to retard their pulsation"; or Bensley allowing "a gleam of understanding" to "appear in a corner of his eye and for lack of fuel go out again" is more than a player described. He is a lesson in comic acting.

The same extension of an assignment, the same complete realization of an opportunity, is shown by Lamb in his notable essays "On the Artificial Comedy of the Last Century" or "On the Tragedies of Shakespeare." In both cases he writes mimetically as a critic should, taking the hint and color from his subject matter. Wycherley or Congreve did not produce prose wittier, more belaced, or of greater sparkle as verbal marquetry than he did when, in playful earnestness, he rose to the defense of their amoralities.

In "Barbara S . . ." Lamb could tell sentimentally, with skillful, hot, forced tears, the one backstage story that has come down to us which Woollcott might have written. To read Lamb, however, on the reasons why Shakespeare's greatest tragedies, in the fullness of their tragic statement, were beyond the posturing, grimacing, and gesturing of actors is to realize the extents to which he could carry theatrical writing. As many have pointed out, Lamb, with his admiration for actors, could of course have taken the other side of the argument with equal felicity. But even Lamb the theatre-lover stood no chance against Lamb the bookman or Lamb the intellectual. As a profound man who doted on the stage, and was more entitled than most to the escapes it offered him, he was too well aware of the theatre's limitations to be limited by them. In a style worthy of his subject he could so enter into Lear's mind that Lear ceased to be a character and became a mortal in agony.

The same Lamb who had abandoned poetry early in his career wrote as a poet when he was at his best as a critic or a correspondent. The stuttering, jesting, smoking, drinking little fellow, valiantly linked to Mary, was little in an abidingly big way. He was big of heart, large of mind, and unique in his endowments. Victim of life though he was, he was never victimized by it. He lived an interior life externally. It was his mind and the abilities out of which he fashioned his style which made his living, on the whole uneventful, eventful for the world no less than for him. Perhaps Pater, another stylist, wrote the best summary of Lamb in these words, "Unoccupied, as he might seem, with great matters, he is in immediate contact with what is real, especially in its caressing littleness, that littleness in which there is much of the whole woeful heart of things, and meets it more than half-way with a perfect understanding of it."

July 4–31, 1948

Spice of Life

*THE STRANGE experience of en-
countering years afterward a teacher
from one's youth, and feeling somehow
older than he and yet as young as one
once was.*

꙰꙰꙰꙰꙰꙰꙰꙰꙰꙰꙰꙰꙰꙰꙰꙰꙰꙰꙰꙰꙰꙰꙰꙰꙰꙰꙰꙰꙰꙰

Out of the Past

HIS NAME, printed on a closed door, caught my eye as I
hurried down the corridor to the office of the faculty
member who was to guide me to my morning lecture.

Let's say the black letters spelled "Ben Emery." They did
not, but that is as near to what they did spell as I care to come.
He would hate me if I used his real name. He was always the
shyest, the most retiring of men.

I looked twice at those letters on the door. I looked at them
with disbelief and excitement. It must be some other Ben
Emery, thought I. It couldn't be mine. It couldn't be the one
who taught me English in prep school. That was thirty years
ago, and I had not heard of him or seen him since. Still it was
worth taking the chance.

"Do you happen to know if the Ben Emery whose office is
down the hall ever taught at a prep school in New Jersey?" I
asked the man who was to guide me around this huge Mid-
western campus.

"I don't think he did. At least I never heard of it."

This did not dash my hopes. It raised them. Such silence
about himself sounded like the Ben Emery I remembered.

"Would you mind asking him?" I inquired. "Because, if he did teach there, I had the good luck to be one of his students."

Left alone, I was almost sorry I had made such a request. I very much wanted to see Ben Emery again. Over the years I had thought of him many times when trying to write or when enjoying this book or that. There were things I wanted to thank him for. But this business of stirring up memories, of confronting the past with the present or the present with the past, is perilous to say the least. Conrad in quest of his youth is Conrad in quest of what cannot be found, as Leonard Merrick and all the rest of us have discovered to our sorrow.

Two voices reached me from the hall. One of them, though very dry and firm, was nonetheless gentle. Unmistakably it was Ben Emery's. I had heard it too often in class, or when as housemaster he would assemble his dozen or so charges in his room at bedtime to read to us, not to recognize it at once. It had not changed a bit.

I wondered, of course, what he would look like. Thirty years for mortals are not merely three decades. They are the equivalent of several geological periods. Ben Emery had always seemed old to me. Not venerable, mind you. Not that at all. Just ageless old; just grown-up old; just old enough to be addressed unquestioningly as "sir" by those of us who were his pupils.

One trouble with seeing people you have not seen for a long time is that they also get to see you. Suddenly, instead of imagining what Ben Emery would look like, I began to wonder what I would look like to him. I had been eighteen when he last saw me. Or was it seventeen? My hair was then red. Not only red and Airedale bushy but complete. My face . . . .

Before I could go further with this dismaying inventory of change and erosion, Ben Emery was in the room.

I would have known him anywhere. Why not? Although there was more of him, more to his face, more to his jowls, and more to his waistline than I remembered, he was the same tense little man he had been thirty years ago. His eyes were the same china-blue, capable of brightening or fading according to his interest. Though rounder, his face, with its small nose and firm but kind mouth, remained moonlit in its pallor. His suit was as rumpled as ever, his colored shirt as wrinkled, and his dark tie gathered into as clumsy a knot. His forehead, to be sure, was a little higher, but his plentiful hair was still sandy. I noticed that at once, with envy.

"Sir," I surprised myself by saying, "Mr. Emery, sir," as I scrambled to my feet. "It's good to see you again. I couldn't believe it would be. . . ."

"So it's you," said he, shaking my hand and disguising by word and manner that he had to look hard to rediscover in me the me he had known. "After all these years." What was passing through his mind, I do not know. He was considerate enough to mask the shock. I know what I was thinking. It was that those who do not teach fail to be protected against the years by that kind cottoning—is it contact with youth?—which can keep teachers young.

We plunged with some embarrassment into talk. Ten minutes is less than a thimble into which to try to pour the accumulation of thirty years. We had our stabs at "Do-you-remember?" We had our quick interchanges of "What-has-become-of-Peter?" and "Have-you-seen-Jim-or-Henry-lately?"

Pleasant as they were, these racing minutes were not easy. I found myself forgetting my age intermittently and, quite foolishly, feeling as if I were eighteen. That is the effect teachers have on us. Neither they nor we can at once outgrow that past relationship. I made my valiant, even my ostentatious, attempts to do so. Or rather my subconscious did. Once I startled myself by calling him "Ben." Right out. Just like that. Right to his face. He did not bat an eye.

The age business bothered me. If this moment I felt young again, at the next I felt old; infinitely older than Ben Emery. Not in years. Years had long since ceased to matter. In exposure; in the lack of that protection from life—indeed, of that insulation against it—which teachers enjoy and campuses create.

In the presence of a third person, it was hard to put into words the gratitude I felt. It would have been hard to thank Ben Emery had we been alone. I wanted to. I tried to—stammeringly. Yet each time I attempted to do so, he pinkened, just the way he used to pinken when he was about to send a boy out of the room, and changed the subject.

Among many things, quickly touched upon, he told me he had given up teaching composition and literature, and moved into some cactus-dry field of research where he was happy. Far from making me happy, this news saddened me. It saddened me no end. I would have as soon heard that Heifetz, because of crushing his hands in an accident, had been forced to give up the violin.

When, as adults, we think of the "great" teachers we have had, we are apt to think, if we are college graduates, of the flamboyant, the full-fledged, figures who dazzled and delighted us by speaking to us for the first time as adults in our college days. If Harvard-bred, and of a fortunate vintage, we have a Kittredge, a Copeland, a Baker, a Lowes, or a Bliss Perry as our ideal. Properly so. Because the flame, however different, blazed in each of these extraordinary men.

Our memories, like our standards, tend to be quite different when it comes to those who have taught us in grade school, high school, or prep school. We have a way of taking them for granted because all too many of them took us and their subjects for granted. We remember the names, the looks, even the personalities of the best of them. And sometimes even the special affection we felt for them, whether it was hopeless puppy love or frank hero worship. The stricter they were, the harder they worked us, the more in retrospect we respect them. By then our escape from their discipline has made this possible. Yet, unless they were exceptional, we are inclined to forget precisely what it was that they taught us. We forget this just as we overlook the difficulties of the teaching assignment they faced.

Theirs is, and always has been, a harder task than that confronting the professors. They have to housebreak us while filling our minds; be policemen and baby-sitters no less than prophets; and second parents, doing all those things for us that parents never get around to doing, at the same time that they function as quite independent guides and stimulants.

Our limitations are their concern; our immaturity is the problem which they, as mature people, cannot overlook and must live with. We come to them too young to enable them to shine as titans. Instead of permitting their minds to gallop ahead, they must hold them in check as pacemakers for our own. They must speak our language rather than indulge to the full in theirs. Their need for patience is greater than their need for scholarship. They are the friends of youth whose mission it is to help us outgrow it. A contagious curiosity or an igniting enthusiasm serves them better in the school-room than all the pyrotechnics, eloquence, wit, and learning which are the staples of those figures who stand out on the campus.

When I knew and studied under Ben Emery, he was a secondary-school teacher who relished what he was doing. His quietness was part of his force. Plainly he felt more than he could phrase. He loved literature with an affection which was epidemic. He knew its beauties and had the carrying gift, that gift so essential to teachers and so uncommon among them. What he cared for, he could make others care for. He was not frightened by the best. Classics for him were simply good books which had never ceased to be contemporary, though written in an earlier age.

He was a well-read man when I studied with him, and not, I suppose, a learned one. His knowledge was not of that juice-less, bloodless, irrelevant, and dusty variety which some scholars acquire out of professional need, and others because by temperament and taste they are themselves juiceless, bloodless, irrelevant, and dusty. He did not read to produce unreadable treatises; he read to enjoy.

An English sentence was something he respected. He treated it as grammar when duty compelled him to break it down into its component parts. Yet he preferred to deal with a sentence as music; a music which with him was instinctive since he possessed an unusually fine ear. No doubt much of what he taught us was as elementary as we deserved and as it had to be. His teaching, however, was blessed with those rare, those needed, virtues. It was eye-opening, ear-quickening, vista-exploring, and exciting. I know it was for me.

To have Ben Emery lost to composition, lost to the history of literature, and devoted to some side-alley subject, seems to me a casualty in a profession where such casualties are costly. That he is good at his new and very specialized subject, I do not doubt. But the gift to teach the living stuffs of English—indeed, the gift to teach at all—is as exceptional as all other creative gifts.

The failure of education to "take" among so many of those exposed to it in this country is a proof of this. In all too many of our colleges, we pride ourselves on the numbers turned out rather than upon what has been taken in. The Ford body may be produced on the assembly belt, but the quickened mind cannot be. Although without dispute teachers deserve more pay, more pay will not necessarily produce good teachers. Teaching to be good needs more teachers like the Ben Emery I remember. Truly he did not teach to live but lived to teach, and in the process added to the living of those he taught.

February 12, 1949

*WHAT JUNE, July, and August can
do to city husbands, accustomed in other
months to having homes and families.*

⥣⥤⥣⥤⥣⥤⥣⥤⥣⥤⥣⥤⥣⥤⥣⥤⥣⥤⥣⥤⥣⥤⥣⥤⥣⥤⥣⥤⥣⥤

Summer Bachelor

A HUSBAND should not lead a double life. Even people who are not moralists know this. Nor should he lead a single one. Yet summer, which is supposed to be the year's Sabbath, forces both of these upon him. At least it does when his wife and family have gone to the country and he is left behind in the city, a bachelor between week ends or until he takes such a vacation as his budget and his bosses permit.

Come June, July, and August, and a husband becomes a displaced person. His town address remains the same. To all intents and purposes he is at home. But what happens to nature when summer greens the landscape does not represent a greater change from winter's bareness than does that wintry blight which overtakes a husband's home in summer.

The cuckoo's singing loud is not the only proof that "sumer is icumen in." Let May steal up on the calendar, and on one unannounced day, between a husband's going downtown and coming back again, his apartment becomes alien territory. The slip covers come out of hibernation. Suddenly the gray furniture in the living room goes green or white. Without warning the pictures on the wall turn into sheeted Klansmen. The draperies are stripped from the windows. Newspapers, neatly folded, obscure the bookshelves. The lamp shades are shrouded in what resembles plastic raincoats. The silver disappears from the dining room. Knickknacks vanish throughout the apartment. Comforters and blankets are hidden beyond finding. Closets, once accessible, are locked against intruders. The floors in every room are left naked, robbed of their rugs. And these rugs, so soft and silencing, are rolled into long and cheerless obstacles at one side of the front hall. What remains is not rubble, but neither is it home.

Naturally the husband cries, "Good Lord!" wondering if his key has opened the right door. Naturally, with a man's dislike of change and genius for forgetting, he demands, "What's happened?"

"Summer, dear," is the changeless answer.

"But why?"

"So much cooler, dear," is the invariable reply. Every female visitor applauds the transformation as surely as every male visitor shudders at it. But all protests against it are in vain.

"You'll like it," the husband is told. "You'll see."

And see he does, even if he never comes to like it.

Why should he? For three long months, whenever he is in town, he camps out—indoors. For three long months he wanders around his domicile like a privileged night watchman in a storage warehouse. He dwells in a mausoleum. He is assigned to active duty with the mothball fleet.

He does not have the run of the whole apartment. He lives his hermit's life on little atolls of pseudo domesticity in a sea of loneliness. He walks past doors shut on empty rooms which are not sealed but "closed," their blinds drawn against the brightening sun. He returns from sea breezes or mountain air to inhale camphor and tar-paper bags, the more redolent because of the city's heat. Nothing looks the same. Nothing is the same. If he would enter a home that is not a victim of the summer, he must dine at the apartment of a year-round bachelor who knows nothing about housekeeping and whose flat, therefore, is undisturbed by the summer's dislocations.

"Those whom God hath joined together, let no man put asunder," says the marriage service. But summer is not a man. It is a season. As such, it does not hesitate to uncouple the happily married and separate the *pater* from his *familias*. It is no respecter of persons or entities. Perhaps inevitably, it holds all fireside units in the warmest contempt. Not only its inclinations but its sympathies are feminist. It coerces the most independent of men into the realization that they are dependents. One of its heaviest and most reliable crops is the gratitude which each year it makes males feel for the women who give order to their lives.

The month of May, with its metamorphoses, is only a storm warning of what is to follow. As a wife explains the new routine on the eve of her departure with the children, it sounds simple enough.

"I've made all the arrangements," she says. "You can get breakfast. That's easy. It would be cooler, I think, don't you, to eat it on a tray by an open window in the living room? You'll have complete peace while reading your mail and the morning papers. A maid, an awfully good maid and a nice person, will come at nine each day. Don't forget her name is Elizabeth. She'll wash the dishes, dust, make your bed, and scrub the bathroom. The laundress will be here every Wednesday. All you have to do is be sure to empty the hamper on Tuesday night, and remember to pay her. A lot of your friends will be in town. I'm sure they'll ask you out for dinner from time to time. Anyway you can always go down to the club or to a nice air-cooled restaurant. I'll bet you have a grand time."

Getting breakfast is easy. In fact it is fun. No coffee is as good as the coffee you make for yourself. To squeeze an orange, boil two eggs, put two pieces of bread in an automatic toaster are not acts requiring the magic of a Ragueneau or a Brillat-Savarin. The process is quickly systematized. Its carrying out becomes as unconscious as tying a shoe. The results taste the better for the childish pride involved. They acquire the merits, known to mountain climbers, of the earned view.

Reading a newspaper—really making a meal on its columns, devouring the most minuscule stories no less than the front-page reports of that misbehavior which at any time is largely current history—has its advantages. The news, however, being what it is, give me interruptions any day. News, good or bad, needs sharing and the interchange of reactions and opinions to take on its full flavor. Without such immediate pooling it is incomplete and often strangely flat. Besides, one wants to be reminded that what the headlines insist is true of humans is not the only truth about them.

Breakfast offers no problem. Neither does lunch or dinner on those days when you happen to be working at home and are functioning as your own cook and dishwasher. Your regular cook, be it instantly confessed, rises higher than yeast in your esteem. How you come to respect her talents and her patience, and marvel not only at her gift for producing peas unscorched and potatoes baked through but for timing her efforts so that the meat and vegetables are ready simultaneously and do not appear like installments of a serial in a magazine! How soon, too, you dispense with such accessories as cream and water pitchers or butter plates and, with the washing up in mind, reduce eating to a one-plate menu! Quite humanly, your ultimate inclination is to feed out of the Frigidaire and nibble from the breadbox.

Those luncheons and dinners downtown at the club or at those chilled restaurants with other deserted husbands are agreeable while they last. But the fact that they will end, that they are only interludes and jail-breaks, hangs over them, Damoclean-wise. Regardless of the front they may put up, those other husbands are in the same fraternity. They are lost souls, widowed by the calendar. They also live in, and must return to, homes which are mere locust shells of themselves. They, too, are waiting for the time to come when they can push their way onto those Friday afternoon trains. They, too, wonder what they can do with their evenings.

Gertrude Stein's Saint Theresa in *Four Saints in Three Acts* eked out what, at best, must have been an uncomfortable existence. She, you may recall, was in a state of constant suspension. She was described as being "half indoors, half out of doors." The position occupied by summer bachelors is no less acrobatic and no more easeful. Such a position has its effects upon these bachelors. As men, they are quite different from what they were, and will be again, between September and May. Plainly, they are mariners who have lost not only their compasses but their ships.

No places are emptier than those which, having housed many, house one. Every male singled by the summer dreads the going home to that apartment of his to which, when it was not his alone, he looked forward to returning. If anything, the slip covers, the rolled rugs, the covered pictures, and the closed doors are more dispiriting by night than by day.

"My wife's gone to the country, hooray!" the old song used to proclaim. General McAuliffe, at the Battle of the Bulge, had the proper reply to that hooray. A summer bachelor can only say "Hooray!" when he has gone to the country, too. One thing, at least, the summer months teach him. His home is not where his house is. It is where his family is.

August 27, 1949

*THE COMPULSIONS which drive
us to use our tongues, with special attention to the attributes which distinguish
conversation from talk.*

Conversation Piece

IN HIS course on Carlyle—a memorable one—Bliss Perry used to take off his glasses, hold them in his left hand, and lean forward on the desk as he told his story. Obviously, he relished it. Obviously, so did all his hearers at Harvard who had New England blood in their veins. It was only those of us who hailed from the loquacious South who found it uncomfortable, if not unbearable.

The yarn in question had to do with an evening—supposedly a wonderful, friendly evening—that Carlyle, not always a friendly man, once spent in Tennyson's company. As I recall it, the two men had descended to the kitchen after dinner, there to sit alone before the large open fire and smoke their pipes. How long they sat puffing away, each pursuing his own thoughts, I do not now remember. But I do know (this is what chilled the blood of Southerners as much as it warmed the hearts of Northerners) that they sat in *silence* for many blissful hours. In utter and undisturbed silence. When the time came for him to leave, Tennyson rose, emptied his pipe in the grate, and said to Carlyle (or was it the other way around?), "Thank you. I don't know when I have had such a happy evening."

To Bliss Perry this speechless communion was the finest proof of friendship imaginable. It was the ultimate compliment that each man could bestow on the other. It meant that the understanding between them was beyond the need of words. It implied a fellowship capable of finding pleasure in mere propinquity. It made silence eloquent.

As a person not ungiven to words, I could, and can, comprehend the point academically. But what even now I cannot understand is why Tennyson, Alfred Lord, should have bothered to leave his home that night and seek out the company of a friend if talk was what he wanted to avoid. Certainly, had such muteness been the ideal communication of all the articulate people from Socrates to Stalin, upon whom we eavesdrop in *The Book of Great Conversations*,* Louis Biancolli would have had no book. That is, of course, unless the voids created on page after page by these golden silences were filled in by some such words as "Compliments of a Friend."

We would have lost much if Michelangelo; Rousseau; Voltaire; Dr. Johnson, that grand old bully with the language; Napoleon; Goethe; Hazlitt; Sainte-Beuve, Flaubert, Gautier, and those other wine-lit but sunbright minds that dined at Magny's; Walt Whitman and his birthday-greeters; Shaw; Chesterton; Wells; and even testy old Carlyle himself had always mistaken mum for the word. We would have lost much, too, if no one with a long memory or a good imagination and Boswellian inclinations had been on hand to write down what these men had said soon after they had said it. Yes, and ours would also have been a real loss had not Mr.

* *The Book of Great Conversations*. Edited by Louis Biancolli. New York: Simon & Schuster. 1948. 570 pp. $5.

Biancolli, with infinite patience and with true skill at setting
the scene and characterizing his people, assembled from an
incredible number of sources these fascinating records of meetings when tongues and minds were exercised and words flew.
Among other things we would have lost a stimulating reminder of how different conversation is from talk.

All of us, who can, talk—even when we don't listen. And
most of us talk too much. The impulse to talk is what strong
men surrender to when they no longer have the strength to
remain silent. What steam is to the kettle, talk is to the average
mortal, the chief difference being that men and women do
not have to come to the boil before releasing it. We talk out
of loneliness, curiosity, or because of emotions, observations, or
recollections which automatically well up into words. We talk
to while away the time. We talk because our spirits demand
constant ventilation. We talk because good talk is one of the
most delicious of man's pleasures, and even poor talk is one
of the most satisfying of his releases.

We talk for a thousand reasons. We talk to transact business, to find our way, to gain the importance that comes from
being the first to carry bad tidings, to ferret out the news of
our friends and tell them ours, to express sympathy or re-
ceive it, to advertise our operations, to salute the weather, to
indulge in gossip, personal or political, or to repeat a joke.
Mainly, however, we talk from the deep-seated, age-old human need to talk. That is one reason why some people, even
when they are alone, can be heard mumbling away to themselves, sadly bereft of listeners but happily free therefore of
the fear of interruption.

Yet much as we use our tongues, the mere fact that we
keep them wagging does not mean that we often achieve

conversation. Mr. Biancolli's absorbing anthology makes this clear. So does the dictionary. It is mercilessly precise on this point. It insists that to speak is to articulate sounds, how-ever disconnected. The act of talking represents a step for-ward. It implies connected colloquy or discourse. Conversa-tion is on a still higher, hence rarer, echelon. "No, sir," grumbled Dr. Johnson, "we had *talk* enough but no *conversa-tion;* there was nothing discussed." Each word in the defi-nition of conversation bears not only underscoring but re-membering. For to converse is to have an *interchange* in talk of *thoughts* and *opinions.* This sounds at once the death knell of those monologists to whom speech is a monopoly rather than a coöperative enterprise. It also exiles, as exile it should, all those whose tongues can be industrious while their minds are quiescent.

"What's that you were saying?" the detective asked Gracie Allen in *The Gracie Allen Murder Case* when, in the midst of her prattle, she had dropped some important clues. "How should I know?" was her reply. "I wasn't listening." This is at once the limitation and the relaxation of most talk. This is why, quite properly, it rejoices in the name of small talk. The source of its universal popularity is that it demands no concentration and requires no effort. Frankly, proudly, pleas-antly, it is a proof of amiability rather than an exercise of the intellect. In leaving the mind untouched, its skill can be enormous. The maintenance of sound is its chief con-cern.

It shoots the breeze; it chews the rag. It is as contented as the chirping of crickets and as thoughtless as the buzzing of bees. The manner and matter of its droning are unimportant. The main thing is to have it continuous. Because small talk,

when it is good, admits no such hiatuses as the pause that
refreshes. It lacks both the courage and the will to pause. Deem-
ing silence a sign of self-consciousness, fatigue, or indifference, it feels about a pause as nature does about a vacuum. "I
must preach and preach and preach," confessed the prophetic
figure in Mr. Shaw's *Too True To Be Good,* "no matter how
late the hour and how short the day, no matter whether I
have nothing to say." Small talkers (and everyone is that
most of the time) are under the same happy compulsion to
keep on small talking. We delight in trivia; we relish the
unimportant; personalities are our substitutes for ideas; silence is our foe. Words, any words, serve us so long as their
flow is constant. Speech for us is a reflex, not an effort. It is
breathing wired for sound. Voices, our own and others', provide the sweetest music we know.

But, as Mr. Biancolli's great conversationalists demonstrate, talk—large or small—is not conversation. The conversationalist, whether he is Dr. Johnson, Goethe, Wilde,
Napoleon, or Shaw, not only expects others to listen to what
he is saying but listens to it himself. He is, so to speak, intel-
lectually pink-coated and mounted and in full cry after an
idea.

He does not have to be serious. Most frequently, he is at
his best when he is not entirely sober. If his tongue is loosened,
so are his mind and spirit. The two of them are liberated in
conjunction; fired by the stimulation of the right company,
the right evening, the right mood, the appealing subject, the
moment's quickening challenge. The potative approach to
such an evening does not hurt. Wine has been known to
help; even hemlock has produced memorable words. Yet, if

small talk can sound like conversation late at night, glass in hand, a sure test of true conversation is that its champagne is not flat the morning after or when decanted in print.

The conversationalist is bound to think quickly. He thrives on instantaneous combustion. If he is among equals, he must be as prepared for the parry as he is for the thrust. He must interrupt and welcome interruptions. These are the joy, the ignition, the life of a conversation. A good conversation (see the Goncourts' accounts of the Magny dinners, or Hazlitt's delectable and justly famous report of a Thursday at the Lambs') is a long series of contributive interruptions. They are, however, interruptions which add to the subject discussed rather than lead away from it.

Since wit is his weapon and ideas are his interest, the conversationalist must use words accurately. This is where language comes into the picture. This is what Madame de Staël had in mind when she contrasted French and German as conversational releases. "No language," wrote she, "is more clear and rapid [than the French], none indicates more lightly or explains more clearly what you wish to say." German, she insisted, accommodates itself much less easily to the precision and rapidity of conversation. "By the very nature of its grammatical construction, the sense is usually not understood until the end of the sentence. Thus the pleasure of interrupting, which, in France, gives so much animation to discussion, and forces one to utter so quickly all that is of importance to be heard, this pleasure cannot exist in Germany. . . . Every man must be left in possession of all the space he chooses to demand." Although Madame de Staël admitted that this might be "more civil" and "better for the purpose of getting to the bottom of things," she deplored the liveliness thus sacrificed.

How reliable the transcripts of these conversations are that Mr. Biancolli permits us to enjoy, there is no way of knowing. Unquestionably, some of them are as deliberately rouged as Laurence Housman's reconstruction, many years afterward, of a dinner with Oscar Wilde in Paris; or as suspect as the account of Napoleon's family reunion in the Tuileries on the eve of his coronation. Even so, the essence and spirit of most of Mr. Biancolli's conversationalists are amazingly present. It is too bad that their facial expressions, gestures, and the tones of their voices could not be reproduced along with their words, since all of these are part and parcel of good talk. They are the scenery, the costumes, and the lighting of colloquy.

For those of us who might like to cease being talkers and become conversationalists, there are several lessons to be learned from Mr. Biancolli's volume. First of all, it is interesting to note the restraint with which the men and women whose speech is worthy of recording have made use of the anecdote. Though the mainstay of after-dinner speakers and traveling salesmen, and often a delight, the anecdote when used as an end in itself is fatal to conversation. Unless it illustrates a point, it derails the main idea. It can, of course, be both apt and amusing. If, however, it is only amusing, it is an irrelevance to which the true conversationalists have refused to surrender. One trouble with the anecdote is that too often it smacks of being a dusty piece exhumed from one's repertoire. Hence it lacks the improvisation essential to conversation.

Another thing. Precious few of Mr. Biancolli's verbalists waste much time talking of their families, stirring memories, or indulging in quotations. They seem to have known without being told that the business of a real conversationalist is not to remember what someone else has said but to say something which someone else will want to remember.

February 19, 1949

*THE "Boys in Blue," meeting as cen-
tenarians for the last encampment of
the Grand Army of the Republic, give
younger veterans food for thought.*

Old Glory

THEY HAVE long since met and gone home, those
wizened reminders of the past who were still able to
travel. The youngest of them was a mere stripling of one
hundred; the most venerable was eight years his senior. From
Portland, Oregon; from Duluth and Pontiac; from Princeton, Kentucky; from Long Beach, California, and Rochester,
New York; by plane, train, or automobile these veterans of
long marches and decisive battles in the Brothers' War had
arrived in Indianapolis, there to be met by trained nurses, by
Red Cross station wagons, and wheelchairs.

Ten more of their comrades-in-arms, who had lived through
and outlived so much history, were still alive. At least they
were still breathing. They, however, were too frail to travel
and face the fatigues of this, the G.A.R.'s last encampment.
The wearied and the aging mind being as relinquishing as it
is, perhaps these ten survivors who could not make the trip
were too frail even to distinguish between Shiloh and Antie-
tam, Vicksburg and Lookout Mountain, those names which
for decades had been at once the milestones and the pivots in
their thinking.

The six who did meet must have felt the loneliness which

progresses geometrically with the mounting years. They must also have been aware of many other changes, although one hopes not too many. In 1890 the G.A.R. had numbered 400,000. For them that had been a big year, comparable to the kind of bumper year the American Legion was celebrating in Philadelphia at the very moment when these six old men were holding their invalids' bivouac in Indianapolis.

Did President Truman, unable to find the time to lay the cornerstone for the U.N.'s new building, discover his schedule was sufficiently free for him to address the Legionnaires in 1949? President Benjamin Harrison in 1890 had traveled all the way to Boston to speak to the G.A.R. Numbers count in a democracy. Seventy-five thousand Legionnaires, veterans of two wars, young men and oldish and still able to get to the polls, had marched by the reviewing stand this August in the City of Brotherly Love. In Indianapolis it was different. What had once been an army—the Grand Army of the Republic— had now shrunk to two squads of very tired, very feeble, very old fellows. From these two squads only a half dozen could be mustered who remained able to march—in wheelchairs.

One of these was a Negro. Born a slave one hundred and five years ago, he had run away from his master to fight at Vicksburg. This was his first encampment. Although blind now, he liked it so much he hoped there would be another. Two others, including the commander in chief, were of a different opinion. They felt "the boys should stay home hereafter and take care of themselves." The commander in chief had his own personal and very human reason for feeling this should be their final reunion. Age apparently does not wither vanity. It leaves pride unscathed. The commander in chief wanted the honor of being the last to bear that title. But there were others who had their eyes on the office. The senior vice commander was one of these. He was the next in line of succession. At one hundred and two he coveted the same honor.

On the first day of their three-day session at the Claypool Hotel, the six old men had discussed such questions amiably. They had exchanged views with the aid of amplifiers and a portable microphone, since all of them were deaf. The arguments pro and con had never become heated. The talkers tired too easily for that. The commander in chief had called for a "yea" or "nay" vote for permanent adjournment. Six quivering voices, broken by age and emotion, were reported to have murmured "yea." "I close this last meeting of the Grand Army of the Republic," said the commander in chief. And that was that—the closing not only of a meeting but of a great page in history.

Before this vote had been taken, the senior vice-commander had asked a very human question. "Commander," he had said, "can I hold the gavel just a little while?" "Sure enough," had been the reply, and for a few minutes the vice-commander had fondled it in his wrinkled hands and then, smiling, given it back.

Another veteran had also spoken. The oldest member present, the ex-soldier whose years number one hundred and eight had bent forward in his dark blue uniform to say a few words. In a quavering voice he had confessed his hope had been that the final encampment of the G.A.R. might be a joint meeting in Washington with the last survivors of the United Confederate Veterans. "It is just a suggestion," he had said. "I know it can never be, but I have lived in the hope that we might see it some day, to prove to the world that we are united states."

Some of the Legionnaires in Philadelphia, between drinks, parades, and business sessions, must have stolen glances at the newspaper stories about the G.A.R. encampment. Some of the vigorous young MP's assigned to pushing these old soldiers in their wheelchairs through the crowds in Indianapolis must have looked at their charges—and wondered. Some of the nonjoining veterans of the Spanish-American War, the Mexican Border incident, World War I, and World War II must, in the freedom of their civilian lives, have read their newspapers and smiled at first, as smile we will at age which is abnormal and warriors who have ceased to be warlike. Then suddenly they must have stopped smiling. For those stories and those pictures out of Indianapolis were at once ridiculous and sobering, ironic and pathetic, and frightening if for no other reason than the hints of prophecy they offered.

"You are me forty years from now," cried Anna to Marthy, the frowsy old woman in O'Neill's *Anna Christie*. All of us pass daily, without recognizing them, older people whose presents are forecasts of what our futures will be like, if only we last to their age. We seldom see ourselves in these passers-by. We do not want to. We live nourished by the illusion that each of us is somehow different. The repeated pattern, being an uncomfortable idea, is something we reject.

The young men to whom Anzio, Iwo Jima, or Normandy are real, personal, and everlasting names have as hard a time believing in the reality and closeness of Château-Thierry and Belleau Wood as their fathers have in comprehending the nearness and actuality of Gettysburg and Chickamauga to those ancients who assembled in Indianapolis. Remember, the oldest of these gray old men was twenty-four when Grant and Lee met at Appomattox, and the youngest a green sixteen. As they grew up, they must have tired of hearing tall tales of Buena Vista and Chapultepec, and a heavy mist must by then have settled on the battles of Lake Erie and New Orleans. The first person lends life to a story, but history heard or read is never the same as history lived. Other people's adventures are bound to lack for us the vividness of our own. Experience, after all, and tragically, is an untransferable commodity.

In their youth these participants in the Civil War could have talked with palsied centenarians who had fought with Washington. (This is the measure of how young our country is.) If they did happen to do so, they must have found it as impossible to see ragged Continentals in the eroded faces at which they looked as we found it impossible to see "Boys in Blue" in the faces of those six G.A.R.'s photographed at their final meeting. From the watch fires of a hundred circling camps to wheelchairs and trained nurses in the Claypool Hotel is more than a sea change.

In a famous paragraph, written when Mrs. Siddons had been unwise enough to come out of retirement and act again, Hazlitt wrote: "Players should be immortal, if their own wishes or ours could make them so; but they are not. They not only die like other people, but like other people they cease to be young, they are no longer themselves, even while living. Their health, strength, beauty, voice, fail them; nor can they, without these advantages, perform the same feats, or command the same applause that they did when possessed of them. It is the common lot: players are only *not* exempt from it."

It is the common lot indeed, and from it veterans also enjoy no exemption. Although they may have volunteered during a war, none of them can escape being drafted by Time. They come home from combat full of youth and impatience with the old, only to grow old themselves. With the passing years they cease to look their words. Their bodies age, sag, soften, fatten, or shrink. They contradict what they have to say and what is said about them.

Where once these men of action were capable of scaling walls, charging up hills, or trudging through miles of mud, they dwindle into men of inaction, no longer able to climb stairs. Their rifles are replaced by canes. Their eyes ultimately fail them; their hearing goes. If only they live long enough, the final Ages of Man overtake them. They may find inner strength and abiding satisfaction in the knowledge that they have had their St. Crispin's day. But should they follow the warlike Harry's counsel and be so foolhardy and so tiresome as to strip their sleeves and show their scars on each anniversary of their big moment, they would discover to their humiliation that their arms are no longer what they were and that their neighbors were running from them.

No one has ever written better about the returned soldiers' fate than Dixon Wecter in his fascinating *When Johnny Comes Marching Home.* From Yorktown to V-J Day, the repeated pattern has certainly been present in all our hours of demobilization. We have no monopoly on it. It must be as old as the history of conflict; as familiar to the troops of Epaminondas as to those of Grant or Eisenhower. The hero soon ceases to be a hero in the public mind and, when the need for him has vanished, little by little he turns into a bore.

When long ago the news of Appomattox reached them, the six old men in Indianapolis must have thought everything was over but the shouting. They could not have guessed how quickly the shouting would be over, too. It always dies down with merciless swiftness. Before all uniforms can be exchanged for civilian clothes, the welcoming debutantes and hostesses at the stations have disappeared and the service clubs have disbanded. *Tommy Atkins*, more than being a complaint written in cockney, is a definitive history of both the soldier and the public everywhere in war and peace.

As Mr. Wecter makes clear, the time comes inevitably when the job hunter, who once would have been asked for his war record, begins to conceal it. All too soon, instead of winning him a position, such a record loses him one by advertising his age. It dates him. Worse than that, if he is cursed with undue longevity, it stamps him as out of date. If he lives too long, he becomes something of a joke; poignant because helpless, touching as a reminder, gallant as a symbol, but laughable as an anachronism.

This is cruel. This is shocking. This is lamentable. This is the ultimate in ingratitude. Yet it is inescapable. And perhaps not without its signs of health. The inrushes of the present in every period are so insistent and confusing that no people could be expected to live in the past. The veteran who makes a career of being a veteran is not an endearing figure. We say too much about what the country owes us and never enough about what we owe the country. The true Welfare State is that in which citizens, instead of assuming that they will be subsidized, take it for granted that they must do everything in their power for the nation's welfare. It would consist of more givers than takers; be made up of the prideful, not the prideless. It would be a country of self-reliant individuals, not dependent groups; of producers rather than extractors.

At moments of danger, military service is an obligation which, when discharged, should not be converted into a profession. If one tires of the reminders of war, it is because one is anxious to get on with the fulfillments of peace. Time marches forward far faster than the fastest troops advancing into battle. Those ever-ready replacements, who are the young, are forever pushing to the front. In the relay race of history, the torch is passed so quickly from older to younger hands that no one ever sees it being passed.

Even the youngest and least reflective of the Legionnaires who met in Philadelphia, if they followed the story of the G.A.R.'s final encampment, must have sensed without pleasure that they too, due to the calendar's inexorability, will someday be condemned to the same kind of shrunken farewell. No doubt, these young Legionnaires were not downed for long by the thought. It is difficult to identify yesterday's sorrows with tomorrow's. Moreover, all things considered, including the urgencies of today's action, it is just as well that people have no inclination to do so.

"Never send to know for whom the bell tolls; it tolls for thee." Life would be insupportable, in fact it would be already death, if we squandered our time cupping our hands to hear that bell. For the G.A.R. it has finished tolling.

September 24, 1949

THE QUAINT American belief that there must be a book to explain every subject, and a new volume on etiquette which will make Emily Post to look to her fourchettes.

R.S.V.P.

"SOMEWHERE there must be a book that tells all about it, where I could go to straighten it out in my mind. But I don't know where the book is, and maybe I couldn't read it if I found it!"

It wasn't a boy anxious to learn how to sail a boat or fly a kite who uttered this lament. Neither was it an urban dowager turned gardener at her newly acquired country place. Nor, for that matter, was it an office-bound older man, facing at last the pleasures of a vacation out-of-doors and hence needing to rediscover golf or fishing.

No, it was a President of the United States, a President speaking right at the White House. As a matter of cold and poignant fact, it was Warren Gamaliel Harding. It was Harding lamenting his lot as Chief Executive, Harding harassed by the cares of high office. It was the same Harding who, in the same setting, could cry, "My God, but this is a hell of a place for a man like me to be!"; the identical Harding who could wail, "My God-damn friends, they're the ones that keep me walking the floor nights!" It was Harding, William Allen White tells

· 118 ·

us in his *Autobiography,* wondering what he should do when he had to take a position on an important tax bill.

The belief that somewhere a book is always to be found which will tell us what we should do or think under any and every circumstance may be both laughable and touching when voiced by a supposed leader. Yet such confidence is undeniably American. In the instance of Mr. Harding it might almost be cited as a proof of his "normalcy."

Among the books certain to be secretly consulted or even openly displayed by all sorts of perplexed Americans during the coming years is a fat volume recently issued by Simon & Schuster. The questions to which it supplies ready answers on page after page may be less momentous than were those which agitated Harding. They can, however, be equally embarrassing, because the tome I have in mind is none other than *Vogue's Book of Etiquette.** Due to Millicent Fenwick's long research and careful writing, it is so complete a guide to traditional forms and modern usage that, ten to one, it will make Emily Post look to her *fourchettes.*

There is bound to be something absurd about all books of etiquette; something humorless, pontifical, snobbish, and silly. Their admonitions have none of the interchange of conversation or the willingness to make immediate exceptions. They take with deadly seriousness what most people feel should be taken for granted. The subjects on which they hand down solemn decisions never seem more trivial than when they are accorded the dignity and finality of print.

Books of etiquette face the problem of being Baedekers written for residents as well as tourists. Their market is bound

* *Vogue's Book of Etiquette.* By Millicent Fenwick. New York: Simon & Schuster. 1948. 658 pp. $5.

to be a mixed audience, composed of those in the know and out of it. It consists of social climbers and *arrivistes* no less than the long-arrived. The very idea that good manners can or need to be codified is ridiculous to those who think they have them, and irritating to those who do not care about acquiring them.

Moreover, "society" is no longer a fashionable word. This, of course, increases our willingness to smile today at volumes concerned with the amenities of social intercourse. Then there is the matter of certainty. Authors of books of etiquette push this to such a point of infallibility that it becomes unbearable. Theirs is the last word on every subject. Compared to them, Macaulay is indecisive and critics undogmatic. Not content with being lower courts, they must function as the supreme court, too. From their verdicts, one gathers, there is no appeal. Yet what they are so grave, and even condescending, about is usually nothing more significant than how to send or accept an invitation or give a party.

All of us, in our time, have smiled when skimming the pages of old books of etiquette. I have before me, for example, a charming little *Hints on Etiquette and the Usages of Society*, which was published first in London more than a hundred years ago and has recently been reissued. In it are to be found such gems of wisdom as, "Do not pick your teeth *much* at table, as, however satisfactory a practice to yourself, to witness it is not a pleasant thing." Or, "Ladies should never dine with their gloves on—unless their hands are not fit to be seen." Although at present we may laugh at these precepts, a lot can be read between the lines of such a book about the manners, the society, the class feeling, the elegance of the great houses, and the shopkeepers then turning into merchants in a changing England.

I must admit I approached Mrs. Fenwick's volume hoping for chuckles of the same kind. What is more, I found them. I could not help smiling to read that "after an active sport such as tennis, when normally they might have worn a brightly colored sweater, men (in mourning) should wear a white sweater instead." I was no less interested to learn, by way of useful information, that "when one is entertaining royalty, the line under the crest (on the menu) reads Diner (or 'Déjeuner' or 'Souper') de Leurs Majestés (or 'Altesses')."

Likewise I was grateful to be told that "the whole question of kissing hands is becoming very complicated" for American girls, since foreigners no longer kiss hands with their old-time consistency. The terrible result is that a "foreigner's nose often gets bumped" by young ladies who had made up their minds that all they could expect was a handshake. I was also pleased to discover that "young girls, no matter how seriously they may be working, spend at least half their free time thinking about men." "And how right they are!" adds Mrs. Fenwick, with more realism than romance. "A good job may not last a lifetime, but it is always to be hoped that a marriage will."

Yet, much as any of us may be tempted to smile at some of the things Mrs. Fenwick is duty-bound to take seriously, I for one am grateful for her book. In spite of all its seeming staidness, it makes its concessions to the present. It is fully aware of what has happened and is happening. To be sure, at times Mrs. Fenwick may appear to indulge in delusions of grandeur, as when she tells us what to tip stewards on a "big yacht" *after a month's cruise;* refers to the domestics in American homes as "the household"; or offers as a suggested menu *Les huitres en coquilles, Le consommé Brunoise, Le pompano Bercy, Le filet de boeuf Richelieu, La sauce Madère, Les pommes soufflées, Les haricots verts au beurre, Le suprême de volaille Jeannette, La salade Russe, La mousse aux fraises, Les friandises*—and all this for *Le* 15 *Décembre,* 1948!

Even so, and in spite of her Trianon-Blenheim-Ward Mc-Alister moments, Mrs. Fenwick has faced the facts of contemporary society. She knows that yachts are no longer plentiful; that the day of the "great houses" is almost gone; and that the chef has been replaced by the casserole, the nanny by the baby-sitter, and the footman by the accommodator. She is intermittently aware that maids are scarce, that prices are soaring, and that most American families (including those who entertain) get along—quite nicely, thank you—with the wife doing the cooking.

Moses contented himself with Ten Commandments; Wilson with Fourteen Points; the Episcopal Church with Thirty-nine Articles. Not Mrs. Fenwick. How could she? The laws she is laying down are ordinances. Her edicts range from glassware and flat silver to engagement presents and writing paper. She is conscious of how paradoxical and absurd etiquette can be. Yet she has the wisdom to realize that, though its "ramifications are trivialities . . . its roots are in great principles." She believes "good behavior is everybody's business, and good taste can be everybody's goal." Whenever egos touch and conflicts of interest arise, says she, common sense demands a system; a system that will make things more agreeable, because easier, for all, once it is accepted. Evidently she subscribes to the sane theory that conventions represent organized common sense in the field of behavior.

I have no way of knowing how other readers of *Vogue's Book of Etiquette* will feel about this or that of its manifold entries. Many will doubtless accept it as Gideon; others as a companion volume to Bennett Cerf's *Shake Well before Using*. But I do know that, in this well-nigh mannerless world, I have a list—not a little list, a long one—of people who would benefit from mastering Mrs. Fenwick's book, particularly her chapters on the responsibilities of hosts and guests and good manners in general. Come to think of it, I could name some nations that could also read it to advantage. Good manners, however despised by those who neither have nor want them, can make their contribution to peace, international no less than intramural.

December 4, 1948

"*The Actors Are Come Hither*"

*THE INSPIRED way in which Alfred
Lunt and Lynn Fontanne demonstrate
that they are not among those married
actors who have found billing a problem
which puts an end to their cooing.*

Acting at Its Best

DISASTERS are supposed to come in three's, but good
things obviously come in two's. The Lunts prove this.
Since Adam and Eve was there ever such a couple? Alfred
Lunt and Lynn Fontanne have this advantage over that other
pair who were the first to taste the fruits of Paradise. They
have never left the garden, which in their case is the theatre.
Moreover, they have labored long and joyously in it without any threat of being driven out. In *I Know My Love* * they
are celebrating their twenty-fifth year together as an acting
team, a fact well known to those who love the Lunts, and
this means almost everyone.

   They were married in 1922 and first appeared together, in
The Guardsman of unforgettable memory, in 1924. I summon these cold statistics with a reason. For plain citizens to

* *I Know My Love*, a play by S. N. Behrman, adapted from "Auprès de Ma
Blonde," by Marcel Achard. Directed by Alfred Lunt. Settings and costumes
by Stewart Chaney. Presented by the Theatre Guild and John C. Wilson.
With a cast including Alfred Lunt, Lynn Fontanne, Geoffrey Kerr, Betty
Caulfield, Katharine Bard, Thomas Palmer, Doreen Lang, Allen Martin,
Noel Leslie, Lily Kemble-Cooper, Henry Barnard, Hugh Franklin, Anne
Sargent, Esther Mitchell, etc. At the Shubert Theatre, New York City. Opened
November 2, 1949.

be man and wife for more than a quarter of a century is in itself something of an achievement in the contemporary world, where there are those to whom marriage obviously seems less a sacrament than a game of leapfrog. Players, however, belong to a race apart. For them to remain married for twenty-five years is in the nature of news, and good news at that. Actors, both on the West Coast and on Broadway, do sometimes enter into matrimony as breathless transients. Since the agitating question of their billing can end their cooing, they are often tempted to be more interested in their liberty than their union. But the Lunts, whom all of us applaud, would also get a hand from Daniel Webster. They have remained one and indivisible all these happy and contributive years.

On the subject of marriage Emerson once indulged in a paradox. "Is not marriage," asked he, "an open question when it is alleged from the beginning of the world that such as are in the institution wish to get out, and such as are out wish to get in?" The only problem (and a sizable one it is) Alfred Lunt and Lynn Fontanne have ever raised by continuing to act together as man and wife is how the countless thousands who wish to get in to see them wherever they are playing can come by the necessary tickets. Their popularity up and down the country is enormous. It is exceeded only by their skill.

The commonplace comment to make about the Lunts is to fall back on a story once associated with Modjeska, and to insist that were they to recite the alphabet audiences would be delighted. To a certain extent they are doing the brilliant equivalent of this in *I Know My Love*. The play which S. N. Behrman has derived from Marcel Achard's *Auprès de Ma Blonde* is scarcely Pulitzer Prize material. I doubt if

it edged M. Achard closer to the *Académie* when Yvonne
Printemps and Pierre Fresnay scored a triumph in it in Paris.
Not that this is important, but it is about as near as a French
dramatist, or Mr. Behrman for that matter, ever came to
writing like Dodie Smith.

Laid now in Boston, it deals with what might be described
as a John Marquandary. It is one of those family cavalcades
which tells how a couple has managed to stay on affectionate
and welded terms for fifty years, in spite of parent trouble,
mistress trouble, children trouble, and grandchildren trouble.
The American version starts off in January, 1939, when the
prosperous Chanlers are celebrating their golden wedding.
Thereafter, with the aid of a machine which thoughtfully
flashes the date of each pivotal scene on the curtain, it leaps
backward in time to 1888, 1902, 1918, and 1920, in order to
catch up with and explain what is here presented as its prologue.

The imagination is not taxed to realize what a holiday of
wig-wearing and costume-changing is provided by a script
which embarks on such a safari through the calendar, or what
raids on the make-up box it necessitates. Although Mr. Behrman's wonderfully crisp and precise mastery of the language
again and again makes itself felt, one trembles to think what
the play he has adapted would be like without such a couple as
the Lunts. One trembles the more upon encountering the hints
given in those moments when the Lunts are not on the
stage.

Since they are present, however, and very much present,
such considerations are beside the point and have nothing
to do with how agreeable and rewarding an evening is offered
by *I Know My Love*. What matters is not what the play is

like as a play but what it becomes as a delectable theatrical experience because of the Lunts.

No one needs to be reminded that, much as the theatre benefits from dramatic literature, it can thrive without it. Fine acting is capable of creating a satisfactory substitute for good writing. Actors of the Lunts' perfection endow shallow scenes with depth and make tarnished situations sparkle. Their faces do the work of words. Their voices, gestures, expressions, stance, make-up, and costumes supply a self-sufficient vocabulary of their own; a vocabulary which can be eloquent, witty, moving, simple or sophisticated, and altogether enjoyable.

Everybody knows that the Lunts have been liberated, not fettered, by their union. Their marriage bonds have set them free, entitling them to audacities beyond the reach of unwedded performers. Although fortunately our theatre possesses its full quota of dazzling players, its good fortune is to possess in the Lunts the finest acting couple, if not in the world, certainly in the English-speaking world. Long, long ago I tried to point out that one of the most ingratiating aspects of their teamwork is that they act to show each other off rather than to show each other up. Their playing is blessedly free from those petty frictions and attention-winning tricks by means of which lesser actors indulge in that special form of grand larceny known as scene-stealing. Their performances are glorious games of give-and-take in which there is no jealousy in the giving and only generosity in the taking.

In *The Guardsman, The Second Man, Reunion in Vienna, Design for Living,* or *O Mistress Mine,* for example, they may have romped and tussled more vigorously around the stage or on couches, but they have never shown greater warmth or tenderness than in *I Know My Love.* Their skill is such that one is willing to believe in them even when, in the prologue as an aged couple, they are asked to say affectionate things to one another in the presence of newspaper photographers which most proper Bostonians would find it hard to get said even in private.

Not unnaturally, theatregoers like to see actors act. Their wishes are often ignored. The Lunts, however, do not fail them. They delight in their profession and make others delight in it, too. In *I Know My Love* they may run the gamut of the years, but whether they are being old, middle-aged, or young they never rely upon their make-up, their wigs, or their costumes to do the real work for them. They are in complete command of all those subtleties and shadings in voice, expression, and physical bounce (or its recession) appropriate to the changing ages.

Watching them impersonate the altering Chanlers includes among its other pleasures the agreeable sensation of turning over the pages in the Lunts' scrapbook, and hence reviving some of the most treasured of our theatrical memories. We are bound to recapture something of our own youth when the Lunts recapture theirs. The calendar presents them with no difficulties. Having removed their white wigs, Mr. Lunt is able to bob up looking as he did in *Outward Bound*, and Miss Fontanne (who is truly the Fontanne of Youth) can appear as she did in *Dulcy*.

The theatre is nowadays said to be in a bad way. There are plenty of facts to support such a statement. Yet, so long as the Lunts are part of it, no one can deny that it still possesses life and vitality, or that it is capable of providing joys to be found nowhere else.

December 3, 1949

*THE INCREDIBLE Mae West re-
seen in these post-Kinsey days, and some
discussion of the undeniable figure she
presents as an actress.*

Mae Pourquoi

O N MY way to *Diamond Lil* * the other night I could
not help wondering what Time, Kinsey, and John
O'Hara might have done to Mae West. Sixteen years ago
when last I saw her (this was when the New Deal was new
and other much-needed relief agencies were mushrooming),
she had already become a national institution.

Since then, however, the ever-changing world has changed
in ways uncountable and with unprecedented swiftness. The
Kinsey Report and the atom bomb have both been dropped.
We are supposed to be tougher now—war-toughened and
peace toughened, too. We are franker in our discussion of
the pleasant blushful subjects. Our approach to the facts of
life is nothing if not factual. We call a spayed a spayed, or
worse. Grandmothers are not unconversant with, or always
ungiven to, the language of GI's. The small talk of the

---

* *Diamond Lil,* by Mae West. Directed by Charles K. Freeman. Settings
by William De Forest and Ben Edwards. Costumes by Paul Du Pont.
Presented by Albert H. Rosen and Herbert J. Freezer. With a cast including
Mae West, Richard Coogan, Charles G. Martin, Walter Petrie, Miriam
Goldina, Val Gould, James Courtney, Billy Van, Sheila Trent, Sylvia Syms,
Ray Bourbon, Mike Keene, Jack Howard, etc. At the Plymouth Theatre.
New York City.

smoking room, more than having become the conversation of the entire car, has invaded the drawing room. Our eyes have grown accustomed to four-letter words which at least simplify the task of typesetting. Even sex, that three-letter word in which Miss West has always had a rather open interest, is being talked, written, and thought about in terms so different from those of sixteen years ago that naturally I approached *Diamond Lil* in an apprehensive mood.

Would—could—La West possibly be and seem the same, thought I. Might not her boldness have become tame, her lustiness anaemic? How could she hope, even granting her superior equipment, to hold her own with the fanciful enlargements of those wind-swept females who are at present plastered across the jackets of historical novels and the covers of cheap reprints? Wouldn't the sand have run out of her hourglass figure? In short, like certain other pounds, weren't hers bound to have undergone a devaluation?

But my worries, though chivalrous, were absurd. They were the sillier because I had forgotten that, in spite of her dedication to what Percy Hammond used to refer to as the "obstinate urge," Miss West has never asked to be taken seriously. Sex itself is for her a cartoon which she delights in animating. If she is a high priestess of desire, she is also its most unabashed and hilarious parodist. When she gets through with the Tenderloin, it is ham—sheer, unadulterated Smithfield.

As an archetype of the predatory female, Miss West is about as sinister as a retrieved copy of *The Police Gazette*. She remains dateless (I mean this, of course, only in the historical sense) because her choice has always been to be an anachronism. For all her contours, and in spite of the dromedary dip with which she walks, the incessant pelvic rotations that punctuate her sentences, and the steaming sultriness of her voice, her chief invitation is now, as it was in the beginning, to laughter. Had she been only a siren, Puritan America could never have been "had" by her. But she is also a *farceur* and a comedienne. And it is these endowments which originally saved her and which continue to endear her.

Sixteen years ago when she was conquering the country as a survival of the most tightly fitted, I tried to point out that she was that rarest of all specimens among contemporary artists. She was a pre-Freudian, than which a Miocene mammal could not be harder to find. Her scarcity value has grown with the years, even as she has. Vocally she is still a hootchy-kootchy artist. Visually she remains as modernistic as a barroom nude. She can still turn the simplest statement into a scorching insinuation. She can still make the most innocent "Hello, boys" sound like a traveling salesman's idea of *The Decameron*. The course she pursues so grandly is still down the midway. Her lack of subtlety remains the most subtle thing about her.

Only the Statue of Liberty has been carrying a torch for a longer time than Mae West. She, moreover, seems no more fatigued by maintaining her chosen attitude than does the iron lady down the bay with her eternally uplifted hand. Always, and proudly, an armful, Miss West is a bigger girl today than she used to be. But what devotee of the madame could object to there being more of her. She would not have had to come from Tennessee or India to be a grandmother by now. Yet few people could bear a more remote resemblance to Whistler's *Mother* or Grant Wood's *D.A.R.* than she does.

No one has ever looked quite like Mae West, or ever will. She fills the eye no less surely than she fills the stage. She is several dreams walking; several nightmares, too. She commands more curves than Christy Mathewson thought of doing. What a poster is to Proust she is to Kinsey, and also to O'Hara, in her own flamboyant person. The dictionary assures us that in mathematics a curve is the locus of a moving point continuously deviating from a straight line. A more accurate description of La West has not and could not be written.

She never deviates into Christendom any more than she wanders within the outskirts of reality. To her, sex is more than an obsession. It is a joke with no primal eldest curse upon it but with the most ancient of blessings. Her voice, like her person and her incredible costumes, disturbs the risibilities far more than it inflames the senses. A nest of attacked vipers could not emit hisses more insistent than are all of her conscienceless sentences. She is an actress who seldom reacts but who is always being reacted to; a soloist in a duet world. Accordingly, she seems lonely even in her thickly populated plays.

Although she is credited with having written *Diamond Lil*, she can scarcely have bothered to use a pen or pencil. After all these years, it persists in being a dreary charade which still sounds as if it were being improvised. That is, of course, except at those plentiful moments when Lil herself is hard at work, as the professional she magnificently is, rasping and undulating, undulating and rasping. Then the evening becomes the ultimate in calculation, the final word in skilled deliberation.

The truth is that, like *The Constant Sinner* and *Sex* before it, *Diamond Lil* is no play at all. It creates a category of its own which can only be defined as a Mae Western. If it is a drama, then so is it a trip to Chinatown on a sightseeing bus. Without Mae West it would be nothing. With her it is Mae West. And that is decidedly something. Miss West is a lesson in geography as well as in acting. Compared to her terrain, that of Hollywood's young sirens (true or false) is what the Appalachians are to the Rockies.

The world may have changed to a terrifying extent, but when it comes to toughness it has not yet caught up with La West. More than being a person or an institution, she has entered the language and taken her place in the underworld of the present's mythology. She is the Bobby Clark of the boudoir. She does not bother with the flowers when teaching about the bees. She continues to be what every playgoer, young and old and in search of a laugh, ought to know.

October 8, 1949

LYNN BELVEDERE as Clifton Webb and vice versa, or the comfort created in a confused world from meeting again a character who has no doubts about anything, including his own perfection.

That Man Again

GALSWORTHY'S contention was that a human being is the best plot there is. But, as *Mr. Belvedere Goes to College* * makes clear, a character who is more—and less —than a human being can also be a plot; that is, if he is vivid, entertaining, and original enough.

Everyone who saw *Sitting Pretty* must remember that Mr. Belvedere was "out of this world." Played once again by Clifton Webb, he remains "out of this world." His unearthly superiority is what makes him hard to resist. No one like him has ever walked this planet. No one like him would be tolerated on it. He is Superman without the red underwear and blue cape; Superman with the tongue of Woollcott and the manners of Sheridan Whiteside; Superman in the nursery, Superman in the library, the kitchen, the classroom, and the stadium.

* *Mr. Belvedere Goes to College.* Screen play by Richard Sale, Mary Loos, and Mary McCall, Jr. Directed by Elliott Nugent. Produced by Samuel G. Engel for Twentieth Century–Fox. With a cast including Clifton Webb, Shirley Temple, Tom Drake, Alan Young, Jessie Royce Landis, Taylor Holmes, etc. At the Roxy, New York.

Apparently there is nothing he cannot do. There is nothing he does not know. There is nothing at which he does not excel. As Mr. Webb plays him, or he plays Mr. Webb, he may look prissy, but he is a man of iron. Irate husbands, bawling children, university presidents, husky athletes, or the untamed inmates of a sorority cannot daunt him. Each and all of them come to heel when he is around.

If fear is alien to him, so too is reverence. Yes, and, for that matter, modesty. Shaw and Oscar Wilde were never more conscious of their genius than he is of his. His arrogance would be unbearable were it not so well founded. We may start out each time by thinking of him as disagreeable, which indeed he is, but we soon begin to marvel at him, then to admire him, and next to like him. We like him in spite of his superciliousness, his imperturbability, his smirking condescension. We like him because he sails or minces through life triumphantly, as a kind of Walter Mitty who lives his dreams instead of dreaming them, and hence awakens Walter Mitty dreams within us.

I doubt if, when she wrote *Belvedere*, Gwen Davenport foresaw what she had started. Lynn Belvedere's knowledge and aptitudes were prodigious in her pages. Since then, however, they have kept on multiplying, Shmoo-wise. Each new scenarist extending his career has added to them. For Mr. Belvedere is obviously the kind of creation (or is it creature?) who cannot, who must not, be confined to one book or film.

He is the stuff of which serials are made. His trim, slim, overelegant person has more lives to live than a cat. He can go on forever; that is, if it is permissible to misuse the language in the bold manner of beauticians who speak of a wave as being "permanent," or the custodians of cemeteries when

they promise "perpetual care." Like the Little Colonel, the
Rover Boys, the Oz group, Mary Poppins, Babar, Peter
Rabbit, the Forsytes, the Jalna tribe, the Hubbards, the
Days, Tarzan, and the characters of Proust, Lynn Belvedere
is too good a property to be used once and then discarded.

In the present-day world he has a special place, just as to
that world he makes a special appeal. Most of us may be
confused. Most of us may be distressed by each hour's
showing-up of our ignorance. Most of us may have been
forced into being specialists and been compelled to hood our
eyes with the blinders of our chosen professions. Not so Mr.
Belvedere. All knowledge is his province; all human activity,
a dominion of his.

Does it take an average college student four long years to
win the skin of that sacrificed sheep? One short year is
enough for Mr. Belvedere's all-grasping mind. He has come
to a university with what for most would prove an academic
handicap. His only previous submission to orthodox education has been "two revolting weeks in kindergarten." Yet
Mr. Belvedere, being Mr. Belvedere, has needed no teachers
since he has walked through life in his own company. Apparently this has amounted to having a full faculty always
at his elbow.

Mr. Belvedere reads all the classics, including the Per-
sonals in the *SRL*. He writes classics too, because as a novelist he has garnered great fame though no fortune. Dead languages come as easily to him as living ones. If he can play
the piano with Iturbi's skill, he can also cook with something
of Alfred Lunt's virtuosity. His gifts are not limited to higher
learning. The altitudes he can achieve at pole vaulting are
equally dizzying. In short, the man is a whole empire of talents.

That is why, though we would run from him in the flesh, we run to him on the screen. In an uncertain universe he not only arouses our envy, he restores our certainties.

Mrs. Davenport may not have had Mr. Webb in mind when she created Mr. Belvedere. One thing, however, is indisputable. Mr. Webb pops into everyone's mind—and eyes—whenever Mr. Belvedere is mentioned. As surely as the Allegheny and the Monongahela merge to form the Ohio, so he and Mr. Belvedere combine to create an unforgettable character.

Mr. Webb has come a long way since he used to prance across the polished dance floor of the Château Madrid in hot pursuit of the Dolly Sisters, with his coattails flying behind him like advertising streamers trailing after a plane. He has come a long way, too, since as a dancer extraordinary he stopped such musicals as *Sunny* with Marilyn Miller or *The Little Show* with Libby Holman. *As Thousands Cheer* first made some of us realize his potentialities as a comedian. On his way to becoming Mr. Belvedere, he appeared on the road, be it noted, as Sheridan Whiteside in *The Man Who Came to Dinner*. This is not without its significance. His Mr. Belvedere is a twin (not identical, though still a twin) of Mr. Webb's notion of Mr. Kaufman's and Mr. Hart's notion of Alexander Woollcott. Sheridan Whiteside served Mr. Webb as his prep school for arrogance and bad manners. His limitless learning he has picked up since; indeed, it has been thrust upon him.

If Webb Belvedere, or Belvedere Webb, is one of the more amusing and reassuring comic inventions of our distressed times, the Messrs. Webb and Belvedere must be thanked for this. Certainly the character they have jointly made famous deserves more loyal support than he is given by his script-writers in <i>Mr. Belvedere Goes to College.</i> Lindbergh, flying the Atlantic, was never more alone than Mr. Webb is in this latest Belvedere exploit. The final tribute to him is that he manages to keep so frail and silly a scenario aloft for the better portion of an evening which he makes diverting.

There is an elaborate subplot involving Shirley Temple and Tom Drake, which is better if followed inattentively. Then, for poor measure, there are those undergraduate types which it pleases Hollywood to assume infest our colleges. They are a vomitous crew: plump freshmen whose heads have only adenoids in them; paddle-flourishing upperclassmen whose own posteriors call for immediate attention, and sorority sisters so rude and strident that they would make a monk of Casanova or Errol Flynn.

Colleges have a hard time of it in American movies and musical comedies. They emerge as junior insane asylums. The wonder is their libraries have any other books in them except comics. Their campuses are peopled by cheer leaders, sweater-wearing loons, bullies, and bra-some babes whose native habitat would be a chorus.

Although the land is almost as dotted with institutions of higher learning as it is with five-and-ten-cent stores, Hollywood never seems to have visited one. Its universities are all Katzenjammer and no culture. They are Ruritanias where everything that is either untrue or only partially true about American youth is king. The wonder is that American educators no less than American undergraduates do not picket the films dealing with them or, in their search for endowments, turn to their law departments for redress.

We, of course, know that what is offered us as a campus in

Mr. Belvedere Goes to College is no campus at all but straight Hollywood. As such, we either yawn or smile at it, and reject it. But what opinion people the world over, looking to us for leadership or teetering on the verge of persuasion this way or that, would form of us or of our educational institutions in the presence of the sillier sequences in such a film is another and a frightening matter. Perhaps it should not alarm us too greatly. At least not so long as Mr. Belvedere is a visitor on such a campus. Assuredly, he must be one of the best friends and most convincing ambassadors that the Marshall Plan and democracy now have. Any country that can produce him must be able to do anything.

May 7, 1949

Of English Origin

SIR LAURENCE OLIVIER brings
Hamlet *to the screen in a production*
which has its fine and stirring features
in spite of being in many ways dislo-
cated by being on location.

Olivier's Hamlet

IF AND when they build houses for us, architects usually reflect our tastes, hence our personalities. Even if they fail to do so, one thing is certain. They determine the physical pattern of our living, once their blueprints, realized in terms of brick and mortar, have become our homes.

The new film version of *Hamlet* * is, of course, billed as Laurence Olivier's. Since he directed it and plays the Prince, it is as the Laurence Olivier *Hamlet* that the picture will always be identified. Yet, while sitting before it, as filled with admiration as with misgivings, I could not help wondering if this cinematic *Hamlet,* so fine in some respects, so unsatisfactory in others, should not more accurately be described as Roger Furse's.

It is Mr. Furse who served the production as its architect.

---

* *Hamlet,* a film version of William Shakespeare's tragedy. Directed by Laurence Olivier. Text editor, Alan Dent. Designed by Roger Furse. Music composed by William Walton and played by the Philharmonic Orchestra. With a cast including Laurence Olivier, Eileen Herlie, Basil Sydney, Jean Simmons, Felix Aylmer, Norman Wooland, Terence Morgan, Stanley Holloway, Peter Cushing, etc. A J. Arthur Rank Enterprise. Sponsored by the Theatre Guild. A Universal-International Release. At the Park Avenue Theatre.

It is he who designed the huge, drafty structure, part conch shell, part labyrinth, part courtyard, part lighthouse staircase, part Simmons-bed window exhibit, part Cloisters, part ziggurat, part Danish pueblo, but mainly movie setting, which is the most recent Elsinore. By so doing Mr. Furse has conditioned the whole performance. He has provided its terrain, created its mood, charted its action, steered its actors, and, sometimes, smothered the play in the *cloche* which is his castle.

Mr. Furse's interest, understandably, is the camera. He would be in the wrong if it were not. Transferring the drama to a different medium, he is bound to have thought in terms of close-ups, long shots, fade-outs, and all those supposedly liberating technical devices which the screen enjoys and the stage does not. His problem, a sizable one, is external. It has been to find an outward form for an inward tragedy. Not such a form, mind you, as a stage designer would have evolved. No, a form three-dimensional, spacious, filmworthy. A form intended to dispense with the scene divisions of the theatre, to occupy the eye, and add those free-ranging elements impossible behind the footlights.

Almost inevitably, Mr. Furse's problem becomes not only Olivier's but ours, too. The final *Hamlet*, if indeed there be such a thing in the case of a text so endlessly self-extending, exists in the mind and achieves its most satisfying visualization in the mind's eye. What Shakespeare wanted to say, what he felt necessary to get said, with all its subtleties, tantalizing depths, and interrelationships, is said by him in his uncut text. How exciting that text can be when its wonders are untampered with, the Maurice Evans production made clear in 1938. The play, in that instance, was indeed the thing; the thing it was plainly meant to be, and in many stirring moments is, in the film. Yet in the film much that is valuable is lost, and needlessly lost, because of the swollen dimensions of Mr. Furse's Elsinore. The paradox is that the screen text finds itself confined instead of freed by the very space now at its disposal.

To have *Hamlet* hacked at in order to compress it within the theatre's regulation playing time is the common experience. Even when so dismembered, the results can be incomparable. Everyone knows this who has responded to the tattered texts acted by Walter Hampden, John Barrymore, Basil Sydney, John Gielgud, or, for that matter, by Mr. Evans in his oddly truncated GI version. To sacrifice great language, however, for meaningless pantomime; to have complexity and innuendo dispensed with in favor of camera angles; and to lose key speeches, characters, or scenes merely because so much time is wasted getting the actors from one part of the castle to another is to encounter a *Hamlet* in many ways dislocated by being on location.

The film runs two hours and thirty-three minutes. In other words, since the performance is continuous, its playing time is about the same as that required for the cut stage versions which, with one or two intermissions, usually take three hours. These cut versions in the theatre, incidentally, have always found room for Rosencrantz and Guildenstern; for so pivotal a speech as "O what a rogue and peasant slave am I"; for the second gravedigger (who is not greatly missed); sometimes, and rightly, for "How all occasions do inform against me"; usually for Fortinbras; and as a rule for many lines or speeches not to be found in this new *Hamlet*.

The film's cuts are not in every instance wise or logical

even in view of the camera's needs. The transposition of "To be or not to be" until after Hamlet's scene with Ophelia does not, I suppose, really matter. But, surely, the Fortinbras sub-plot and the scene of Hamlet's embarkation for England, in addition to contributing to our understanding of the Prince, are compounded of ideal stuffs for the movies. Certainly, too, it makes little sense to have the First Player express his willingness to learn a "speech of some dozen or sixteen lines" for the play-within-the-play and then have that play acted entirely in dumb show.

One trouble with the picture is that it squanders at least forty precious minutes in stage crosses, in slow fade-outs, in travelogues up and down the stairs of Mr. Furse's palace, or in such a long and pointless sequence as the concluding one in which, after a superb duel and a very moving death scene, the Prince's body is carried up endless flights of steps for no good reason (except perhaps to honor Cecil B. de Mille) to the castle's highest tower. In short, the film is as conditioned in its physical movements (hence in the scope of the text it uses) by Mr. Furse's ungainly setting as we are in our daily living by the blueprints of our architects. This is why I, for one, hold Mr. Furse responsible for some of the picture's more perplexing omissions rather than Mr. Olivier or his able script-editor, Alan Dent.

All this, however, is more than enough of reservations. It is overlooking, and most unfairly, the fact that even a lame man can also claim a leg which is both good and strong. What matters in the case of Mr. Olivier's *Hamlet* is its virtues. These are many. They are sufficient to live down the sad and utterly unnecessary introductory moment when, as a prologue to the film and in the worst radio-narrator manner, Mr. Olivier's voice is heard explaining, "This is the tragedy of a man who could not make up his mind." That is a depressing and disastrous start. Nevertheless the merits of this *Hamlet*, considering its intentions, compensate for the lacks.

Mr. Olivier's production is meant for the "groundlings"; for people who come to it fresh. In other words, it is intended for moviegoers and radio listeners far removed from theatrical centers; people unconcerned with too many niceties and unhaunted by memories of Barrymore's dynamic brilliance, Gielgud's vibrant neuroticism, or Evans's eloquent justification of a prince legionnaire in spirit.

For such an audience Mr. Olivier's *Hamlet* is certain to be an eye opener as well as an experience. It has a bounce, an urgency, a fascination, and an emotional impact which are hard to resist. Measured by the Shakespeare the majority of Americans see, when they are lucky enough to see any pretending to be professional, it is a masterpiece. Compared to most films, childish as they are in intelligence, range, taste, or ambition, it is as full grown as was Pallas Athena at birth. Every schoolteacher in the land should be grateful for it. So should every student not entirely hostile to learning.

Even when seen on Manhattan at previews attended by persons freighted with recollections, it commands, word for word and scene for scene, that utter silence which is the perfect tribute to its compulsion. Make no mistake about it. It is a film not to be missed, regardless of what the long-memoried, the captious, or informed hopefuls may miss in it.

Mr. Olivier's *Hamlet* is bound to raise comparisons with his *Henry V*. His *Henry* was one of the best pictures I have ever seen or expect to see. It had a magnificent sweep. It combined personalities and pageantry so that neither was lost sight of. Its spirit was as stirring as the drums summoning a regiment to battle in bygone days. The love duet in which England's Harry wooed Katherine of France was played with such miraculous skill that it managed to cap in interest even the glories of Agincourt. As for Mr. Olivier, he was so complete a Harry, both as a man and an ideal of kingship, that England's victory, like the film's, was easy to explain.

But there's the rub. The qualities of manliness which made Mr. Olivier Henry "cap-a-pie" are not necessarily attributes fitting him for Hamlet. The Dane is a man condemned to vacillation. Were he as resolute as Mr. Olivier and his will the servant of so firm a mouth and buttressed a chin, *Hamlet* would be a one-act play. Mr. Olivier brings no new understanding of the Prince to his interpretation. His innovations stop with the bleaching of his hair. They do not come from within. He does not reverse tradition as Mr. Evans did when he bounded into Elsinore as an extrovert princeling. Neither does he heighten tradition as did Mr. Gielgud when he laid bare the torments of a neurotic prince. He takes Hamlet as the single speeches come instead of integrating them into an original pattern of his own planning.

Though this represents a deficiency, the simple and exciting truth is that no player now alive can read Shakespearean verse as he does. He is a master of the pause, of underscoring, of illumination. He may at times be tempted to throw lines away, regrettably, as when he rushes to the end of the great hall to scream "The play's the thing." He may surrender to acrobatics and send his body hurtling to the floor more often than necessary. Once or twice, too, his very virtuosity may mislead him into spewing forth more words than a single breath can hope to project. But, even when Mr. Olivier is by temperament at odds with what he is saying, he remains a great actor.

To judge how inspired is his reading, one has only to read to oneself the introductory verses thrown on the screen while Mr. Olivier's voice is heard reading them aloud. What he does with them, to break them, to give them meaning, to explore and ignite them, would have caused Elia to swallow his harsh words about the losses Shakespeare suffers when performed.

In spite of his lack of a definite interpretation; in spite, too, of the way in which his own temperament may clash with Hamlet's, Mr. Olivier achieves his extraordinary single moments. These include his delivery of "To be or not to be" (here, as in the other soliloquies, the illusion of eavesdropping on his thoughts is suggested by our hearing his voice on the sound track and yet seeing him move his lips to speak only an occasional line); the easy naturalness of his speech to the players; his uninhibited ribaldry with Ophelia at the play; his acid humor in all his dealings with Polonius, and with the King when referring to the dead counselor's whereabouts; his entire relationship with Horatio; his apostrophe to Yorick; his asking forgiveness of Laertes; and the athletic fury of his duel.

As a director, Mr. Olivier faces a far more difficult task than he did with *Henry V*. The tragedy of *Hamlet* is internal; its final action within the mind. If this interior struggle is not totally realized in the film, the melodrama—the grand, gory, breath-taking melodrama which is also *Ham-*

let—is made the most of. When not slowed down by Mr. Furse's setting, Mr. Olivier and his fellow players keep it lunging on its bloodstained way.

As in the case of his *Henry*, all the members of the supporting cast speak Shakespearean verse uncommonly well. When it comes to their characterizations, that is a different matter. Personally I was disappointed in Felix Aylmer's Polonius. He seemed to be lacking in humor, if for no other reason than that he took no pleasure in his own garrulity. Unaccountably but typically, the famous "tragedy, comedy, history, pastoral" speech was not even spoken by him as if he were a windy old man toying with words. Instead, it was read by him supposedly from a handbill taken from the Players.

I was disappointed, too, in Peter Cushing's Osric and was especially distressed to see him, when backing and swishing his way out of Hamlet's presence, fall downstairs in order to win a laugh. Eileen Herlie I found too young for the Queen. To me she appeared to be playing by rote rather than from passion. Her Gertrude had none of the tempting wifeliness Mady Christians brought to the part. Nor could I understand why Mr. Olivier, as a director, should have elected to have Gertrude and Claudius wander throughout almost the whole play as attached to their crowns as if they were a playing-card queen and king.

But for Basil Sydney's superlatively well-read and deftly drawn Claudius I felt unbounded admiration. I was touched by the sweet innocence and plausibility of Jean Simmons's Ophelia, though I could not help wishing for her sake that the Court of Denmark had boasted a different hairdresser. I found genuine satisfaction in Norman Wooland's sympathetic Horatio, Terence Morgan's manly Laertes, and Stanley Holloway's Gravedigger.

Mixed in its merits this *Hamlet* may be, but this seems clear. Even Mr. Furse's setting cannot imprison Shakespeare's text. In spite of what is arguable in the production or the cutting and notwithstanding many severe disappointments, the film always aims at the best and sometimes achieves it thrillingly.

October 2, 1948

WHY SOME of us prefer reading As
You Like It *to seeing it, even when the
Rosalind is Katharine Hepburn, who in
her person supplies poetry that is easy
to scan.*

☙☙☙☙☙☙☙☙☙☙☙☙☙☙☙☙☙☙☙☙☙☙☙☙☙☙☙☙☙❧

That Forest of Arden

IN HIS reviewing days (and what days they were!) Mr.
Shaw insisted that the wrestling scene was for him always the main attraction of a revival of *As You Like It*.*
His reason? Simply his conviction that "it is so much easier
to find a man who knows how to wrestle than to find one who
knows how to act."

Dodging the Gorgeous George aspects of this generality
and limiting myself to matters histrionic, I must agree that
Charles the wrestler has an easier time of it in Shakespeare's
comedy than anyone else in the cast. He is thrown when the
first act is but two scenes old and carried off speechless. The
others, however, who are as talkative as they are amorous,
must quit the wicked Frederick's court and hie themselves
to the Forest of Arden. There, amidst plots, subplots, and

* *As You Like It*, by William Shakespeare. Directed by Michael Benthall.
Settings and costumes by James Bailey. Music by Robert Irving. Presented
by the Theatre Guild under the supervision of Theresa Helburn and
Lawrence Langner. With a cast including Katharine Hepburn, William
Prince, Ernest Thesiger, Bill Owen, Aubrey Mather, Cloris Leachman, Judy
Parrish, Pat Englund, Whitford Kane, Jay Robinson, Frank Rogier, Ernest
Graves, etc. At the Cort Theatre, New York City. Opened January 26, 1950.

disguises which could fool only their wearers, they must create the illusion of hunting in a lyric way, of loving no less lyrically, and in general of living a life in which Yale's ever-vocalizing Whiffenpoofs have somehow bobbed up as Robin Hood's Merry Men, carrying *The Oxford Book of English Verse* in their hands instead of cudgels.

The assignment is not an easy one. That there are lovely scenes in *As You Like It*, that there are speeches of pure song and moments of enchantment, no one can deny. But for some of us who were brought up surrendering to the play, the comedy has of late, in *Twelfth Night's* fashion, lost its magic when encountered in the theatre. Where once its sylvan atmosphere, its picnic laughter, and springtime innocence used to beguile us, these nowadays elude us. We find that they resist embodiment behind the footlights.

They are still there in the library. They are there because as readers our minds are free. Arden is then a forest only of the imagination. Those who dwell in it are not real persons but the products of our fancy. We do not see them except with our mind's eye. Their words have no need to be spoken since they speak for themselves. When we come to what bores us in the text, we can skip, racing ahead to what delights us. We are not bothered, much less irritated, by the silliness—indeed the downright asininities—of the story told. Ours is not a questioning mood because on the printed page our idealizations are unchallenged by flesh-and-blood individuals.

That those of us who feel this way are in the minority is made clear by the success of the current revival of *As You Like It*. It proves that audiences in droves remain as anxious to see the comedy as players without number (for reasons which escape me) have always been anxious to appear in it.

Certainly the production which Michael Benthall has directed
for the Theatre Guild has been staged unstintingly. In many
respects it is as competent a revival of *As You Like It* as our
theatre has seen within the last quarter of a century. Its
secondary characters are not entrusted, as so frequently happens, to actors who are palpably tertiary. Whether impersonating courtiers or bumpkins, philosophers or clowns, they
speak clearly. They even attempt to make probable the improbable people Shakespeare drew. This is a measure of their
industry.

If, as a designer, James Bailey has broken with tradition
by introducing us to a wintry Arden before allowing us to
see the forest in the full ripeness of its summer foliage, the
text supplies him with justifications. It also justifies the kind
of settings he has supplied. Quite properly, these have the
quality of backgrounds for a toy theatre. They capture what
is childlike in the play by being childlike in their own way.
Their theatricalism is unashamed. In their more artful and
very pleasing fashion they can claim kinship with the kind
of make-believe at which Skelt excelled and with which Benjamin Pollock's descendants to this day brighten the luckier
of the world's nurseries.

There is one speech which I dread in every revival of *As
You Like It*. I dread it for the actor's sake no less than for
the audience's. This speech, of course, is "All the world's a
stage." Apparently it is the only speech in the comedy that
playgoers know. They take to it as they do to the "Toreador
Song" in *Carmen*. Once Jaques is launched upon it the house
is stilled by a reverent hush of recognition. This is broken
only when those out front, whose lips are ostentatiously form-
ing the words, get so carried away by their knowledge that

they begin to recite aloud. By the time "sans teeth, sans eyes, sans taste, sans everything" is reached, spectators are sans control. Up go their hands and out comes a thunderous barrage of applause—for Shakespeare, for the actor who knows what they know, and for their own erudition. Ernest Thesiger does not seem to mind the ordeal. He approaches it with patience and grave resignation. But where he finds the courage to clear his throat, assume a properly sententious expression, and plunge into a speech so school-contaminated and worn treadless by repetition I, as a mere aisle-sitter, will never know.

To recall how enraptured we once were even by Rosalinds who in their Ganymede moments looked more like brood mares at pasture than foresters at play is difficult enough. It is still more difficult to fight off the faint nausea with which at present we read the automatic lyricism of some of the bygone critics. Take William Winter, for example. In his more or less empty *Wallet of Time* on the subject both of *As You Like It* and Rosalind, words spill out of him like flour from a broken barrel.

"As we ramble through those woodland dells," says he of the comedy, "we hear the mingled voices of philosophy, folly, and humor, the flying echo of the hunter's horn, the soft music of the lover's lute, and the tinkle of the shepherd's bell. The sun shines always in the Forest of Arden; the brooks sing as they glide, and the soft, happy laughter of a sweet woman floats gaily on the scented wind."

Much more of this leads Mr. Winter by-and-by to Mary Anderson's Rosalind. Then he is off again. "Care had not laid its leaden hand upon her heart. Grief had not stained the whiteness of her spirit. The galling fetters of convention had not crippled her life. Accumulated burdens of error and folly had not deadened her enthusiasm and embittered her mind. . . . For her the birds of morning were singing in the summer woods, while her footsteps fell not on the faded leaves of loss and sorrow, but on the blown roses of youth and joy. Strong in noble and serene womanhood, untouched by either the evil or the dullness of contiguous lives, not secure through penury of feeling yet not imperiled through reckless drift of emotion, rich equally in mental gifts and physical equipments, she seemed the living fulfillment of the old poetic ideal of gypsy freedom and classic grace that Byron saw in his 'Egeria' and Wordsworth in his 'Phantom of Delight.' " Etc., etc., *ad infinitum*.

I cannot say that I wish Miss Hepburn had inspired me to write about her in the same vein. Whether or not she hears birds of the morning singing in the summer woods as she strolls through Mr. Bailey's scenery, I am not in a position to state. I do know, however, that her Rosalind's physical equipment is exceptional. No one playing the part since I was old enough to sit up unstrapped in a baby-buggy has been lovelier to look at or blessed with a figure which takes so readily to a jerkin and tights. If Miss Hepburn does not fill the bill, she does fill the eye. She does this in spite of being unflatteringly lighted; in spite, too, of wearing make-up and a coiffure that do scant justice to her beauty.

Mr. Shaw, in the dramatic opinion already referred to, pretended the popularity of Rosalind is due to three main causes: (1) she speaks blank verse only for a few minutes, (2) she wears a skirt only for a few minutes, and (3) she makes love to the man instead of waiting for the man to make love to her. Subject to dispute as such reasoning may be, there are two indisputably good reasons why Miss Hepburn's Rosalind deserves its popularity. Both of these at their lower extremities are encased in her slippers. For, regardless of how much prose she may utter, Miss Hepburn's legs are always poetry, and poetry that is easy to scan.

As a fan of Miss Hepburn since *The Warrior's Husband*, *Morning Glory*, and *Little Women*, I wish I felt she took to Arden as naturally as William Winter took to his *Thesaurus*. I admire her gifts. I enjoy her looks. I like her chiseled cheekbones and find pleasure in her twangy voice. She has grace, breeding, and a sort of matter-of-fact elegance which is not without its own very special glamour. Even so, as Rosalind she does seem to me to be something of a Connecticut Yankee at Duke Frederick's court. Although she has her excellent moments and tries valiantly to give the play its song, I cannot help feeling that she mistakes the Forest of Arden for the Bryn Mawr campus.

When I happened to see *Adam's Rib* just after having seen *As You Like It*, I was the more aware of Miss Hepburn's charms but the less convinced of her talents as a comedian. Though her intelligence is beyond question, the laughs she wins are won by the lines she speaks without the aid of her facial expression or her inner spirit. Her approach to comedy is essentially dead-pan. It is as earnest as a Junior Leaguer's molestation of the poor.

If I may fall back once again on Mr. Winter, Miss Hepburn's performance needs more of the soft music of the lover's lute in it; more, too, of Arden's scented wind. In fact, it needs a great deal more of the song and sunshine which are at the comedy's heart. Heresy though it may be to say so, for me the abiding trouble with Rosalind lies with Shakespeare.

March 18, 1950

*SHAW PROVES his wisdom by rushing
in where Shakespeare dared to tread, with
the result that the applecarts of both
history and historical drama are upset in
a manner brilliantly Shavian.*

Hail, Caesar—and Cleopatra

SHAKESPEARE got there first with his *Julius Caesar*
and his *Antony and Cleopatra*. But did this intimidate
Shaw? It did not. Most fortunately, it did not. Instead, it
served him as a come-on. The Bard has always enjoyed a
priority among G.B.S.'s irreverences. He took to the challenge
like a cat to catnip. He was no more dismayed by his late
arrival on the scene than Napoleon was by Alexander's having
reached the Nile before him.

When in 1898 Shaw decided to invade Egypt, to come to
grips with the mighty Julius, and as a vegetable-fed Puritan to
run the risks of Cleopatra, he had something very much his
own to say, which, as usual, he managed to get said in his own
way. He was the first to admit the value of what he had written. The fact that Walkley and the critics who originally re-
viewed *Caesar and Cleopatra* * had described it as *opéra bouffe*

* *Caesar and Cleopatra*, a comedy by Bernard Shaw. Directed by Cedric
Hardwicke. Settings and costumes by Rolf Gerard. Presented by Richard
Aldrich and Richard Myers in association with Julius Fleischmann. With a
cast including Cedric Hardwicke, Lilli Palmer, Ralph Forbes, Arthur
Treacher, John Buckmaster, Nicholas Joy, Bertha Belmore, Ivan Simpson,

· 160 ·

did not depress Shaw. To him prophecy is routine employment. "In 1920 *Caesar* will be a masterpiece," he wrote in 1908. Readers have long since agreed with him. It was not, however, until the current and brilliant revival of his play that American theatregoers, too young to have seen Forbes-Robertson in it, have realized how right Shaw was.

Certainly Gabriel Pascal's screen version with Vivien Leigh and Claude Rains did no justice to Shaw's work. The film, though well meant, was a colossal bore. It misplaced the play in the pageant, allowed the Shavian wit to evaporate in limitless expanses of Technicolor sky, and reduced G.B.S. himself to the equivalent of a scenarist for Cecil B. de Mille. The Theatre Guild's production of *Caesar and Cleopatra* in 1925 failed, even with Helen Hayes and Lionel Atwill, to project the text's real qualities. It was a stuttering, static affair, the inadequacies of which become all the clearer in retrospect when compared to the excellences of the present performance. The exciting truth is that, as now staged with an admirable cast headed by Lilli Palmer and Sir Cedric Hardwicke, Shaw's play, written more than fifty years ago, seems as fresh as if it had been written today. At last behind local footlights, its humor is released, its wisdom communicated, and its stature preserved.

Shaw, being Shaw, did not hesitate to offer *Caesar and Cleopatra* to the public as an improvement on Shakespeare. "Better than Shakespeare" was the title he chose for his preface. By this, he pointed out with surprising modesty, he did not mean that he professed to write better plays than Shakespeare. He did, however, claim the right to criticize

---

Harry Irvine, etc. At the National Theatre, New York City. Opened December 21, 1949.

Shakespeare, to discard and discredit his romantic notions of passion and history, and to substitute new ideas and a new approach born of a new age.

The first change, an inevitable one in Shaw's case, was that where Shakespeare had written a tragedy Shaw wrote a comedy. The side of Shaw which is John Bunyan pretended to be shocked by Shakespeare's Cleopatra. He dismissed her as a Circe who, instead of turning heroes into hogs, turned hogs into heroes. He would have nothing to do with the mature woman, a tawdry wanton as he saw her, whose lustfulness had transformed a world leader into a strumpet's fool. For that matter, he would have nothing to do with the youthful Cleopatra who, according to history, had a child by Caesar. In her place he preferred to draw, and drew delectably, the portrait of a kittenish girl who under Caesar's tutelage flowered into a queen. His Cleopatra's youth was more than a puritanic evasion. It was a Shavian device by means of which superstitions could be mocked and Caesar, the conqueror, humanized by being seen through the irreverent eyes of a child. In other words, it was Shaw's characteristic way of taking the starch out of the stuffed-shirt approach to history.

As for Shakespeare's Caesar, Shaw had only contempt for him. His contention was that Shakespeare, who knew human weakness so well, never knew human strength of the Caesarian type. Just why Shaw, also a man of words, felt that he had a greater claim to understanding the inner workings of a man of action, is something he did not bother to explain. But that he succeeded with his Caesar where Shakespeare failed with his, few would deny.

In his preface to *Caesar and Cleopatra* G.B.S. described himself as a crow who has followed many plows. Surely none of

these has led him down stranger furrows than his flirtations
with the dictator principle. The champion of the superman,
who was fascinated by Napoleon and who has had kind words
to say about Stalin and even Mussolini, was bound sooner or
later to be drawn to Caesar.

The major source for his Julius was not Plutarch. As he confessed, it was Mommsen, the nineteenth-century German historian. He liked Mommsen's account of the Egyptian visit and
agreed with his estimate of Caesar. Shaw also admitted his
debt to Carlyle for his concept of the historical hero capable of
bearing "the weight of life" realistically rather than suffering
from a passion to die gallantly.

The Caesar Shaw drew would not have been recognized by
Suetonius or Plutarch, neither of whom liked him. But the
man who wrote *The Gallic War* would have recognized this
Shavian Julius—with gratitude and relief. The clemency and
statesmanship, the largeness of mind and spirit, which for the
sake of the record he had been careful to establish as his, are
qualities that shine in Shaw's Caesar. Caesar's self-love could
not have been greater than Shaw's almost romantic infatuation
with the benevolent despot he depicted.

But there was a difference—an immeasurable difference.
Where Plutarch was dignified, Suetonius scurrilous, Caesar de-
terminedly official, and Shakespeare rhetorically athletic, Shaw
was Shavian. This in itself represented a complete abandon-
ment of the orthodox ways of writing not only history but
historical plays. It meant that, more than upsetting an apple-
cart, Shaw had brought about a one-man revolution in the
theatre and in literature.

He approached the past unawed, anxious to see it in contemporary terms, eager for a laugh, and with a wit which,

though impudent, was wonderfully humanizing. The effects of his innovations are still with us, though in lesser hands they have never achieved the same dimensions and have sometimes been downright sophomoric. Quite rightly, it has been pointed out that what is widely thought of as Lytton Strachey's method was something for which Shaw prepared the way. But what is often overlooked is that G.B.S., regardless of his impertinences, was never a debunker. His spirit was always too positive for that, his intellect too superior.

Caesar and Cleopatra is a proof of this. However flippant or hilarious its means may be, its concerns are serious and sizable. For Shaw's real interest, so gaily presented in a very funny play, is nothing less than a study of the anatomy of earthly power and greatness. Although his Caesar may laugh and be laughed at, he is palpably a great man misunderstood by those around him and even by the Cleopatra he has instructed in queenship. If in delineating this greatness Shaw deliberately substitutes colloquial prose for what he had once condemned as the melodious fustian and mechanical lilt of Shakespeare's blank verse, he is nonetheless able in speech after speech to rise to a glorious eloquence of his own.

Caesar's apostrophe to the Sphinx is a sample. It is with this, and neither of the alternate prologues, that the present production opens. Other samples are the wisdom of Caesar's "He who has never hoped can never despair" and his "One year of Rome is like another, except that I grow older whilst the crowd in the Appian Way is always the same age." Or the beauty of his leave-taking of Cleopatra, when he describes Mark Antony to her in these words, "Come, Cleopatra: forgive me and bid me farewell; and I will send you a man, Roman from head to heel and Roman of the noblest; not old and ripe for the knife; not lean in the arms and cold in the heart; not hiding a bald head under his conqueror's laurels; not stooped with the weight of the world on his shoulders; but brisk and fresh, strong and young, hoping in the morning, fighting in the day, and reveling in the evening." In almost every instance the organ plays full and strong, only to be interrupted by a jest. Even so, the sense of greatness is not lost. Moreover, it is part and parcel of the current revival.

Sir Cedric Hardwicke is no plaster-bust Caesar. He is the perfect embodiment of the Shavian conqueror: patrician, accustomed to command, and no less used to meeting the harder challenges of thought. Although his majesty is genuine, his simplicity is equally real. If he can make a joke, he can also take one. His manner is quiet. His eyes twinkle with amusement at the foibles of those lacking his qualities. His humor is kindly, not condescending. It is born of his patience, even as that patience is backed by an iron will. One believes in him not only as a general but as a thinker. More than acting with his body, he acts with his mind. Instead of speaking Shaw's lines as if he had memorized them, he speaks them as if he had thought them. The wit of Shaw's Caesar is his. So is the eloquence; so is the wisdom.

Surely, Lilli Palmer must be the most eye-filling and eye-haunting Cleopatra the stage has known. After seeing her one is bound to feel a new sympathy for Mark Antony. She is blessed with all the physical attributes that one likes to associate with Egypt's queen, but her endowments do not stop there. Hers is a truly exciting personality. What is more, she acts Cleopatra as perfectly as she looks her, changing with great skill from the kittenish girl of the earlier scenes to the violent and imperious monarch of the later ones.

As a director, Hardwicke equals his success as a player. His touch is inventive, understanding, and hence always contributive. He is aided by Rolf Gerard, who, though he has set and costumed the production strikingly, has not been tempted to kill a comedy by turning it into a spectacle. The secondary performances, such as Bertha Belmore's impregnable Ftatateeta, Arthur Treacher's droll Britannus, and Ralph Forbes's stalwart Rufio, are all admirable. But outstanding among them is John Buckmaster's brilliant characterization of Apollodorus.

The happy truth is that this revival of *Caesar and Cleopatra* succeeds in living up to Shaw's comedy. It makes the past provocative, history human, and greatness gay.

January 14, 1950

*THE CONFUSIONS of the modern
world as T. S. Eliot adds to them in a
verse play everyone seems to understand until asked to explain it.*

꩜꩜꩜꩜꩜꩜꩜꩜꩜꩜꩜꩜꩜꩜꩜꩜꩜꩜꩜꩜꩜꩜꩜꩜꩜꩜꩜

Honorable Intentions

THEY WERE there, the faithful and the devout, for the
opening of *The Cocktail Party*.* They were there, carrying their reverence with them much as pilgrims might carry
candles in a procession. They were there, filled with a sense of
the night's eventfulness; confident, because Mr. Eliot, *their*
Mr. Eliot, was the dramatist, that before final curtain time
they would enjoy, as he once put it, "a tremor of bliss, a wink
of heaven." That they were rewarded with both the tremor
and the wink, I am in no position to deny. Even those to whom
T. S. Eliot is a man and not a religion could not fail to be
grateful for certain of the evening's qualities.

Beyond dispute actors of extraordinary excellence were
being seen. What is more, they were being heard. With the
exception of Irene Worth, they were English actors. They
were such gifted English actors as Alec Guinness, Cathleen

---

* *The Cocktail Party*, a play by T. S. Eliot. Directed by E. Martin Brown.
Settings supervised by Raymond Sovey. Presented by Gilbert Miller by ar-
rangement with Sherek Players, Ltd. With Alec Guinness, Cathleen Nesbitt,
Robert Flemyng, Eileen Peel, Ernest Clark, Grey Blake, Irene Worth, Avril
Conquest, and Donald Bain. At Henry Miller's Theatre, New York City.
Opened January 21, 1950.

Nesbitt, Robert Flemyng, Eileen Peel, and Ernest Clark. Moreover, all of them (including Miss Worth, an American who has become as British as the rest) were playing with that finish and authority and that genius for handling the language at which the English are unrivaled.

Beyond dispute, too, there were proofs that the mind responsible for the dialogue these actors were speaking so well was no ordinary mind. It was subtler, lonelier, colder, stouter, more questing than that lying behind most playwriting. Yet I could not help wondering, as I watched the absorption of the devout in what I doubt they at all times understood more clearly than I did, what their reactions would have been if, instead of being hallowed by T. S. Eliot's name, this play in verse had been written by some unknown dramatist.

"You don't expect me to know what to say about a play when I don't know who the author is, do you?" asks Bannal, one of the critics, in the Epilogue to *Fanny's First Play*. It helps a lot, of course, to know that T. S. Eliot is the author of *The Cocktail Party*. No living writer is more revered or has been written about more extensively than he. One has only to turn to *T. S. Eliot: A Selected Critique* and read such worthies as Conrad Aiken, Richard Aldington, E. M. Forster, Mark Van Doren, Paul Elmer More, Malcom Cowley, John Crowe Ransom, Stephen Spender, William Butler Yeats, or Allen Tate to learn what one should—and should not—say about Mr. Eliot. The dicta and dogma of these gentlemen have taken their place among the flora and fauna of the present's higher browed criticism.

A relative of Mr. Eliot may once have described him to me as being "the best British poet ever to have been born in St. Louis," but no one else would dream of being so lacking in piety. Mr. Eliot is a Nobel Prize winner. His scholarship is enormous. His critical contributions are vastly respected. His poetry is widely acclaimed by thousands whether they comprehend it or not. Campuses ring with his name. Intellectuals, young and old, here and abroad grow bright-eyed when he is mentioned. *The Waste Land* is usually cited as being an event no less than a poem. Indeed, such is his pre-eminence that few statements made by any literary figure in our time have provoked more consternation or applause than his declaration that he was "an Anglo-Catholic in religion . . . a classicist in literature and a royalist in politics."

Though he has excelled at poetry and the essay, he has not limited himself to them. As a close student of Euripides, Seneca, the Elizabethans, the Jacobeans, Dryden, and the theory of poetic drama, the theatre has also attracted him. His *Murder in the Cathedral,* a play about Becket's martyrdom, relied heavily upon its choral interludes. Slow in starting as it was, it rose to moments of high beauty, became dramatic almost in spite of itself, and brought poetry back to a prosaic stage.

Since then, Mr. Eliot has written two other plays in verse, *The Family Reunion* and *The Cocktail Party.* In the first of these he made some use of a chorus; in the second he has dispensed with a chorus entirely. In both of them he chose to place his action in modern settings. If he has turned his back on dramas laid in the past, it is because, as he has confessed, he now wishes to write only plays about contemporary life. His conviction is that "if poetic drama is to establish itself again, after three hundred years, it has got to show that it can deal with what appears to be the most refractory material." It must concern itself with such "men and women as we know, in the usual clothes that they wear today, in the same perplexities, conflicts, and misunderstandings that we and our acquaintances get involved in, and uttering no lines that are not relevant to the situation, the mood, and the dramatic action."

Mr. Eliot has admitted that he is working as an experimentalist. To him the iambic pentameter is an anachronism. He rightly refuses to don Elizabethan tights in order to deal with his own times. In the anarchy of the present, when there is no one accepted verse form for poetic drama, he is seeking to find the right contemporary form for himself, even as he believes all other poets drawn to the theatre must nowadays endeavor to do. Mr. Eliot is not of the trombone and oboe school. He does not want his verse to call attention to itself. He is willing to have an audience mistake it for prose when the action is not intense. He wishes by the rhythms in his casual speeches, rhythms perhaps unnoticed by playgoers, to prepare for those crises when his characters have been lifted into poetry by the intensity of their feelings. A first-rate drama, he thinks, should make us believe that there are moments in life when poetry is the natural form of expression of ordinary men and women.

So much for Mr. Eliot's theory as stated by him in a very frank and disarming address delivered in London to the Poets' Theatre Guild. The theory, as theory, makes sound sense and is easy to follow. But, as *The Cocktail Party* once again proves, practice and theory are not always brothers, much less twins. In spite of its intervals of communicated tension; in spite, too, of the fine felicity and beauty of its occasional phrases, the sharpness or wit of scattered lines, and the dazzling brilliance of its performance, it is obscure, not clear.

Mr. Eliot's new play starts as trivially as if he were writing a flat sequel to the highly successful "Yatata, Yatata" scene in *Allegro,* and ends in a pea-soup fog of mysticism. Its poetry is a secret almost too well kept. It is optical rather than auditory. Although on the printed page it looks like poetry, when spoken it seldom explains why it has been set as verse. This is as true of most of its intense climaxes as it is of its calmer stretches.

I approach Mr. Eliot's verse with proper caution. When, in the same address referred to above, Mr. Eliot noted the need of training professional critics of poetic drama and added that very few dramatic critics are especially equipped at present for this task, he was not pointing at me but he might have been. I have my other reasons for being shy about discussing Mr. Eliot's text in detail. He is a great one for playing solemn jokes upon his public—to the delight of his academic devotees. It amuses him to interlard his own creations with lines borrowed here and there from the works of others, as a test of his readers' scholarship. Edmund Wilson, for example, pointed out that in *The Waste Land,* a poem of only 433 lines (to which are added seven pages of notes), Mr. Eliot managed to include "quotations from, allusions to, or imitations of at least thirty-five different writers (some of them, such as Shakespeare and Dante, laid under contribution several times)—as well as several popular songs; and to introduce passages in six foreign languages, including Sanskrit."

I remember the late Theodore Spencer smiling happily when he told me that a speech which I had admired of one of the knights in *Murder in the Cathedral* had been snipped as a merry jest from A. Conan Doyle's *The White Company.* Whether or not Mr. Eliot has been indulging in any such playful appropriations in *The Cocktail Party*, I do not know. I only remember Shaw's warning to critics when, for fun, he rewrote his novel *Cashel Byron's Profession* as a play in blank verse called *The Admirable Bashville*. Shaw confessed he had purposely stolen or paraphrased lines from Marlowe and Shakespeare (not to mention Henry Carey) so that, if any man dared to quote him derisively, he should do so in peril of inadvertently alighting on a purple passage from *Hamlet* or *Faustus*.

In the instance of *The Cocktail Party*, therefore, I do not presume to say whether Mr. Eliot is writing *solo* or *ex libris*. Speaking only as a member of the theatregoing laity, I must nevertheless observe that in my opinion the drama is a medium which seems to resist his advances. Notwithstanding his aroused interest, his honorable intentions, and his vast erudition in the field of dramatic literature, he and the professional stage (at least as most of us know and enjoy it) do not make a congenial couple.

In *The Cocktail Party* Mr. Eliot, if I understand him clearly, and I am not at all certain that I do, is writing about a group of Mayfair sophisticates as interslept as if they were the interchangeable sixsome in Benn Levy's *Clutterbuck*. Mr. Eliot's approach, however, proves ultimately as portentous as Mr. Levy's is farcical throughout.

In the most high-minded way, he is interested in the emotionally maladjusted. His pivotal character is a psychoanalyst who serves not only as a doctor but as a priest to those of little faith. Among these count the husband and wife and the husband's mistress, who turn for help to this psychoanalyst. The love of which these three people are capable exists on planes as different as are their spiritual potentialities. The husband and wife are earth-bound. They represent the unloving and the unloved. Bringing them together again is merely a matter of psychiatric readjustment. But the mistress is made of finer stuffs. She has a sense of sin and is worthy of a saintly atonement. Sent to what she thinks is the doctor's sanitarium, she is dispatched as a nurse to the Far East, where she finds redemption by dying, crucified by natives near a colony of ants.

Mr. Eliot's play begins and ends with a cocktail party. It is against the background of such trivia that his characters, nervous products of a nervous age, are explored. In revealing their problems and their natures, Mr. Eliot is at his most effective in the scenes dominated by the psychoanalyst, and at his least witty and most tedious when trying to write the brittle chitchat of the drawing room. The vigor of his mind and his precise command of language are most strongly felt when his touch is both sardonic and serious. Even so, the difference between dialogue and talk (and far too much talk at that) is something that he does not appear to have mastered any more than he has managed to endow deliberately conversational verse with the lift or song of dramatic poetry.

If we cannot applaud Mr. Eliot for bringing about a new poetic age in the theatre by writing *The Cocktail Party*, we must sincerely thank Gilbert Miller, as producer, and E. Martin Brown, as director, for permitting us to enjoy players who are capable of acting as if that new age had already been achieved. Few plays in prose and none in modern verse that I can think of have been blessed with so notable a cast.

The actors in *The Cocktail Party* are a joy to watch and listen to. The most spectacular performance may be Alec Guinness's wonderfully trenchant and dynamic playing of the psychoanalyst. But Robert Flemyng as the husband, Eileen Peel as the wife, Irene Worth as the mistress, and Cathleen Nesbitt as the older woman are all admirable. They rise triumphantly to meet the challenges of a difficult script. They do their best —and a shining best it is—to protect it from its obvious and sometimes irritating shortcomings. But, exciting as is their contribution and extraordinary as is their skill, they cannot hide the fact that Mr. Eliot in *The Cocktail Party* has not yet found a plot, a poetic idiom, or a dramatic method which realizes his dreams or our hopes.

February 4, 1950

THE TURN OF THE SCREW *as
it continues to conscript the imagination
in play form, and the irony of Henry
James's posthumous success in the
theatre.*

᪥᪥᪥᪥᪥᪥᪥᪥᪥᪥᪥᪥᪥᪥᪥᪥᪥᪥᪥᪥᪥᪥᪥᪥᪥᪥᪥᪥᪥᪥

Haunted Children

HEN TWENTY years ago Heywood Broun wrote an
introduction to the Modern Library Edition of *The
Turn of the Screw* he may have shed little light on a story
which has been variously explained. But one thing he did do.
With unashamed accuracy he described the terror which seized
him when first he submitted himself to the thralldom of
Henry James's ghostly yarn. It is a terror we have all known
as we have read or reread James's story, racing through each
of its pages breathlessly, yet almost dreading to turn to the
next. Broun was well aware that his introduction, purely personal as it was, would not be the last. Many more prefaces will
be written, many more editions will be printed, he concluded,
before *The Turn of the Screw* will have "spent its capacity to
conscript the human imagination."

Conscript the imagination—that is precisely what *The Turn
of the Screw* does and will continue to do so long as men have
eyes to read or vertebrae to unhinge. But its spell, so overpowering on the printed page, is no longer limited to the
library. To the surprise of most of us who would have sworn
that James's story would defy transference to the stage, it is

now conscripting the imagination in play form under the title of *The Innocents*.*

No one, I venture to say, would be more amazed or pleased than Henry James himself by the success which of late has come his way behind the footlights, first with *Berkeley Square* based on *The Sense of the Past*, next with *The Heiress* derived from *Washington Square*, and now with *The Innocents*. It is one of the ironies of authorship that what he so longed to do for himself had to be done for him by others.

He might mutter about the "vulgarities and platitudes" of the stage. He might condemn playwriting as "a most unholy trade." He might dismiss a dramatist as a writer who must hold "the maximum of his refinement" down to meet "the minimum of intelligence of the audience"; in other words, to the intelligence "of the biggest ass it may conceivably contain." He might in his theatregoing sometimes embarrass his companions by whispering diabolical comments in all-too-audible tones. He might even on occasion walk out halfway through a play, groaning, "I can't bear it any longer." But Henry James was always stage-struck; and had been since, as a boy of eight, he was taken by his parents to see *The Comedy of Errors*. If he haunted playhouses, the theatre haunted him. He not only wrote plays from time to time throughout his whole career, but at one point interrupted his work as a novelist to devote five years almost exclusively to playwriting.

The urgency of Henry James's interest in the theatre has been made clearer than ever before by two books which have

* *The Innocents*, a new play by William Archibald. Based on Henry James's *The Turn of the Screw*. Directed by Peter Glenville. Setting by Jo Mielziner. Costumes by Motley. Music by Alex North. Presented by Peter Cookson. With Beatrice Straight, Isobel Elsom, Iris Mann, and David Cole. At the Playhouse, New York City. Opened February 1, 1950.

appeared within the past two years. One of these, edited with true skill and affection by Allan Wade, is *The Scenic Art*. It is a fascinating collection of James's critical writings from 1872 until 1901 (and what an admirable critic he was!) on such players as Madame Ristori, Henry Irving, Salvini, Coquelin, and Bernhardt, and such dramatists as Augier, Dumas Fils, Ibsen, and Rostand. The other is *The Complete Plays of Henry James*, a volume which runs to more than eight hundred double-columned pages. This is a monumental record of brave tries and lost hopes, which gains in both interest and value because of the brilliance of Leon Edel's foreword and detailed introductory notes.

There is a definite connection between James's writing for the theatre and his writing of *The Turn of the Screw*. Mr. Edel establishes this in as full and engrossing an account of what happened before, on, and after a stormy first night as I have ever read. The anguishes of that evening only add to the ironies of James's posthumous success in the theatre. They explain why Henry James would be the more moved, regardless of what he might miss of his story, by the absorbed silence with which *The Innocents* is followed and the applause which thunders at the curtain's fall. These very marks of favor would force him to think back to quite a different experience he once had in the theatre. This was in 1895 and turned out to be an ordeal which he remembered as "one of the most detestable incidents" in his life.

After a year's postponement George Alexander was then presenting *Guy Domville*, one of James's four plays to reach the stage. The period sets and costumes were exquisite, the cast was good, the audience itself more than stellar. But Henry James was "lonely and terrified." As Mr. Edel makes clear, he had decided to beguile the "tremulous hours" between eight-thirty and eleven by going to see *An Ideal Husband* in spite of being no admirer of Oscar Wilde.

James grew increasingly nervous as the evening progressed. He was ignorant of what had been happening at his own theatre when he arrived at the stage door during the last minutes of his play. He did not know that, though the first act had gone well and the third was to have its admirers, trouble had broken out during the second. He did not realize that the baffled gallery gods were in a sullen mood. Or that when Alexander had said, "I am the last, my lord, of the Domvilles," a cockney voice coming from near the roof had screamed, "It's a bloody good thing y'are!"

No doubt it was the first bursts of applause when the actors were taking their curtain calls which induced Alexander to make the fatal mistake of leading Henry James onto the stage, when cries of "Author! Author!" were heard from the stalls. "The forces of civilization" (as James described them) applauded long, hard, and gallantly. But the "roughs" would have none of him. They yelled and booed and hissed. For a few torturing seconds which seemed like eternity he stood there "thunderstruck." His cheeks were pale; his dark beard framed his half-opened mouth. Lacking the mind and body of "vulcanized rubber," which Maxwell Anderson once insisted a playwright must possess, unendowed with Wilde's effrontery, and not relishing verbal clashes in Shaw's manner, Henry James was stabbed to the heart. "Green with dismay" (to quote one witness), he turned and fled to the wings. His wounds were to prove abiding. Neither the loyalty of his friends nor the championing of such a critic as Shaw could heal them.

No wonder he came to the conclusion, "I may have been meant for the Drama—God knows!—but I certainly wasn't meant for the Theatre." Or that, as Mr. Edel points out, the very first notes James jotted down after the unfortunate opening of *Guy Domville* were for a tale of horror. The nightmare story upon which he went to work, with the jeers of the first-night audience still ringing in his ears, had been told him by the Archbishop of Canterbury. In its finished form this became the story which shivering readers have long delighted in as *The Turn of the Screw*.

In daring to dramatize it William Archibald has had to muster his courage no less than his skill. There are those who like to believe *The Turn of the Screw* contains horrors more horrible than the ones which meet the governess's or the simple reader's eyes. They claim it is a study in abnormal psychology and that its ghosts are not ghosts at all but the hallucinations of the governess's disordered mind. This young woman, they maintain, is a spinster suffering from sexual repression. She has fallen precipitously in love with the guardian of the children entrusted to her care. In her loneliness at Bly, the country house to which she has gone, they insist she dreams up the ghosts of the redheaded Quint and the no less evil woman who preceded her in the job of governess as figures terrible enough to cause the guardian, who has not wished to be disturbed in London, to hasten to her aid.

Those who have interpreted *The Turn of the Screw* in this fashion are capable defenders of their theory. If not watertight, as they advance it, it is almost ghostproof. Their subtleties are endless. They are even willing to swallow their sense of humor and point out that there is a valid Freudian significance in the fact that the male apparition first appears on a tower and the female on a lake. As I say, however, theirs is a reasonable enough interpretation of a story weird in its perils, vices, and disorders. It may even be the right one, though no one really knows, since Henry James failed to be explicit about his intentions.

Such a devious, intellectual view is not shared by Mr. Archibald. *The Turn of the Screw*, as he has turned it into *The Innocents*, is a ghost story, neither pure nor simple, but a ghost story nonetheless. Mr. Archibald's emphasis is on fright rather than Freud. Not only the governess, the housekeeper, and the children see the specters in his version, but so do we. Since our seeing them is vital to the fear we feel and want to feel, Mr. Archibald's is no doubt the most sensible of theatrical solutions. Certainly it is one that creates almost insupportable tension and that freezes the blood.

In every dramatization something is bound to be lost. In the case of *The Turn of the Screw* the loss of James's style is a sizable subtraction. Although there are all too many people who write, the number of writers is small whose mastery of their tools is such that they deserve to be described as authors. James is one of these. Sentence by sentence, word by word, his language in *The Turn of the Screw* is a joy. It is rich-textured, accurate, varied, very much his own, and yet uncursed with the involutions which were later to bog down his prose. If we believe in the tale as one being read from the governess's manuscript, we delight in it because it is told as only James could tell it.

In spite of the manifestations of James's prowess which are bound to be lost in play form, *The Innocents* is extraordinarily effective in its own right. To a degree one might have thought impossible, it succeeds in re-creating the story's shuddery suspense and in duplicating all that is portentous and frightening in its atmosphere.

Jo Mielziner's share in this achievement cannot be over-praised. If ever there was a script demanding space it is *The Turn of the Screw*. A huge and empty English country house, the gardens, the woods, and the lake outside—these are the scenes of its itinerant terrors. Yet Mr. Mielziner has managed to confine the whole action within a single interior. No doubt, with its circular staircase and its great curtained French windows opening on a terrace and the lake beyond, Mr. Mielziner's interior is not the kind of room, detail by detail, one would have found at Bly. This, however, is an irrelevance. Mr. Mielziner makes us believe not only that we could find such a room at Bly but that the whole of Bly is somehow in it. It seems endless in its dimensions. If it is a place to alarm the living, it is because palpably it is so hospitable to the returning dead.

Terror is no easy emotion to sustain. It is bound to be shadowed by laughter. The frightening can readily become the absurd. Luckily this never happens in *The Innocents*, owing to the taste and driving skill of Peter Glenville's direction. The production is as fortunate in its casting as in its background and staging. Isobel Elsom is admirable as Mrs. Grose, the housekeeper. Beatrice Straight, who has grown immeasurably as an actress, interprets with a charm and intensity matched only by her skill the difficult part of the governess who feels she must fight the dead in behalf of the living.

But the evening's most astounding performances are given by Iris Mann and David Cole as the haunted sister and brother. They are not child actors whose talents stop at behaving without self-consciousness in public, although that is hard enough. They are young actors in full command of the stage, playing with a technical skill and a sense of characterization beyond the power of most veterans. It is through them, and not only by means of the ghosts who are handled with ingenuity, that the mystery, the evil, and the terror of Bly are communicated. The two of them, as they sing their songs, play their games, or talk, are absorbing enigmas. If neither is quite the child Henry James drew, each adds enormously to the strong tensions of Mr. Archibald's play. Both contribute their full and amazing share to this success which Henry James has scored in the theatre, that "almost impregnable fortress," as he described it, which he has captured posthumously.

February 25, 1950

Pelops' Line

*THE STRANGE yet noble pleasures
of high tragedy, and the tragic pattern
as the contemporary world and modern
man have tended to alter it.*

American Tragedy

IT WAS the year of the Depression, though that had nothing to do with the depression which engulfed Joseph Wood Krutch when he was writing *The Modern Temper*. Mr. Krutch, one of the most penetrating and far ranging of our critics—indeed, one of the few genuine critics we have in the big, proud sense of the word—is more cheerful now. His book *The Twelve Seasons* proves this on its every thoughtful page. It is a delectable account of country living, so all-embracing in its philosophy that even city slickers feel a part of Nature. But Mr. Krutch's mood was different when, at the close of the Twenties, he contemplated Man, Love, Life, and Death. He was woeful then; woeful to such an extent that there were those who, in spite of their admiration, were forced to wonder if the apter title for his volume might not have been "The Modern Distemper."

On no subject was Mr. Krutch more despairing than on the tragic fate which, as he saw it, had overtaken contemporary tragic writing *because* it had overtaken modern man. Mr. Krutch held tragedy, real tragedy, to be among the many good things which had vanished from the earth. He felt it to be an expression of the great ages, the Greek and Elizabethan. For this very reason he would grant it no connection with our own. He saw the world in which he found himself a shrunken place. It had lost touch with the heroic. Its vision of life was not of that ample and passionate kind which had animated Shakespeare or Sophocles. According to Mr. Krutch, God and Man and Nature had somehow dwindled during the centuries since these dramatists had had their say. Mr. Krutch took as the measure of our littleness not the realistic creed of modern art which had led our writers to seek out mean people, but the meanness of the vision of life which had made such a credo acceptable. "A tragic dramatist," he observed, "does not have to believe in God, but he must believe in Man." One gathered that Mr. Krutch, like the modern dramatists he lamented, had misplaced his faith in both.

Mr. Krutch's lament, as I say, was uttered in 1929. Although it made its melancholy points brilliantly, it was guilty of a strange omission. Eugene O'Neill was not even mentioned. Had an historian of the New Deal or the war years written of them without referring to Roosevelt, the omission could not have been stranger. For O'Neill was already fullstream in his career as a tragic dramatist. Ten years had passed since the writing of *Beyond the Horizon;* eight since *The Emperor Jones, Diff'rent,* and *The Straw;* seven since *Anna Christie* and *The Hairy Ape;* five since *Desire under the Elms;* four since *The Great God Brown;* two since *Strange Interlude,* and one since *Dynamo.*

No matter what our opinion may have been of this or that of O'Neill's dramas; no matter how small the biggest of them may have proved compared to the masterpieces of Shakespeare and the Greeks; no matter how tarnished most of them have become by 1949, it was excitingly clear twenty-five years ago when *Desire under the Elms* was produced that in America, of all surprised and surprising places, a dramatist had emerged who was tormented and inspired by the truest sensing of the tragic which the modern world has known.

Few dramatists of his importance have written more unevenly than O'Neill. Few capable of rising as near to the heights as he has soared have sunk into the mire of more pretentious or deplorable mediocrity. Yet even the poorest of his dramas have been enriched by the courage of the man and by that fierce willingness to grapple with the imponderables which has made his best works memorable. What has enlarged the most unsatisfactory of his scripts, and made his career at once heartening and unique, has been the largeness of his concerns. No one, may I quickly add, has attested to this fact with greater warmth or discernment than did Mr. Krutch himself when, in a more cheerful mood, a short four years after his requiem for tragedy, he wrote a preface to a collection of O'Neill's plays welcoming their author to the select company of tragic dramatists.

Like Yank in *The Hairy Ape*, O'Neill's central characters have wanted to "belong." They have been visible cogs in the invisible machinery of the universe. Whatever the crimes into which their passions may have led them, they have cared passionately about the forces controlling their being and their undoing. Not only that, these forces have not been indifferent to them.

This high concern in play after play, regardless of its individual merits, has given to the body of O'Neill's work a significance at once solitary and touched with grandeur. Most dramatists in America and elsewhere during this past quarter of a century have at their moments of greatest seriousness gone no further than to oppose their characters to their neighbors or the social systems under which they have lived. Not so Mr. O'Neill. The barricades his people have assailed have been of a kind unfound in city streets. The altitude of his reach has been the measure of his magnitude and more outstanding than any of his plays. It has set him apart, granted him a deserved pre-eminence, left him lonely but a rallying point. For the forces at war with his people or controlling their fates he has in his evolution found various names—"the great angry eye of God," "the ironic life force," "Mother Dynamo," or "Christ the Crucified." At his best, however, he has handled these elemental conflicts, unfrightened by their savagery and equal to their passion.

To achieve the tragic view, O'Neill was compelled to outgrow the surrenders to irony, crude melodrama, bathos, and pain for pain's sake which cursed his fledgling efforts. Before he could write with the high intensity attained in *Desire under the Elms,* and even more especially in the first two parts of *Mourning Becomes Electra,* he also had to realize that outward naturalism—in other words, those details devoted to documenting the physical life of the body—has little to do with, and could only serve as an impediment to, the interior and spiritual stuffs out of which true tragedy is wrought.

As early as 1922, two years before he wrote *Desire under the Elms,* O'Neill made for a Philadelphia paper an immensely revealing statement of his awareness of high tragedy as the Greeks and Elizabethans had written it and of his attitude toward life and his own works. "Sure I'll write about happiness," said he, "if I can happen to meet up with that luxury, and find it sufficiently dramatic and in harmony with any deep rhythm in life. But happiness is a word. What does it mean? Exaltation; an intensified feeling of the significant worth of man's being and becoming? Well, if it means that —and not a mere smirking contentment with one's lot—I know there is more of it in one real tragedy than in all the happy-ending plays ever written. It's mere present-day judgment to think of tragedy as unhappy! The Greeks and the Elizabethans knew better. They felt the tremendous lift to it. It roused them spiritually to a deeper understanding of life. . . . They saw their lives ennobled by it. A work of art is always happy; all else is unhappy. . . . I don't love life because it's pretty. Prettiness is only clothes-deep. I am a truer lover than that. I love it naked. There is beauty to me even in its ugliness."

I have a reason for quoting this mention of the Greeks and the Elizabethans, and the ennobling lift, the exaltation, the odd but incontestable happiness created by true tragedy. My reason? Because this statement appeared nine years before O'Neill, at the apex of his powers, was to write *Mourning Becomes Electra*. In it he chose not only to retell a Greek story in terms of Civil War New England but to house his Mannons in a great, chaste, Greek-Revival home, columned as if it were a temple. In spite of his barroom, farmhouse, waterfront, or tenement backgrounds; in spite of his prostitutes, his stokers, outcasts, misfits, alcoholics, or sanitarium inmates, and the pungent Americanism of his dialogue, O'Neill did not have to wait for that setting in *Mourning Becomes Electra* to demonstrate that his best plays were Greek-Revival in their spiritual architecture. The worthiest of them, and even some of the less successful such as *The Straw,* followed what in the great periods of the past has been the tragic blueprint.

Religions may change. God may pass under as many names as O'Neill has selected to identify the agents controlling his characters. Yet tragedy in the classic sense has always been, and remains, a kind of religion in its own right. It has sought to impose a pattern upon the patternless; to create an independent logic by relating cause and effect where actual living is most frequently illogical; and to wring ecstasy from misdeeds and tribulations.

Assuredly, tragedy is one of the strangest as well as the noblest of man's gropings for expression. Its subject is anguish, and anguish is the source of the pleasure it gives. No one can explain precisely what Aristotle meant by "through pity and fear effecting the proper purgation of these emotions." But everyone in the presence of an exalted tragedy has an intuitive comprehension of that elusive definition. For true tragedy, regardless of its subject matter, includes those who are adult enough to realize that all men, however happy, are doomed to die and that even a tranquil life, if survived long enough, is bound to be a shorn one.

Even so, tragedy is not concerned with the span of the years. In the vigorous or the old, it is concerned only with the intensity of the testing moments. It holds dying cheap and the death of its heroes and heroines a release for those who have achieved a certain tranquillity, a certain sublime and transfiguring peace, not merely from but because of the agonies they have endured. None of us would be cruel enough to stay their deaths or to deny them their final ecstasies and self-realization. We know that Death, when he at last appears to collect them, will have to be worthy of his conquests. In tragedy the body is almost an irrelevance; the spirit everything. This is why the wounds of the dying spill no blood. This is why, in the concluding acts of all the great tragedies (as once I tried to point out) no expiring character at the supremest moment of pain, whether he has stabbed himself or been stabbed, taken poison, fallen like a Roman on his sword, or been the victim of snake bite (more classically known as asp bite), has ever surrendered to the mortal luxury of an "ouch."

O'Neill's own tragedy, and ours, has been that though he possesses the tragic vision he cannot claim the tragic tongue. "The spirit of inquiry meets the spirit of poetry and tragedy is born," W. Macneile Dixon pointed out in as fine a book as has been written on the subject of tragedy. O'Neill's spirit has always been inquiring and protesting, but neither his inquiry nor his protest has led him to poetry. Although he has been able to feel and plan the great scenes, he has been unable to write speeches which would have made them great. His poetry has been less than prose, his prose no substitute for poetry. Effective as his lines can be in the theatre, they have little or nothing to say when taken out of context. They dramatize pain and exaltation without orchestrating either. The glorious and needed music of the Greeks and Shakespeare is lacking. The result is that, in spite of the attempts of his tragedies to soar, they fly with one clipped wing even when they are not earth-bound. For O'Neill, like all of us, is a victim of an age of prose, and prose confronts the tragic writer with an almost insuperable obstacle.

Maxwell Anderson has been acutely aware of this. He, too, is mindful of the tragic blueprint, the example of the past, and the need for poetry. Indeed, poetry has found no more stalwart champion in the modern theatre than Anderson. He has despised its deliberate inarticulateness and those climaxes in which the only eloquence has been a gesture or a moment of meaningful silence. Again and again, and unfortunately as if by rote, he has tried to escape from the strait jacket of contemporary realism. If his practice has not lived up to his theorizing, at least he has been haunted by the quickening dream.

Too often for his own good and the theatre's, he has turned to the past in his verse plays, succumbing romantically to kings, queens, and costumes, especially Tudor. When he wrote *Winterset*, however, fourteen years ago, he tried to establish a new convention by seeking to do what "the great masters themselves" never attempted. This was "to make tragic poetry out of the stuff of their own times."

It was in *Winterset* that he came nearest to achieving the hopes and aims so eloquently stated in his prefaces. His contributions as a dramatic poet may be indifferent, but no one can deny that in theory the religion which is tragedy finds him among the faithful. This explains why he is so fond of likening the theatre to a cathedral. To him as a thoughtful, sometimes despairing man, science is not enough. "It may answer a few necessary questions . . . but in the end science itself is obliged to say that the fact is created by the spirit, not the spirit by the fact." Anderson's faith, not a very positive or heroic one, is that man must have a faith. Perhaps his old rabbi in *Winterset* stated this belief for him most singingly when, just before the final curtain, he said:

On this star,
in this hard star-adventure, knowing not
what the fires mean to right and left, nor whether
a meaning was intended or presumed,
man can stand up, and look out blind, and say:
in all these turning lights I find no clue,
only a masterless night, and in my blood
no certain answer, yet is my mind my own,
yet is my heart a cry toward something dim
in distance, which is higher than I am
and makes me emperor of the endless dark
even in seeking!

If tragic times were alone required for the incubation of great tragedies, the years of the Depression, the war, and this unpacific peace would have yielded many of them. But, instead of aiding in the writing of tragedy in the older sense and on the older pattern, these tragic times have, if anything, added to the difficulties.

A period of realism and an age of prose are not the only hindrances. The lost or dwindling religious faith of many people; the encroachments of such a materialistic and earth-bound theology as Marxism; an increasing uncertainty as to accepted or acceptable standards; our living with the threat of possible mass annihilation; great changes in the stresses and basic concepts of our economic and social life; the emergence of the "little man" as the new hero for hero worship; the shrinkage of the individual's importance under the pressures of superstates or ever-growing bureaucracies; indeed, not only the notion but the realization that the century belongs to the common rather than the exceptional man—all these are factors, widening or limiting, which have altered tragedy along with everything else. Because of them, one wonders if the tragic blueprint, cherished for so long as an ideal, has not, at least in part, become a glorious anachronism.

Not that tragedy is dead or will ever die. Or that Man has lost his touch with the heroic. No one who has watched men, women, and children rise to the terrible trials of the war years can maintain that Man has become mean. The bigness of the so-called "little man" in the face of such trials and of daily living is one of the most hopeful facts of recent history. It is simply that the heroic has become different in scale and kind, and for this very reason tragedy needs to be rediscovered for our own times and in our own terms.

We have come a long way since "gorgeous Tragedy in sceptred pall" came sweeping by. Thebes, Pelops' line, or the tale of Troy divine, and even the kings and courtiers of Shakespeare are not as close to all of us as they once were. But tragedy in the tenement rather than the palace, tragedy different as it may be in speech, action, and outlook, retains some of its old characteristics. It refuses to become merely a play with an unhappy ending. As Arthur Miller pointed out in some prefatory notes he prepared for *Death of a Salesman*, "tragedy implies more optimism in its author than does comedy. . . . Its final result ought to be the reinforcement of the onlooker's brightest opinions of the human animal."

This is why, much as we admire and are engrossed by such a play as Tennessee Williams's *A Streetcar Named Desire*, we deny it the name of tragedy. It is violent, powerful, and touching; written without mercy and without illusions. No study in disintegration to have come out of our theatre has been more skillful or unflinching. But its people, though fascinating, are too small-spirited to be tragic. They do not grow by suffering; they merely decline. There is no exaltation in them.

There is, however, exaltation in *Death of a Salesman*. At first seeing, it may be obscured by the bruising impact of this story of a "little man" who is sentenced to discover his smallness rather than a big man undone by his greatness. Yet the exaltation is there nonetheless, as the second or third seeing makes clear. It is not strong; it is not meant to be. The play, however, is far from being as negative as some have mistaken it to be. A positive belief in Man underwrites its compassion and lies behind its sorrows.

What Mr. Miller's future will be, no one can say. We can only hope. But it is encouraging to have him divorce the pathetic from the tragic, in those same prefatory notes I have already mentioned, and to have him state his belief that "the common man is as apt a subject for tragedy in its highest sense as kings were." Our need for tragedies, written from and of our times, is great today. For, surely, never before have we so needed to be reminded of the dignity and worth of man the individual.

August 6, 1949

THE DEEPLY moving tragedy of the ebb-tide years and of a little man who lives by the wrong dream and is fated to discover his own smallness.

≈≈≈≈≈≈≈≈≈≈≈≈≈≈≈≈≈≈≈≈≈≈≈≈≈≈≈

Even as You and I

GEORGE JEAN NATHAN once described a certain actress's Camille as being the first Camille he had ever seen who had died of catarrh. This reduction in scale of a major disease to an unpleasant annoyance is symptomatic of more than the acting practice of the contemporary stage. Even our dramatists, at least most of them, tend in their writing, so to speak, to turn t.b. into a sniffle. They seem ashamed of the big things; embarrassed by the raw emotions; afraid of the naked passions; and unaware of life's brutalities and tolls.

Of understatement they make a fetish. They have all the reticences and timidities of the overcivilized and undemonstrative. They pride themselves upon writing around a scene rather than from or to it; upon what they hold back instead of upon what they release. They paint with pastels, not oils, and dodge the primary anguishes as they would the primary colors.

Their characters belong to an anaemic brood. Lacking blood, they lack not only violence but humanity. They are the puppets of contrivance, not the victims of circumstance or themselves. They are apt to be shadows without substance, surfaces without depths. They can be found in the *dramatis personae* but not in the telephone book. If they have hearts, their murmurings are seldom audible. They neither hear nor allow us to hear those inner whisperings of hope, fear, despair, or joy, which are the true accompaniment to spoken words. Life may hurt them, but they do not suffer from the wounds it gives them so that we, watching them, are wounded ourselves and suffer with them.

This willingness, this ability, to strike unflinchingly upon the anvil of human sorrow is one of the reasons for O'Neill's pre-eminence and for the respect in which we hold the best work of Clifford Odets and Tennessee Williams. It is also the source of Arthur Miller's unique strength and explains why his fine new play, *Death of a Salesman*,* is an experience at once pulverizing and welcome.

Mr. Miller is, of course, remembered as the author of *Focus*, a vigorous and terrifying novel about anti-Semitism, and best known for *All My Sons*, which won the New York Critics Award two seasons back. Although that earlier play lacked the simplicity, hence the muscularity, of Mr. Miller's novel, it was notable for its force. Overelaborate as it may have been, it introduced a new and unmistakable talent. If as a young man's script it took advantage of its right to betray influences, these at least were of the best. They were Ibsen and Chekhov. The doctor who wandered in from next

* *Death of a Salesman*, a new play by Arthur Miller. Directed by Elia Kazan. Setting and lighting by Jo Mielziner. Costumes by Julia Sze. Incidental music by Alex North. Presented by Kermit Bloomgarden and Walter Fried. With Lee J. Cobb, Arthur Kennedy, Mildred Dunnock, Howard Smith, Thomas Chalmers, Cameron Mitchell, Alan Hewitt, Don Keefer, Winnifred Cushing, Ann Driscoll, Tom Pedi, Constance Ford, and Hope Cameron. At the Morosco. Opened February 10, 1949.

door might have been extradited from *The Three Sisters*. The symbolical use to which the apple tree was put was pure Ibsen. So, too, was the manner in which the action was maneuvered from the present back into the past in order to rush forward. Even so, Mr. Miller's own voice could be heard in *All My Sons*, rising strong and clear above those other voices. It was a voice that deserved the attention and admiration it won. It was not afraid of being raised. It spoke with heat, fervor, and compassion. Moreover, it had something to say.

In *Death of a Salesman* this same voice can be heard again. It has deepened in tone; developed wonderfully in modulation, and gained in carrying power. Its authority has become full-grown. Relying on no borrowed accents, it now speaks in terms of complete accomplishment rather than exciting promise. Indeed, it is released in a play which provides one of the modern theatre's most overpowering evenings.

How good the writing of this or that of Mr. Miller's individual scenes may be, I do not know. Nor do I really care. When hit in the face, you do not bother to count the knuckles which strike you. All that matters, all you remember, is the staggering impact of the blow. Mr. Miller's is a terrific wallop, as furious in its onslaught on the heart as on the head. His play is the most poignant statement of man as he must face himself to have come out of our theatre. It finds the stuffs of life so mixed with the stuffs of the stage that they become one and indivisible.

If the proper study of mankind is man, man's inescapable problem is himself—what he would like to be, what he is, what he is not, and yet what he must live and die with. These are the moving, everyday, all-inclusive subjects with which

Mr. Miller deals in *Death of a Salesman*. He handles them unflinchingly, with enormous sympathy, with genuine imagination, and in a mood which neither the prose of his dialogue nor the reality of his probing can rob of its poetry. Moreover, he has the wisdom and the insight not to blame the "System," in Mr. Odets's fashion, for what are the inner frailties and shortcomings of the individual. His rightful concern is with the dilemmas which are timeless in the drama because they are timeless in life.

Mr. Miller's play is a tragedy modern and personal, not classic and heroic. Its central figure is a little man sentenced to discover his smallness rather than a big man undone by his greatness. Although he happens to be a salesman tested and found wanting by his own very special crises, all of us sitting out front are bound to be shaken, long before the evening is over, by finding something of ourselves in him.

Mr. Miller's Willy Loman is a family man, father of two sons. He is sixty-three and has grubbed hard all his life. He has never possessed either the daring or the gold-winning luck of his prospector brother, who wanders through the play as a somewhat shadowy symbol of success but a necessary contrast. Stupid, limited, and confused as Willy Loman may have been, however, no one could have questioned his industry or his loyalty to his family and his firm. He has loved his sons and, when they were growing up, been rewarded by the warmth of their returned love. He loves his wife, too, and has been unfaithful to her only because of his acute, aching loneliness when on the road.

He has lived on his smile and on his hopes; survived from sale to sale; been sustained by the illusion that he has countless friends in his territory, that everything will be all right, that he is a success, and that his boys will be successes also. His misfortune is that he has gone through life as an eternal adolescent, as someone who has not dared to take stock, as someone who never knew who he was. His personality has been his profession; his energy, his protection. His major ambition has been not only to be liked, but well liked. His ideal for himself and for his sons has stopped with an easy, backslapping, sports-loving, locker-room popularity. More than ruining his sons so that one has become a woman chaser and the other a thief, his standards have turned both boys against their father.

When Mr. Miller's play begins, Willy Loman has reached the ebb-tide years. He is too old and worn out to continue traveling. His back aches when he stoops to lift the heavy sample cases that were once his pride. His tired, wandering mind makes it unsafe for him to drive the car which has carried him from one town and sale to the next. His sons see through him and despise him. His wife sees through him and defends him, knowing him to be better than most and, at any rate, well intentioned. What is far worse, when he is fired from his job he begins to see through himself. He realizes he is, and has been, a failure. Hence his deliberate smashup in his car in order to bring in some money for his family and make the final payment on his home when there is almost no one left who wants to live in it.

Although *Death of a Salesman* is set in the present, it also finds time and space to include the past. It plays the agonies of the moment of collapse against the pleasures and sorrows of recollected episodes. Mr. Miller is interested in more than the life and fate of his central character. His scene seems to be Willy Loman's mind and heart no less than his home.

What we see might just as well be what Willy Loman thinks, feels, fears, or remembers as what we see him doing. This gives the play a double and successful exposure in time. It makes possible the constant fusion of what has been and what is. It also enables it to achieve a greater reality by having been freed from the fetters of realism.

Once again Mr. Miller shows how fearless and perceptive an emotionalist he is. He writes boldly and brilliantly about the way in which we disappoint those we love by having disappointed ourselves. He knows the torment of family tensions, the compensations of friendship, and the heartbreak that goes with broken pride and lost confidence. He is aware of the loyalties, not blind but open-eyed, which are needed to support mortals in their loneliness. The anatomy of failure, the pathos of age, and the tragedy of those years when a life begins to slip down the hill it has labored to climb are subjects at which he excels.

The quality and intensity of his writing can perhaps best be suggested by letting Mr. Miller speak for himself, or rather by allowing his characters to speak for him, in a single scene, in fact, in the concluding one. It is then that Willy's wife, his two sons, and his old friend move away from Jo Mielziner's brilliantly simple and imaginative multiple setting, and advance to the footlights. It is then that Mr. Miller's words supply a scenery of their own. Willy Loman, the failure and suicide, has supposedly just been buried, and all of us are at his grave, including his wife who wants to cry but cannot and who keeps thinking that it is just as if he were off on another trip.

"You don't understand," says Willy's friend, defending Willy from one of his sons, "Willy was a salesman. And for a salesman, there is no rock bottom to the life. He don't put a bolt to a nut, he don't tell you the law or give you medicine. He's a man way out there in the blue, ridin' on a smile and a shoeshine. And when they start not smilin' back—that's an earthquake. And then you get yourself a couple spots on your hat, and you're finished. Nobody dast blame this man. A salesman is got to dream, boy. It comes with the territory."

The production of *Death of a Salesman* is as sensitive, human, and powerful as the writing. Elia Kazan has solved, and solved superbly, what must have been a difficult and challenging problem. He captures to the full the mood and heartbreak of the script. He does this without ever surrendering to sentimentality. He manages to mingle the present and the past, the moment and the memory, so that their intertwining raises no questions and causes no confusions. His direction, so glorious in its vigor, is no less considerate of those small details which can be both mountainous and momentous in daily living.

It would be hard to name a play more fortunate in its casting than *Death of a Salesman*. All of its actors—especially Arthur Kennedy and Cameron Mitchell as the two sons, and Howard Smith as the friend—act with such skill and conviction that the line of demarcation between being and pretending seems abolished. The script's humanity has taken possession of their playing and is an integral part of their performances.

Special mention must be made of Lee J. Cobb and Mildred Dunnock as the salesman, Willy Loman, and his wife, Linda. Miss Dunnock is all heart, devotion, simplicity. She is unfooled but unfailing. She is the smiling, mothering, hard-worked, good wife, the victim of her husband's budget. She is the nourisher of his dreams, even when she knows they are only dreams; the feeder of his self-esteem. If she is beyond whining or nagging, she is above self-pity. She is the marriage vow—"for better for worse, for richer for poorer, in sickness and in health"—made flesh; slight of body but strong of faith.

Mr. Cobb's Willy Loman is irresistibly touching and wonderfully unsparing. He is a great shaggy bison of a man seen at that moment of defeat when he is deserted by the herd and can no longer run with it. Mr. Cobb makes clear the pathetic extent to which the herd has been Willy's life. He also communicates the fatigue of Willy's mind and body and that boyish hope and buoyancy which his heart still retains. Age, however, is his enemy. He is condemned by it. He can no more escape from it than he can from himself. The confusions, the weakness, the goodness, the stupidity, and the self-sustaining illusions which are Willy—all of these are established by Mr. Cobb. Seldom has an average man at the moment of his breaking been characterized with such exceptional skill.

Did Willy Loman, so happy with a batch of cement when puttering around the house, or when acquaintances on the road smiled back at him, fail to find out who he was? Did this man, who worked so hard and meant so well, dream the wrong dream? At least he was willing to die by that dream, even when it had collapsed for him. He was a breadwinner almost to the end, and a breadwinner even in his death. Did the world walk out on him, and his sons see through him? At any rate he could boast one friend who believed in him and thought his had been a good dream, "the only dream you can have." Who knows? Who can say? One thing is certain. No one could have raised the question more movingly or compassionately than Arthur Miller.

February 26, 1949

Out of the Night

THE HENRY VIII that Holbein drew, that actors must resemble, and that Maxwell Anderson has sought to speak of and for in a verse drama.

༈ ༈

Harrison Rex

"MAY THE King come in?" asks a servant at one of the many moments that Henry VIII appears in *Anne of the Thousand Days*.* Enter, of course, he does. Not because he has a sovereign's rights nor because Henry in the flesh was a monarch beyond stopping; but because, in Maxwell Anderson's most recent excursion into history, Rex Harrison takes Tudor possession of the stage.

Every actor playing Henry VIII is Holbein-haunted. Few canvases have so dictated the make-up, costume, and stance of performers as those made by the younger Hans when, as Henry's "servant" with thirty pounds sterling a year for wages, he was commanded "to take" the "physiognomy" of his royal patron. Did Sir Joshua, when painting *The Tragic Muse* print his name at the edge of Mrs. Siddons's skirt because of his gallant resolve to go down to posterity on the

---

* *Anne of the Thousand Days*, by Maxwell Anderson. Directed by H. C. Potter. Setting and lighting by Jo Mielziner. Costumes by Motley. Music by Lehman Engel. Presented by the Playwrights' Company and Leland Hayward. With a cast including Rex Harrison, Joyce Redman, Percy Waram, John Williams, Viola Keats, Charles Francis, Robert Duke, Louise Platt, Margaret Garland, Monica Lang, Russell Gaige, Wendell K. Phillips, Harry Irvine, George Collier, etc. At the Shubert. Opened December 8, 1948.

hem of her garment? Well, Henry VIII has come down to us on the tip of Holbein's crayons and brushes. The King's skirmishes with Rome are not unremembered, nor are the number and fate of his wives forgotten. But the Henry we see when his name is mentioned, and the Henry we expect to see on stage and screen, is the Henry Holbein saw and drew.

The fringe of feathers on the rakish hat which is all up-turned rim. The balancing fringe of downturned whiskers, hiding the jowls and veiling the sizable chin at the bottom of that square-rigged head. The thin eyebrows, almost plucked or penciled, arching upward. The decisive puffs above those cruel, imperious, and naked eyes. That long, thin, arrogant nose, which even Hazlitt would have had to salute as a proper "rudder" for such a face. The strongly marked, passionate indentation above those tightly pursed, cynical lips, and the mandarinlike mustaches which frame them. The mingled power, amusement, and haughtiness of that gross, willful face. The great broad shoulders, made the broader because of the paths of fur edging the cape. The magnificently bejeweled sleeves. The doublet, also jewel-studded, stretched across that solid body. The fleshy, ringed fingers; the right arm akimbo, the left hand resting on a sword. The long, muscular legs. And the slippered feet, widely spread, with the toes turned out for balance. All these Holbein details create for us the visual image of Henry VIII which we expect every actor to re-create.

Mr. Harrison does not disappoint us. His Henry is younger by some fifteen years than the monarch Holbein immortal-ized. He is more dapper, less portly. Even so, he is Holbein's Henry made flesh. But—and this is the notable merit of his notable performance—he does more than look and dress and stand like Holbein's king. Most actors who have mastered their make-up boxes can, with a costumer's aid, suggest that Henry. To capture his spirit as Holbein caught it and history has recorded it is, however, another matter. At this Mr. Harrison succeeds more completely than any player who on a stage or before a camera has undertaken to impersonate the king within our time.

Until Mr. Harrison turned Tudor, the most widely remembered contemporary performance of Henry was Charles Laughton's. Although acted with skill, Mr. Laughton's Henry was deliberately a coarse fellow. He was a leering, lecherous, greasy man. He was proud, fat, bumptious, and evil. In Falstaff's fashion he was a "great tub of guts." In his lack of amiability, however, he more closely resembled Captain Bligh than Falstaff. If he dressed like a Holbein portrait, he behaved like a Hogarth caricature. His table manners were those of a hog. He had authority, but it was not a king's. The crown seemed as foreign to him as a napkin or a finger bowl.

It is a relief to turn from such a gross interpretation to Mr. Harrison's. His king has all the faults with which history cursed Henry and he cursed history. As a monarch able to mistake his earthly lust for his divine right, he is cruel, remorseless, and headstrong. He is selfish, too, and gruff and commanding. He is to the palace born. The hot blood in his veins is royal. Haughty though he is, his eyes are lighted by wit. Formidable when he is crossed, he is charming when having his way.

Mr. Harrison manages to suggest weight without being fat himself or resorting to undue padding. He also succeeds in suggesting the physical changes which overtake Henry in the ten years' span of Mr. Anderson's drama. He does this in such subtle ways as stance or gesture. But, most of all, he manages to capture the fatal vitality of the sovereign he is playing.

Mr. Harrison's mind is as much a part of his performance as his appearance. If the verse he reads were Shakespeare's, he could not take greater pains to preserve the music of what he has to say. He speaks with wonderful clarity, creating the illusion of significance in line after line by Mr. Anderson in which, unfortunately, the significance like the music is often no more than an illusion.

Joyce Redman brings the same resonance and intelligence to her reading of the fiery Anne, who, in Thomas Wyatt's phrase, was "wylde for to hold." Her redhead is a termagant with a will to match Henry's own. She humanizes Anne, giving her both dignity and fire, even if she is somewhat monotonous, a little shrill, and if at moments she acts Anne with that shadowy indirectness with which the Player Queen in *Hamlet* is always acted.

Mr. Anderson has many reasons for being grateful to Miss Redman and to Mr. Harrison. Chief among these is the simple fact that the two of them are blessed with voices capable of making rhythmic prose, however meager in its profundity or melody, sound like poetry. Such other gifted performers as Percy Waram, who is Wolsey; Harry Irvine, who acts Bishop Fisher; John Williams, who is the Duke of Norfolk; and Robert Duke, who is Percy, the young Earl of Northumberland, in varying degrees possess this same talent. It is a talent which proves sorely needed; as sorely needed, in fact, as it is to have a real musician fiddling in the wings when an actor who cannot play a violin is asked on stage to impersonate Paganini.

Of all American dramatists Mr. Anderson is the hardest to do critical justice to. Regardless of what anyone may think of this or that of his poetic plays, it cannot be denied that his aims are of the highest. His is a splendid, lonely courage. The theatre of which he dreams is the theatre at its noblest. No one has written more eloquently than he about the theory of tragic exaltation, or understands it more completely. With Goethe, he is convinced dramatic poetry is man's greatest achievement so far; with Shaw, that the theatre is essentially a cathedral of the spirit. He despises "the starvation diet of prose" on which we are ordinarily fed. Prose, as he sees it, is the language of information; poetry, the language of emotion. His hope is "strong and chronic . . . that the theatre in this country will outgrow . . . journalistic social comment and reach occasionally into the upper air of poetic tragedy."

It is not Mr. Anderson's fault if his ambitions outrun his talents. That is the common lot. Most of us are doomed to live with the anguish and embarrassment of knowing what is first-rate in this field or that without being able to produce it. Luckier than most, Mr. Anderson has had the satisfaction of making his distinguished contributions. *What Price Glory?*, written with Laurence Stallings, was one of these. So was the father-daughter scene in such a realistic drama as *Saturday's Children*. Certainly Mr. Anderson's *Winterset*, in spite of its shortcomings, had its sizable and redeeming merits as a reaching for poetic tragedy in modern speech and dress. His *High Tor* was a delectable fantasy. And *Elizabeth the*

Queen and *Mary of Scotland* were historical romances which benefited by his eagerness to expose audiences to a kind of brave, colorful language which in our naturalistic theatre is rarely heard.

Why is it then, notwithstanding single speeches of interest in such of his other plays as *The Masque of Kings, Valley Forge,* or *Key Largo,* that Mr. Anderson does not wear well as a poetic dramatist? Why is it that a good many of us approach his plays with less anticipation than we once did and sit through them with less pleasure? Why is it that, even when as in *Anne of the Thousand Days* he is writing more tightly and strongly than he has written of recent years, we feel no real enthusiasm?

Is it because we are onto the trick? Is it because the horrid conviction is bound to overtake us that what Mr. Anderson prints as poetry, and what his actors speak as such, is not poetry at all but a sort of singsong in which very simple thoughts are ornately stated? Or is it because, by undertaking what he has the courage and idealism to essay, Mr. Anderson raises our hopes as high as his own—and then leaves us hoping?

Anne is serviceable enough as theatre. It may add nothing to the story it retells, but at least it follows that story with fair fidelity. Most assuredly, from the point of view of interest, history is on Mr. Anderson's side. To be dull about Henry VIII's love for Anne Boleyn would be difficult. Their passion was tremendous in its political and religious repercussions, and disastrous to Anne. Mr. Anderson touches upon all these ramifications. He employs a flashback technique, having both Henry and Anne on the night of Anne's execution

recall the key events in the tempestuous course of their court-
ship and marriage.

One listens and looks, pleased by the swift movement of
H. C. Potter's direction, charmed by the beauty of Motley's
costumes, and enthralled by such a performance as Mr. Harrison's. One listens and looks, not minding the play too much
but not admiring it either. Those happiest at *Anne* are bound
to be those who do not listen too carefully. The sound (or its
illusion) is there. So is the fury. These, however, do not sig-
nify what they would or could or should. What Mr. Anderson wanted to be, and we hoped would emerge as, history sung
and illumined by a poet turns out to be an actor's evening. It
is not Shakespeare that we must measure Mr. Anderson by.
Alas, it is Sheridan Knowles.

December 25, 1948

HOW PARIS is saved by a daffy countess in an enchanting fantasy which can boast the best mad tea party since Lewis Carroll's.

≈≈≈≈≈≈≈≈≈≈≈≈≈≈≈≈≈≈≈≈≈≈≈≈≈≈≈

Inspired Madness

TO THE jokesters "the little man who wasn't there" has long been a stock figure. In the theatre, night after night and week after week, the big thing that isn't there is apt to be imagination. Its lack, however, is no joke. We come to our playhouses, season in and season out, summoned by the hope that we will find it. As poor substitutes for it, we often encounter competence, slickness, and the same old things said well enough in the same old tired, literal ways. But imagination, the kind of imagination which is quickeningly at work in *The Madwoman of Chaillot*,* is a rarity, and trebly welcome for that very reason.

That the world is in a bad way; that nothing is free, including the fruits of a fruitful earth; that men, who could be happy, condemn themselves to unhappiness by their lust for power and money; that the good, harmless, joy-loving

* *The Madwoman of Chaillot*, by Jean Giraudoux. Adapted by Maurice Valency. Directed by Alfred de Liagre, Jr. Settings and costumes by Christian Berard. Lighting by Sam Leve. Presented by Mr. de Liagre. With a cast including Martita Hunt, Estelle Winwood, Nydia Westman, Doris Rich, Clarence Derwent, Vladimir Sokoloff, John Carradine, James Westerfield, Martin Kosleck, etc. At the Belasco. Opened December 27, 1948.

people are frequently trampled upon by the cruel, the conscienceless, or the avaricious; and that love is the essential emotion for blissful living—all of these are, as observations, commonplace enough to be dismissed as bromides. At least they are when so phrased. Yet they are all made to seem as new and diverting in Jean Giraudoux's dramatic statement of them as if they had never been put into words before.

Coleridge defined imagination as the "modifying power." This is a talent Giraudoux possessed to a remarkable degree. It remains the beguiling source of his strength, the fountainhead of the fun and stimulation he provides in *The Madwoman of Chaillot*. If the stage sustained a loss when he died four years ago, it is because he was blessed with this transforming gift. Both as an observer of human behavior and as a thinker, he was an alchemist. When seen through his eyes, the mundane regains its wonder, the expected becomes unpredictable.

The basic truths are simple and no doubt as limited in number as the basic plot ideas. Like these plot ideas, however, they are capable of being expressed in an infinite variety of forms. The originality of the result depends in either case upon the originality of the mind dealing with them. Let an intellect as unconventional as Giraudoux's come to grips with the stalest of notions, and these notions are bound to emerge all glittering as if freshly minted.

In *The Madwoman of Chaillot*, which New York has at last been permitted to see because of Alfred de Liagre's courage as a producer, Giraudoux is writing in a manner decidedly his own about a sorry universe which (in his script at any rate) is easily bettered. His scene is Paris—a Paris as different from the city most Parisians know as is William Saroyan's

Fresno from the town known to the less fanciful people who dwell there.

It is a Paris endangered by the presidents of crooked corporations. They are dishonest and unsentimental men who, in their search for oil, are determined to dig up and destroy the city. These unscrupulous profiteers, however, are thwarted by the mad countess who gives the play its name. From the King of the Sewer Men she learns that in the cellar where she lives there is a secret door which opens on steps leading deep into the bowels of the earth. It is down this oubliette that she sends not only the hopeful profiteers but their press agents and their molls. Then—presto—she springs the trap. And the world, because of this good riddance, becomes instantly a better, happier, more habitable place.

The means whereby Giraudoux's countess disposes of "the pimps who little by little have taken over the world" may seem as uncomplicated as those by which the Pied Piper rid Hamelin of its rats and robbed it of its children. But do not be misled by the simplicity of Giraudoux's basic story into thinking that *The Madwoman of Chaillot* must be a simple little allegory. Its real action lies in its surprising and incessant play of mind. It is centered in the delectable and unforeseeable fashion in which it makes sense by standing sense on its head, and achieves sanity by toying deliciously with madness.

Giraudoux writes with a love for man, a faith in his goodness, and an understanding of his hunger for happiness every bit as radiant as Mr. Saroyan's. In essence he may be saying in *The Madwoman of Chaillot* what Mr. Saroyan said with a dewy magic of his own in *My Heart's in the Highlands*. Furthermore, he may be saying it in much the same terms of the misfits and the oddities of the race. Yet, though Giraudoux's heart is fully as sizable as Mr. Saroyan's, it becomes clear in no time that his intellect is roomier; far, far roomier.

He is as sophisticated as Mr. Saroyan is naïve, and as much an expression of the decencies surviving in a disillusioned Old World as Mr. Saroyan is of the unfaded and youthful virtues of the New. Where Mr. Saroyan, so to speak, may have been brought up on Maxfield Parrish and Pollyanna, Giraudoux has plainly been exposed to Toulouse-Lautrec and Proust. Even so, his belief in man's goodness and dependence upon the wealth he carries within himself is untarnished.

Giraudoux's sharp Gallic mind protects his fantasy from the sentimentalities which might easily destroy it. His wit offers his comedy an identical protection. So, too, does the fact that, in a very French way, he is blessed with something of that genius for sensible nonsense and inspired topsy-turvydom which Lewis Carroll could claim and which is the glory and delight of *Alice*.

Like many another, Giraudoux appears to suggest that, in a world as mad as our own, sanity may well be the possession of the insane rather than the sane. Certainly, it is the countess and her no less daffy crones from three other Parisian *quartiers* who speak, however irrationally, with the sweet voice of reason in *The Madwoman of Chaillot*. If the countess has her followers; if the waiters, the street singer, the flower girl, the ragpicker, the shoelace peddler, and the gendarmes at a café in Chaillot compose her court, and despise the profiteers, it is because she has never lost her love of life or her respect for, and interest in, those with whom she comes in contact. Addle-pated she may be, but dangerous she is not.

She lives by her illusions, allowing others to be nourished by theirs. Does her friend, the madwoman of Passy, prefer to think that her dog, Dickie, is still alive? Very well. The countess is perfectly willing to enter into the spirit of the game and pretend to believe, in the most hilarious and maddest tea party given since the Dormouse, the March Hare, and a certain Hatter entertained Alice, that poor dead Dickie, though as invisible as Harvey, is present, begging for attention, pleading to be taken up on someone's lap.

Is the news in the daily journals depressing? Not to the countess. Her solution is a brilliant one which she advises her friends to follow. She reads a newspaper every day, but always the same faded copy of the same old paper. It is one she chose because, instead of frightening her with all the news that's fit to print, it brings her just such stories as she finds pleasant to peruse. This may mean that she is somewhat out of touch. Nonetheless it keeps her cheerful.

"What a funny watch!" remarked Alice, when the March Hare had taken it out of his pocket, looked at it, dipped it into his cup of tea, and looked at it again. "It tells the day of the month, and doesn't tell what o'clock it is!"

"Why should it?" muttered the Hatter. "Does *your* watch tell you what year it is?"

"Of course not," Alice replied very readily, "but that's because it stays the same year for such a long time together."

"Which is just the case with *mine*," said the Hatter.

Alice, we are told, felt dreadfully puzzled. "The Hatter's remark seemed to have no meaning in it, and yet it was certainly English. 'I don't understand,' she said as politely as she could."

Unquestionably, there are those who, Alice-wise, will be dreadfully puzzled, if not downright irritated, by *The Mad-*

woman of Chaillot. The violent division in opinion between New York's morning reviewers (who praised it highly) and evening reviewers (who damned it roundly) indicates the heat of the discussions it is bound to provoke.

It is not everyone's play. This is one of its virtues. If it were everyone's play in the sense, say, that *Born Yesterday* is, that *Harvey* is, that *Edward, My Son* is, or, for that matter, that *Mister Roberts* is, it would not, could not, possess its unique merits as an adventurous and imaginative work. One thing seems clear. However much it may annoy those allergic to it, it will occupy a very special place in the affections and respect of the many whose play, and kind of play, it is.

Much as I admire and enjoyed *The Madwoman of Chaillot,* and grateful as I am to Mr. de Liagre for having been able to see it, I cannot pretend to think the full quality of Giraudoux's script has as yet been projected in the New York production. For American consumption, the text still needs cutting. The first act is slow in getting under way. The oil men talk far longer than is necessary to communicate the drollery of Giraudoux's idea. The sidewalk characters at the café are not only too stiffly grouped but remain Americans pretending to be Parisians without having been translated in spirit. Yet, once the madwoman has entered, the production leaps into life.

That life, brilliant and fascinating, lasts, save for the brief interruption of the dream scene in which the countess sees her former lover in the young man she is protecting, until the end of an evening that is as different as it is delightful. Beyond question it is there—irresistibly there—in James Westerfield's playing of the King of the Sewer Men. Certainly, it is present—wonderfully present—in every giddy and glorious moment of the mad tea party given by the countess for her three crazy friends.

Moviegoers cannot have forgotten Martita Hunt's spider-webbed and inflammable Miss Havisham in *Great Expectations*. Nor are theatregoers apt to forget her madwoman of Chaillot. She is as haunting as Toulouse-Lautrec's Marcelle Lender, whom she so closely resembles. She is a harridan, chalk-pale of face and crowned with mounds of dyed red hair, who is dressed from a trunk in the attic. Yet she is a queen, too. Her manner is both imperious and gracious. She may wander into the land of the living from the realm of the dead, but she brings life with her. Her being so odd a spokesman for it only makes her the more persuasive. Estelle Winwood's madwoman from Passy is equally arresting as a fantastic creation. If the superbly stylized and selective settings by Christian Bérard which Mr. de Liagre has imported from Paris are to the needs and mood of Giraudoux's play what John Tenniel's drawings are to *Alice*, so, too, are the performances of these two gifted women.

"Probably *The Madwoman of Chaillot* ought to be rehearsed by a company of well-blended geniuses for a year before the curtain is raised for the public," wrote Brooks Atkinson in the *Times*. No doubt, in an ideal world it would be. There are not many recent scripts worthy of such devotion. In my opinion *The Madwoman of Chaillot* is one of the most interesting and rewarding plays to have been written within the last twenty years. Mr. Atkinson is right when he says "what we have is not perfect." But with him I agree that what Mr. de Liagre has enabled us to enjoy is "original, inspired, and high-minded, and also a creative work of art." That is something; indeed a great, great deal; and another proof of how welcome imagination is on those rare occasions when it blazes behind the footlights.

January 15, 1949

*ANGRIER THAN most at not having
found Hollywood a cross between Brook
Farm and the Moscow Art Theatre,
Clifford Odets returns to write, like
many another, a bad play about his profitable experiences there.*

Biting the Hand

R UTH GORDON was wiser. When in *Years Ago* she
wrote a comedy about a young girl's leaving home to become an actress in New York, she did not attempt to disguise
that it was about herself. Her heroine was identified as either
Ruth Gordon Jones or "Me." *The Big Knife* * might have
been a better play had Clifford Odets followed Miss Gordon's
example.

He, too, is writing about himself; writing bitterly and
angrily about Hollywood and the years he spent there. But,
instead of speaking for and through himself as a disenchanted
dramatist on the Coast, he has elected to make his central
character an actor rather than a playwright. He has done
this in spite of the fact that his script is as personal as a first
novel. The substitution proves a fatal one.

* *The Big Knife*, by Clifford Odets. Directed by Lee Strasberg. Setting by
Howard Bay. Costumes by Lucille Little. Presented by Dwight Deere Wiman.
With a cast including John Garfield, Nancy Kelly, J. Edward Bromberg,
Paul McGrath, Reinhold Schunzel, Joan McCracken, Theodore Newton,
Leona Powers, Mary Patton, Frank Wilson, etc. At the National Theatre.
Opened February 24, 1949.

That actors may be idealists, that some of them have strong political beliefs, that they follow careers which mere money-seeking can blight, and that they must all face difficult personal problems, I do not deny. But that the inner anguishes of the average screen star are of the same size and kind as those which torment a writer of Mr. Odets's convictions and intensity, I do question.

Ideas are not the first concern of players. Their job is to make the thoughts and characters of playwrights live, and at this they excel. Their best thinking is apt to be done about and within their own profession. In spite of their humanitarian impulses, they are, as a rule, more enlightening when the "System" they discuss is Stanislavski's, not the capitalistic.

If for these very reasons Mr. Odets weakens *The Big Knife* by building it around an actor instead of a dramatist, he makes his play the more unconvincing because of the type of actor he has chosen to write about. His central character, through whom he ventilates his hatred of Hollywood, is a figure for whom it is impossible to feel either sympathy or respect.

Supposedly, he is a man who has retained his "integrity," even though his great talents have been wasted by the studios. Just what this integrity amounts to, it is hard to discover. When drunk, he has run over and killed a child and, in order to hold his job, he has not only permitted his studio to hush up the whole affair but allowed his best friend to take the rap and go to prison for him. Yet, thereafter, he never once seems to think about the child he has slain or to do anything for its parents. The way he rewards his blindly trusting and self-sacrificing friend is to sleep with this man's wife. Nevertheless, we are expected to feel sorry for him, callow, egocentric, and verminous as he is. This sympathy would be difficult to muster in any case. It becomes the more difficult when the major dilemma confronting Mr. Odets's actor appears to be whether he should or should not sign a fourteen-year contract that would yield him some three million dollars, that guarantees him a bonus of twenty-five thousand dollars for each picture he makes, and that grants him the right to refuse any script which he deems unworthy of his genius.

Mr. Odets's lesser characters, in other words his additional means of expressing his loathing of Hollywood, include a sulphurous, semiliterate producer who is an utter egomaniac; a female gossip columnist of the nationally syndicated variety; an oily and ruthless henchman who combines the more anti-social features of Dracula and Richard III; a blackmailing chippy whom the studio's big shots have determined to "erase" since she knows the real story of the star's killing of the child; a playwright given to speeches so literary that the ink still seems wet on them; a none too scrupulous agent; the weakling who is the actor's stand-in in jail, the Kinsey queen to whom he is married; and the actor's wife who is as liberal in her thinking as she is in her doses of sleeping pills.

It is people such as these, the scum of the earth, who inhabit Mr. Odets's Hollywood. The play they infest is as active as a trayful of Mexican jumping beans. Almost as pointless, too. It is a silly, overwritten, and turbulent affair. Yet it is not without its interest. Again and again flashes of the old, the welcome, the exceptional Odets talent shine out. In spite of the inadequacy of his story and his characters, there is a communicated, almost frightening sense of Mr. Odets's own unhappiness. Few scripts have made me more uncomfortably aware of the inner despair of the authors; few have left me more apprehensive about their writers' immediate future.

Lee Strasberg has staged *The Big Knife* admirably. Howard Bay has set it sumptuously. John Garfield obviously takes its actor hero as seriously as Mr. Odets does. Such players as Paul McGrath, Reinhold Schunzel, and Joan McCracken acquit themselves creditably, and J. Edward Bromberg, as the wicked studio magnate, gives a performance piloted by his usual authority and skill. But the drama, a problem play leading to its hero's suicide in the bathroom, raises many problems Mr. Odets fails to answer.

Among these is just why Mr. Odets should himself, as an intelligent adult, have been so surprised and scandalized by Hollywood. When he elected to go West, he must have known that he was not heading for the Garden of Eden. There were those returned travelers who had circulated such a report even before, fat contract in hand, he arrived there. Hollywood did not need a war to become one of the world's most blitzed capitals. Since its studios first mushroomed, bombloads of abusive words have been dropped on it. Novelist after novelist has attacked it, usually in books as feeble as the films they were making fun of. Dramatist after dramatist has mocked it in plays that were failures, or in a few successes which laughed rather than frowned at it.

Mr. Odets did not have to go to the Coast. He chose to go. What in the Thirties were thought to be his leftist interests did not prevent him from cashing the capitalist checks Hollywood unquestionably paid him. Certainly, he was too knowing a man to persuade himself that any lot on which he found himself would be a combination of the Group Theatre, the Moscow Art, the Old Vic, Utopia, Brook Farm, or Coleridge's and Southey's dream of Pantisocracy. He must have heard of the place's *Snake Pit* aspects. Having made his own compromise, he must have been prepared for further compromises.

That Hollywood has its faults, can be Mad-Hatter mad, produces more bad pictures than good ones, is not peopled exclusively with angels or intellectual titans, and is not as great a cultural center as the Sorbonne, everyone knows. But Mr. Odets appears to have had an even bitterer experience than the thousands of others who, quite voluntarily, have made the same profitable trek. He must have got in with the wrong set. There are plenty of self-respecting, intelligent, decent, and amusing people to be found out there, Evelyn Waugh notwithstanding. They just happen to be utterly realistic about their jobs. Mr. Odets seems to have been not only unrealistic about his but strangely ungrateful, too.

March 19, 1949

A PROUD Britisher and a Zulu preacher, both fathers, discover they have more in common than they guessed when each is faced with the loss of his son.

☙☙☙☙☙☙☙☙☙☙☙☙☙☙☙☙☙☙☙☙☙☙☙☙☙☙☙☙☙

Lost in the Stars

MY COMPANION wept almost uncontrollably throughout the evening. So did the woman next to her. She, too, was moved, and deeply moved, by *Lost in the Stars*.* At every performance of the play which Maxwell Anderson has derived from Alan Paton's *Cry, the Beloved Country* there will be many whose hearts will be so torn that (to borrow a famous phrase of old Thomas Kyd's) their eyes will be "no eyes but fountains fraught with tears." Indeed, one person has already reported that she was made so happily unhappy by *Lost in the Stars* that she felt like dropping in at *Death of a Salesman* just to cheer herself up.

I envied my neighbors in the theatre. I envy those countless people who will be as carried away by what they see at the

---

* *Lost in the Stars*, a musical tragedy, based on Alan Paton's novel *Cry, the Beloved Country*. Words by Maxwell Anderson. Music by Kurt Weill. Directed by Rouben Mamoulian. Settings by George Jenkins. Presented by the Playwrights' Company. With a cast including Todd Duncan, Leslie Banks, Warren Coleman, Inez Matthews, Julian Mayfield, William Greaves, Frank Roane, Sheila Guyse, Herbert Coleman, etc. At the Music Box, New York City. Opened October 30, 1949.

Music Box as I was when I read Mr. Paton's novel. I wanted to be moved. I did not enjoy being excluded. When the heart is an evening's target, your rightful wish is to have yours hit too. "What's Hecuba to him or he to Hecuba" is not a rewarding attitude. It becomes less so when you know all too well what the relationship really is. There was so much to admire in Kurt Weill's music, in the singing, the acting, and the staging that my detachment surprised me. It became a sorrow in itself.

At first I fancied the line of demarcation between the dry-eyed and the wet was a simple division of playgoers into those who had or had not read the book. Since then, however, I have learned that such an explanation, like most pat answers, is far too easy to be true. I have encountered many persons with an enthusiasm for *Cry, the Beloved Country* as deep-seated and abiding as my own who feel that *Lost in the Stars* does full justice to the spirit and the power of Mr. Paton's book.

As I say, I wish I could share such a feeling. I gratefully admit that Rouben Mamoulian's direction of this tale of parental loss and racial animosities in South Africa is as dynamic as was his handling of Catfish Row in *Porgy and Bess*. I recognize the sweep and beauty of Mr. Weill's music. I realize how intelligent and forceful a performance Leslie Banks gives in the difficult and shadowy part of the British father whose son has been killed. I can only applaud the contagious charm of such a young and exuberant Negro actor as Herbert Coleman. I appreciate the effortless richness of Frank Roane's singing as the choral leader. I acknowledge that few settings of recent years have equaled George Jenkins's in their stunning powers of suggestion. I grant that Julian Mayfield, as the trapped Absalom, represents a triumph of felicitous casting. I concede that Todd Duncan, as his bewildered father, is the epitome of benevolence and sings with uncommon skill. And I am not unaware that Maxwell Anderson, writing with the deepest sympathy, has denied himself those indulgences in the ornate which often tempt him. Yet, even so, though I kept hoping for them, I missed behind the footlights those final qualities of radiance and simplicity which are so irresistible and unique a feature of Mr. Paton's novel.

As critics and readers have agreed, few contemporary books have been blessed with the virtues which distinguish *Cry, the Beloved Country*. Its pages have an uncorrupted innocence. Something of the Bible's sonority is in them; something of its rhythm, too. Their statement of cruel circumstances and tragic wounds is wonderfully simple. The sweet music of a folk song is in Mr. Paton's prose, even though his story is composed of many interwoven themes.

Its contrasts are incessant. The comfortable, if uneasy, life of the rich whites in South Africa as opposed to the poverty of the Negroes; the unsmudged goodness of country people confronted with the corruptions of urban living; the deep-seated conflict of racial animosities as set against the anguish of two fathers, one white, one black, whose sufferings are the same when each loses his son; the irony of an Englishman's being inadvertently killed by a Zulu youth (the parson's boy) when this young white man has chosen to dedicate his life to the Negroes' cause; the faith of a believer shining amidst the cynicism of the unbelieving; the sneers of Shantytown delinquents employed as a foil to the spiritual growth of the preacher's son, who finds redemption by choosing to hang for

· 229 ·

a crime he never meant to commit; the present seething racial antagonisms of South Africa and the fervid hopes for a more decent future—these are among the varied materials which add to the richness of Mr. Paton's exceptionally moving and seemingly uncomplicated book.

Naturally, Mr. Anderson has had to omit characters, telescope scenes, sacrifice subtleties, and skeletonize the story. He could scarcely have faced a more difficult assignment than trying to turn *Cry, the Beloved Country* into a play. If in his script he seems (to me, at least) at times to have made a sow's ear out of a silk purse, it is not because Mr. Anderson's writing lacks honesty or intensity. It is mainly because by the very nature of both the stage and Mr. Paton's novel a certain clumsiness has been thrust upon him.

One of the sources of the book's power is its indirection. Another is its understatement. It preaches without preaching, and is therefore the more convincing. Its compassion comes from within; it exists between the lines no less than in them. Its pages gain their warmth from unuttered thoughts, inward responses, and strong though often unphrased emotions. What makes Stephen Kumalo so persuasive a character is not what this Zulu parson says but what he feels. In the library ours is the illusion of having looked into his heart. On the stage we can only hear his words. This is a genuine loss, a loss because in the theatre incidents which once filled chapters have no other choice than to be reduced to captions.

Lost in the Stars fails in other ways to retain for me the dissolving yet lovely qualities of *Cry, the Beloved Country*. Take, for example, Todd Duncan. As I have noted, his is a remarkable singing voice. He has a kind face too, illumined by something of that benevolence of spirit essential to the Reverend Kumalo. Yet to me, good actor though he is, he has little or no relationship to the parson Mr. Paton created. Although supposedly a simple fellow from the hills, Mr. Duncan's minister is very much a city man. He is sophisticated, not naïve. He exudes prosperity rather than poverty. He is as neat and spruce in his well-cut gray suit as if he shepherded the richest of Anglican parishioners in the most fashionable of churches. If there is little about him of the old country parson described by Mr. Paton as wearing "black clothes . . . green with age" and a collar "brown with age or dirt," there is also nothing of the Zulu.

The staging raises another question. That Mr. Mamoulian has done a stunning, stylized job I have already admitted. In Mr. Anderson's fashion he, too, runs head-on into sizable, if not insoluble, problems. Unable to make use of Mr. Paton's narrative style, Mr. Mamoulian has had to reach inescapably for a theatrical substitute. What he offers is a treatment similar to that he employed unforgettably in *Porgy and Bess*. Although his Negro choruses, carefully posed against the proscenium, are effective, they are far too studied to serve as equivalents for Mr. Paton's prose. His strivings for the simple are strangely elaborate. They are not art seeming to be artless, but art at its most deliberate, hence artful.

Admirable as the production of *Lost in the Stars* is, it was no doubt such aspects as these which I have touched upon that left me interested but unmoved. Mine, I am happy to emphasize, is a minority report. Only a few of my confreres appear to have shared my reservations. We, the dry-eyed, find ourselves in a position similar to Shaw's when an enthusiastic audience called him onto the stage at the conclusion of the first night of *Arms and the Man*. There was one loud and resolute "Boo" from the balcony. Shaw's classic quip was, "My dear fellow, I quite agree with you, but what are we two against so many?"

November 26, 1949

SOME OVERLOOKED differences
between Chekhov's Russians and our
Southerners which may explain why
The Cherry Orchard *cannot be trans-*
planted, and some sage advice from
Stanislavski.

Louisiana Chekhov

" ALL BLAME for the existence of *The Wisteria Trees*," *
explained Joshua Logan in the *Times* on the Sunday
before the New York opening, "I lay at the feet of Miss Helen
Hayes. One day two years ago she said to me, 'I'd like to do
The Cherry Orchard.' I had always thought that Chekhov's
play is as much the story of Louisiana's plantation life as it was
that of the great Russian estates.

"We agreed that I was to try to transpose the Russian play
to my home state. Parallels were obvious. In both countries
slavery had been abolished at about the same time. The decline of power in the landed gentry of both countries took
place during the same years. The agonies of change are uni-

* *The Wisteria Trees*, a play by Joshua Logan, based upon Chekhov's *The*
Cherry Orchard. Directed by Mr. Logan. Setting by Jo Mielziner. Costumes
by Lucinda Ballard. Musical arrangements by Lehman Engel. Presented by
Leland Hayward and Mr. Logan. With a cast including Helen Hayes, Kent
Smith, Walter Abel, Peggy Conklin, G. Albert Smith, Maurice Ellis, Alonzo
Bosan, Bethel Leslie, Georgia Burke, Ossie Davis, Douglas Watson, etc. At
the Martin Beck Theatre, New York City. Opened March 29, 1950.

versal, we felt. That's how Helen got me into trouble, but how she got me out of trouble is another story."

It is easy enough to understand why *The Cherry Orchard* in American dress beckoned both Miss Hayes and Mr. Logan. Miss Hayes would not be the fine actress she is were Madame Ranevsky a part which held no fascination for her. Certainly, Chekhov's drama is one of the few unchallengeable masterpieces of the modern theatre. The tragedy of change and decay to which it gives so magical a statement is a tragedy timeless in its truth and universal in its application, however Slavic in its setting. Moreover, most of us had long been persuaded (at least we had until we saw *The Wisteria Trees*) that the Russian landowners in *The Cherry Orchard* were close enough in mood and spirit to be interchangeable with the fading aristocracy of our own South at the century's turn.

The parallels seemed to run even deeper than those suggested by Mr. Logan. Southerners of a certain kind and class possessed their unmistakable Chekhovian characteristics. Many suffered from the same sadness. They were subject to the same sense of frustration and futility. They were the victims of the same poverty in the midst of proud reminders of gentility. They, too, were aware of being helpless and condemned. Theirs was an identical willingness to live nostalgically in the past without doing anything about the present. They were symbols and expressions of an old order passing and a new one taking over.

No one had stated these parallels more eloquently than the late John Anderson when, as long ago as 1930, he had contributed an article to *Theatre Magazine* called "Look Away, Dixieland." I know that I was one who agreed with Mr. Anderson when he said the analogy is so close "that such plays as *The Cherry Orchard* and *The Sea Gull* could be transplanted with few changes to the remote country houses of Virginia, Georgia, Alabama, or Mississippi and leave the essentials intact." The ex-serfs, he had indicated, would turn color. Old Firs would become "a woolly-headed Uncle Tom." Yet the trueness of the characters would remain undimmed. "Nations apart," he concluded, "these gentle people touch hands."

These resemblances, as I have hinted, had struck some of us as being beyond challenge until Miss Hayes and Mr. Logan, sharing this belief, sought to give *The Cherry Orchard* a Louisiana background. However, there was a factor—the vital one as we have been taught by *The Wisteria Trees*—which had been lost sight of by those of us who believed the South to be completely Chekhovian. This was an elusive feature. Even now, it is hard to capture and make tangible.

Undeniable as are the similarities between Chekhov's Czarist Russia in its twilight years and the late post-bellum days of the South, these prove to be more superficial than I, at least, had suspected. What some of us had overlooked is a question involving inner intensity. It has to do with race, a subject which foolishly (though out of a wise respect for dangerous generalities) is now held to be all but unmentionable. That Chekhov's estate owners and their contemporary Southerners, who were also doomed to lose their plantations, were equals in inertia, no one can deny. Nonetheless, as a comparison of *The Cherry Orchard* and *The Wisteria Trees* demonstrates, the two peoples were inert in very different ways.

Although Southerners were then, as they are now, capable of strong emotions, they did not share the Russians' passion for introspection. If they fed their minds on memories and dreams, they were, I suspect, Anglo-Saxon enough to be reticent about Life with a capital "L." Climate may have made them languid. Cheap labor, which had once been slave, may have made them indolent. Living on the bitter diet of defeat may have left them maladjusted and contributed to their melancholy. But, unless present-day Southerners are a totally different breed, which I doubt, and unless my memories of the older generation mislead me, the South's men and women who correspond to Madame Ranevsky and her intimates did not plunge into metaphysical depths. Wisely, gaily, or ruefully, they prattled on about the surface of subjects. They were happier when discussing people, clothes, food, or events than abstract ideas. Theirs was a fierce family or sectional pride. It was the conditions of their life, past or present, which interested them more than the exploration of their psyches. Their troubles were many, but the "soul" in the Russian sense was not one of them.

Chekhov's people were different. Passive as their outward lethargy may have been, their inward activity was unceasing. A critic such as Matthew Josephson may, in current fashion, dismiss "the mysterious Slavic soul" as a form of *blague*, but to Chekhov's characters this same "soul" was a matter of constant concern. Their preoccupation with it supplies a special energy to the most becalmed of Chekhov's speeches.

His plays substitute interior action for outward happenings. Although his people may be trivial, life in its largest sense speaks through them. Gay as they can be, and gay as they must be to preserve the comedic richness of Chekhov's sorrowful scripts, at heart (more accurately, in those "Slavic souls" of theirs) his characters are sad. In oversimplified terms, the intensity which distinguishes their sadness from that of their Southern counterparts can perhaps be suggested by comparing the sheer sorrow of "Massa's in de Cold, Cold Ground" (which is accepted as being Southern) with the fateful, almost electric melancholy of "The Volga Boat Song."

The vibrancy which underlies the seeming languor of Chekhov's Russians is missing in *The Wisteria Trees*. Mr. Logan cannot be blamed for this. His Southerners, as I have come to realize, would be Russians if they possessed it. Yet the lack of it is sorely felt. All the fine talents involved in the production cannot compensate for its absence.

Before the curtain has gone up the evening presents another difficulty. The program describes *The Wisteria Trees* as "a new American play written and directed by Joshua Logan." Then, a few lines down in parentheses it adds, "The play is based on Anton Chekhov's *The Cherry Orchard*." The problem immediately arises how a script can be at once new and old, original and derived, foreign and domestic, transplanted and native, borrowed and created.

Obviously, the only persons equipped to accept *The Wisteria Trees* as a new play are those who have never seen or read *The Cherry Orchard*. But, as Mr. Logan has himself confessed, such playgoers are harder to come by than one might think. For those who have read or seen it and who cherish the faintest recollections of *The Cherry Orchard*, *The Wisteria Trees* is bound to suffer from a cruel disadvantage. Palpably it is *The Cherry Orchard*, yet just as palpably it is not. It is a work haunted by a masterpiece. It not only has to live up to *The Cherry Orchard* but to live it down. In other words, it starts off its supposedly independent life as handicapped as the son of a great father.

In its major essentials the story Mr. Logan tells is the same story Chekhov told. Often his single speeches are Chekhov's speeches, even as his scenes are suggested by Chekhov's scenes and his characters are cut from the general pattern of Chekhov's originals or are adaptations of them. But the alterations forced upon Mr. Logan by a new locale and people belonging to a different race subtract from the old play's greatness without creating a satisfactory new play. Pruned of their "Slavic souls," denied their sudden eruptive outbursts of autobiography, unable of necessity to speak tangentially, and forced to address one another with American directness, Chekhov's characters lose their depth. The story itself shrinks in significance. Where once it managed to speak for a whole condemned generation, indeed to symbolize the anguish of all change, it now seems no more than the chronicle of a very silly woman who deserves to lose her plantation.

Our theatre does not boast individuals more respected and endowed than those who have collaborated on the production of *The Wisteria Trees*. Jo Mielziner's single setting is a room rich in beauty and decay. Its elegance, though tarnished, is unmistakable. As a children's parlor, it is filled with poignant reminders of the days that were. Its great French windows, with their broken shutters, open on a bower of wisterias with which Mr. Logan, in a moment of inspiration, has supplied Mrs. Ransdell as a substitute for Madame Ranevsky's cherry orchard. We see these wisterias, first in full and glorious bloom, then bare and gnarled when their clutching branches seem to reach out to threaten the Ransdell home. In line, form, color, and detail Mr. Mielziner's setting succeeds, as the rest of the production fails, in stating in Southern terms the Chekhovian essence of the play itself.

Miss Hayes gives one of the best performances of her career as Mrs. Ransdell. It is a glowing performance, radiant and moving, which comes from both the heart and the head. The spell it casts is genuine. Yet, in spite of Miss Hayes's excellence, Mrs. Ransdell in her de-Russianized form is no match for Madame Ranevsky. As her impractical brother, Walter Abel not only plays with charming sensitivity and skill but manages to make his listening as telling as his talking. Kent Smith, a good actor who continues to get better and better, is admirable as the poor-white-grown-rich who purchases the plantation. Although there are many other performances of merit, I, for one, wish that Mr. Logan had not pushed some of his capable Negro actors—including Alonzo Bosan, the Firs of the occasion—so perilously close to caricature.

Mr. Logan, as goes without saying, is one of the most adept and brilliant people in our theatre. His skill and ingenuity do not desert him in his writing and directing of *The Wisteria Trees*. Plainly, his is a labor of love which yields its fine single scenes here and there. Even so, it seems to me a labor that is largely lost if for no other reason than that Chekhov's Russians and our Southerners prove to have less in common than most of us had thought.

Throughout the evening I found myself thinking of the advice Stanislavski had given Mr. Logan in 1931. Mr. Logan, as he tells in his introduction to Stanislavski's *Building a Character*, had left Princeton in the middle of his senior year to make a pilgrimage with the late Charles Leatherbee to study at the Moscow Art Theatre. The two young men were starry-eyed in their admiration for Stanislavski. Stanislavski became interested in them the minute they told him about the University Players and their plans to establish with college students a permanent repertory theatre in the United States. His face fell, however, when Mr. Leatherbee confessed their hope was to duplicate the Moscow Art Theatre in America.

"You must not duplicate the Moscow Art Theatre," said Stanislavski. "You must create something of your own. If you try to duplicate, that means that you merely follow tradition. You are not going forward."

"But your System," protested Mr. Logan, "the Stanislavski System! We have read so much about it, talked so much about it. We have traveled so many miles to study it first hand."

Stanislavski's answer was, "Our methods suit us because we are Russian, because we are this particular group of Russians here. We have learned by experiment, by change, by taking any concept of reality that has become worn and substituting something fresh, something always nearer and nearer the truth. You must do the same. But in your own way, not ours. . . . You are here to study, to observe, not to copy. Artists must learn to think and feel for themselves and find new forms. They must never be content with what someone else has done. You are American, you have a different economic system. You work at different times of day. You eat different food and your ears are pleased by different music. You have different rhythms in your speech and in your dancing. And if you want to create a great theatre, all these things must be taken into consideration. They must be used to create your own method, and it can be as true and as great as any method yet discovered."

Mr. Logan's productions of *South Pacific* and *Mister Roberts* prove how right Stanislavski was.

April 15, 1950

Freedom's Battle

*SOME VITAL problems of education
in a divided world as very differently
approached by the heads of two universities, the one real, the other imaginary.*

☙☙☙☙☙☙☙☙☙☙☙☙☙☙☙☙☙☙☙☙☙☙☙☙☙☙☙☙☙

Two College Presidents

IT MAY seem odd to approach such an agreeable, if machine-
made comedy as Fay Kanin's *Goodbye, My Fancy* * with
a copy in hand of James Bryant Conant's *Education in a
Divided World.*† To write about the magpie or the humming-
bird in terms of the eagle or the owl might appear no less far-
fetched. The connection between the play and the book is
nonetheless there. The differences in attack, depth, range,
medium, and manner do not remove it. It persists if for no
other reason than that Mrs. Kanin's serviceable Broadway
concoction and President Conant's profound and important
volume touch upon what in essence is the same subject. This is
academic freedom, one of the many freedoms threatened in
the present-day world.

To be sure, if Dr. Conant were the college president in

* *Goodbye, My Fancy,* a new play by Fay Kanin. Directed by Sam Wanamaker. Setting by Donald Oenslager. Costumes by Emeline Roche. Presented
by Michael Kanin in association with Richard Aldrich and Richard Myers.
With a cast including Madeleine Carroll, Conrad Nagel, Shirley Booth, Sam
Wanamaker, Lillian Foster, George Mitchell, Bethel Leslie, Sally Hester, Ger-
rianne Raphael, Eda Heinemann, Joseph Boland, Lulu Mae Hubbard, Mary
Malone, etc. At the Morosco. Opened Nov. 17, 1948.

† *Education in a Divided World.* By James Bryant Conant. Cambridge:
Harvard University Press. 1948. 235 pp. $3.

Goodbye, My Fancy, Mrs. Kanin would have no play. The point of her comedy, and the keystone of its plot, is that it deals with an educator who has so lost the courage he once possessed that Mrs. Kanin's heroine, a famous female war correspondent turned congresswoman, decides she cannot become his wife though she has been in love with him since her undergraduate days. Instead, when she has returned to her alma mater to get an honorary degree, she marries a hard-boiled and eccentric *Life* photographer, with whom she has had an affair during the war. She chooses him because he is a liberal whose liberalism has not faded.

There are college presidents—no doubt too many of them —who have become intimidated by their reactionary trustees. In order to hold their jobs, they have surrendered their beliefs. They have made compromises which have unmade them as men worthy of respect. President Conant is not one of them. His liberalism, like his courage, is beyond question. No college president in this country has a more realistic knowledge of the world as it is than he has gained by his membership on the National Defense Research Commission and his other invaluable governmental services. None has a more positive faith in what is beckoning and abiding in the principles of democracy. None has met more unflinchingly the intellectual challenges of Communism, or written more eloquently about the dangers which everywhere imperil that enlightened and untrammeled inquiry necessary for teaching which is to be true, honest, and in the great tradition.

President Conant remains unconfused in the confusions of the present. He is full of confidence where others have become the prey of easy and tempting negations. He is a leader, not a follower. Analytical though his mind is, his spirit is constructive. He does not believe in running from the ugly facts. His signal contribution is his awareness that the uglier they are, the more unblinkingly they must be faced.

In *Goodbye, My Fancy* the college president has ossified into a benevolent mouther of platitudes. As acted, and very well acted, by Conrad Nagel, he can claim all those façade qualities which create an impression of pleasing dignity. He has, however, shriveled into a mere locust shell of what he formerly was. His courage has gone. He is the tool of his trustees. Even on his own campus he solves issues by side stepping them. Education in a free world has for him apparently dwindled into a matter of safeguarding fat endowments.

If the congresswoman, who had hoped to marry him, is compelled to acknowledge his weakness, after forcing this college president into a tardy show of strength, his daughter is no less aware of his shortcomings. To her shame and heartbreak, she has seen through her father. Indeed, she has seen through him as completely as Mrs. Kanin has allowed audiences to do. His spinelessness is revealed in two ways; first, by his failure to back up a member of his faculty accused of being a "radical"; then, by his refusal to let his students see a documentary film making clear the full horrors of war. The film in question had been assembled by the congresswoman in her days as a combat correspondent. The president has favored its showing until a conservative trustee objected to it on the ground that, when he saw it at a private preview, he felt like asking his wife to turn her head away at certain moments.

The theatre being the theatre, and Broadway being Broadway, the issues in *Goodbye, My Fancy* have no other choice than to be somewhat diluted and to take the form of entertainment, amusing if synthetic, and cannily contrived with an eye on the box office. Plot; romancing, probable as well as improbable; comedy; scenes, big and little; campus atmosphere skillfully captured both by the players and in Donald Oenslager's interior with its "Dormitory Gothic"; and good, sharp wisecracks delivered by Shirley Booth as the congresswoman's secretary with the devastating accuracy at which Miss Booth excels—all these combine to jostle the play into liveliness as an acceptable comedy, even when Mrs. Kanin has serious things to say.

In getting these said she is aided not only by the punch and drive of Sam Wanamaker's direction but by the general competence of her actors. Most particularly, she is aided by Mr. Wanamaker's own drily sardonic performance of the *Life* photographer and by Madeleine Carroll's radiant playing of the congresswoman. Miss Carroll's is no easy assignment. She must be beautiful, good, courageous, capable, liberal, successful, and all-conquering. Not many actresses could meet these difficult demands without being smug, coy, conceited, and generally intolerable. Miss Carroll, however, manages to suggest all of the needed attributes, effortlessly, without affectation, and with irresistible charm.

What the stage makes acceptable by saying indirectly in *Goodbye, My Fancy*, President Conant says directly, and with fine clarity and force, in his *Education in a Divided World*. Unimpeded by plot and the diverting irrelevances out of which plays must be made, he thoroughly explores a subject which, behind the footlights, is no more than touched upon. His hopeful, lucid, and fact-facing pages are the more encouraging because they demonstrate that there are college presidents who have nothing in common with the one about whom Mrs. Kanin writes.

Dr. Conant does not mince words. He is well aware that the fundamental cleavage in the contemporary world is the sharp and unbridgeable division between the democratic and totalitarian ideologies; in short, between the American and Soviet philosophies. He knows how unpacific is the peace in which we now find ourselves. As a realist, he believes that "in planning the future of the United States we must assume, at best, an armed truce until the middle Fifties and a divided world for a long time to come."

The question which concerns him—and all of us—is the effect that such an armed truce, in a world so divided, will have upon education. Yes, and the all-important constructive role which education can play in a free society in order to make that society the more secure in its freedoms.

Dr. Conant is fully conscious that reactionaries are going to use the tensions inescapable in such a truce as an excuse for attacking ideas held to be radical or even liberal. But, as he sees it, "those who worry about radicalism in our schools and colleges are often themselves either reactionaries who themselves do not bear allegiance to the traditional American principles or defeatists who despair of the success of our own philosophy in an open competition." Dr. Conant is not the victim of such despair. He writes as a man who has no doubts about the superiority of the democratic beliefs he is defending. It is this unshaken and unshakable belief which makes him unafraid.

One condition, as he sees it, is essential—"freedom of discussion, unmolested inquiry." Our tolerance, which to the Soviets may seem a sign of democratic weakness, is to Dr. Conant a proof of our strength. The pivotal dilemma in such troubled times is for us not to be so misled by our fears that, in our eagerness to protect our basic ideas, we destroy them. "The first requirement," insists Dr. Conant, "for maintaining a healthy attitude in our universities in these days . . . is to get the discussion of modern Marxism out into the open. . . . Studying a philosophy does not mean endorsing it, much less proclaiming it. We study cancer in order to learn how to defeat it. We must study the Soviet philosophy in our universities for exactly the same reason. No one must be afraid to tackle that explosive subject before a class."

As I have said, had the college president in *Goodbye, My Fancy* held such beliefs, Mrs. Kanin would have had no play, which would have been a pity. What seems equally undeniable, however, is that, unless more and more college presidents, teachers, and trustees share Dr. Conant's enlightenment, we may have no democracy to defend. There is nothing to be gained, and everything to be lost, by dodging the truths and challenges of the present.

January 8, 1949

SOME ENCOURAGING proofs of Hollywood's willingness to stop producing films dealing with nothing and to come to grips with some of the appalling and humiliating realities of American life.

Land of the Free

IT ALL depends upon the point of view and what movie-goers want of the movies. In other words, it all depends upon what their patrons not only expect but permit the movies to be. Shortly after *The Barkleys of Broadway* had opened in New York, the *Daily News* saluted this Fred Astaire–Ginger Rogers picture with an editorial which, supposedly, expressed the attitude of many American film fans. The editorial was headed, THIS IS MORE LIKE IT, HOLLYWOOD. It maintained that one reason for Hollywood's box-office troubles was that U.S. moviegoers had been "stuffed to the gills with pictures bearing pious, noble, but sleep-producing 'messages.'" It insisted that people were tired of "laying down their dough" for what they had hoped would be an evening's entertainment but which "too often turned out to be a long, dreary, 'socially significant' treatise about how you really should feel sorry for Willie the Mugger, on account of he was just misunderstood."

There, in language especially designed for *News* readers, is one point of view. There, toughly and honestly stated, is what Matthew Arnold would have identified as the Philistine approach. There, given editorial sanction, is the eternal alibi advanced by Hollywood's bigwigs to justify the puerility, the emptiness, and the unreality of most of the West Coast's offerings.

That the public is entitled to entertainment, that preachments are dreary, that propaganda can be irritating, and that good "messages" generally result in bad art everyone will admit. But, surely, no one who both likes and respects the movies would maintain that all films must be as delectably about nothing as is *The Barkleys of Broadway,* welcome though it is.

Entertainment is a big word. In its largest meaning, it is sizable enough to include the most serious plays or films. It is not limited either to escape or laughter. Tragedy, though painful, can give a special pleasure of its own. To be effective, works of protest and reminder must also be entertaining. None of these types excludes the others. There is plenty of room for them all. Not only room, but need.

My suspicion, more accurately my conviction, is that one of the reasons Hollywood has had its troubles at the box office is that its public has tired of films dealing with *nothing.* It is because the better European films have dared to deal with *something* that so many Americans have turned to them with admiration and relief. The recognizable anguishes of life and war and peace have been in these movies. This is what has kept them from being alien, however foreign. Instead of separating themselves from their audiences by saying, "You will like this because it did not and could not happen," these films from overseas have won their audiences by saying, "This is not what happened in a story or a studio. This is what did happen or could happen to you." In these importations such nearness to reality has been one of the sources of their strength. They have dared to be adult for an adult public and refused to insult that public by condescending to it.

There have, of course, been American films, such as *The Snake Pit, The Best Years of Our Lives, The Search, The Lost Weekend, Gentleman's Agreement,* or *Crossfire,* which have come courageously to grips with problems or situations rooted in reality. But there has not been enough of them. Indeed, they have been pitifully few. To their thin ranks, however, must be added *Home of the Brave.** Whatever its faults, this movie can claim the virtue of being most decidedly about something. Since its concern is the insults and indignities to which an American is subject if he happens to be a Negro, few Americans, white or black, can sit before it without recognizing what is at once disquieting and shaming in its truth.

When *Home of the Brave* was seen as a play on Broadway three seasons back, its central figure was a Jew. Now he is a Negro. And the story, though otherwise unaltered, is strengthened by the change. Once again it is told in terms of flashbacks, as an Army psychiatrist in a field hospital cures a soldier of the paralysis which has robbed him of the use of his legs. The doctor effects this cure by persuading his patient to relive the episodes in war and peace which have provoked his illness.

* *Home of the Brave,* screen play by Carl Foreman based on the play by Arthur Laurents. Directed by Mark Robson. Produced by Stanley Kramer for Screen Plays, Inc. Released through United Artists. With a cast including James Edwards, Douglas Dick, Steve Brodie, Jeff Corey, Lloyd Bridges, Frank Lovejoy, Cliff Clark, etc. At the Victoria, New York. Opened May 12, 1949.

Moss, the Negro soldier in question, had gone on a dangerous mission to a Japanese-held island with four white men, all of whom, in ways blatant or small, conscious or unconscious, had shown their prejudice against Negroes. Although the mission had succeeded, one of the white men, Moss's friend since boyhood, had been killed by a sniper. Moss's illness has been brought on by the psychological shock he had suffered because of the death of his friend and the needless sense of guilt that had welled up within him. He had been inundated by this sense of guilt because of having felt happy at being alive even though his friend was dead. His emotions were the more complicated because his friend had died with an involuntary insult to the Negroes on his lips. But in essence, as the Army doctor laboriously proves, what Moss has blamed himself for feeling was no more than the pleasure common to all soldiers at finding themselves among the spared.

The psychiatry in *Home of the Brave* may be childishly obvious, the battle scenes may take place in a jungle which is more hothouse than Pacific, and the ending, in which a white man and the Negro go off arm-in-arm to open a restaurant, may oversimplify a problem that is anything except simple. Yet the movie has a hard-hitting power the play could not claim. It is a power born of the courage with which it faces its subject. The scenario may still tell two stories which refuse to be soldered. One and only one story leaps from the screen, however. This is the story of the sufferings a black man must endure, in or out of uniform, in a free land for no other reason than that he is black.

Home of the Brave has been vigorously and intelligently

directed by Mark Robson. It is capably played, too, in an offhand, soldierly fashion by Lloyd Bridges, Frank Lovejoy, Steve Brodie, and Douglas Dick. But what one remembers, indeed what one cannot forget, is James Edwards's performance of the Negro. Mr. Edwards is a fine-looking man, clean-cut, sensitive, and proud. He has an athlete's body, genuine grace, and an intelligent face. To watch him, wincing, suffering, and reacting to the taunts and obscenities to which his people are heir merely because of their color, is to feel a proper embarrassment for the white man and his civilization. One of the better features of *Home of the Brave* is that it does not preach tolerance and decency directly. It does not have to. The lines of Mr. Edwards's face are more eloquent pleas for enlightenment than any scenarist could hope to write.

When *Gentleman's Agreement* was new, I remember recording the grateful shock with which one heard such everyday words as "Catholic," "Jew," and "Protestant" emerge from a sound track in a darkened movie palace. This shock, as I tried to point out, was not a compliment to the motion pictures. Instead, it was a comment—and a sad one—on the kind of fare upon which they ordinarily starve us. The effect, I noted, was as startling as if a backward child had suddenly begun to quote verbatim the whole of John Stuart Mill's *Essay on Liberty*.

Home of the Brave is even more outspoken. "Dirty nigger," "nigger lover," "yellow-bellied nigger" are among the words thundered at the audience. To the ears of moviegoers they are new words. At least they are new to moviegoers while in a motion-picture theatre. They have never sounded crueler or more indecent than when blown up on a sound track and spoken publicly before an audience of attentive and well-behaved Americans, both black and white.

More than being an exciting picture, *Home of the Brave* is an encouraging one. It shows what the movies can do when they put their fears behind them, when they discard their childish taboos, and state a major problem for grownups in a grown-up way. I do not see how anyone, North or South, could object to such a film. With Bosley Crowther, of the *New York Times,* I wholeheartedly agree that "the only people who will scorn it are those who would segregate truth."

June 11, 1949

THE TRUE and shaming story of the cruelties to which a white-skinned Negro doctor was exposed when, as an American, he sought to serve his country in wartime.

Eyes That Blind

"YOU CAN put me down as an expert on being a colored American, with thirty years of experience at it. And just like any other colored person with sense enough to look around him and understand what he sees, I know that life in these United States can be mighty tough for people who are a little different from the majority—in their skin, color, or the way they worship their God, or the way they spell their names."

Almost anyone could identify these words as Jackie Robinson's. Almost anyone, too, North or South, East or West, would have to admit their bitter, bruising truth. Mr. Robinson's statement before the House Un-American Activities Committee was a masterpiece of its kind. Even in his career as one of the most artful of the Dodgers, he has never made a cleaner hit. His were words in the fight against discrimination and for democracy which deserve to find their way into the anthologies. For his people and the country he performed a service equal to Paul Robeson's disservice to both. Mr. Robinson was not fooled. He knew he had had "a chance open to very few Negro Americans." Yet he spoke as an American and not as a Communist dupe.

The problem he discussed is the problem which provides *Lost Boundaries* * with its theme and point. The terrible, the appalling, the recognizable touch of truth is upon this Louis de Rochemont film. It is there in the effective episodes no less than in the weak ones. It makes itself felt as an anguish beyond a scenarist's contrivance, with the reality characterizing a documentary. No doubt its presence is explained because the story it tells is based upon the account W. L. White wrote two years ago for *The Reader's Digest* of a real Negro doctor and his family who were accepted as white in a small New England town.

To look white but not to be wholly white must, if anything, be more terrible for an American than to be manifestly black. The black American lives confronted by facts, outrageous and humiliating. The white American whose looks belie that he has any Negro blood lives not only with the full knowledge of these facts but, if he has "passed," with the constant fear of being found out. He goes through life weighted down by that heaviest and most intolerable of burdens—a secret. In addition to being exposed to all the agonies of

---

* *Lost Boundaries*. Screen play by Virginia Shaler and Eugene Ling. Based on W. L. White's true story of the same name published in *The Reader's Digest* and issued in book form by Harcourt, Brace & Co. A Louis de Rochemont production released by Film Classics, Inc. Directed by Alfred L. Werker. Photography by William J. Miller. Screen adaptation by Charles A. Palmer. Musical score by Louis Applebaum. Additional songs by Albert Johnston, Jr. With a cast including Beatrice Pearson, Mel Ferrer, Richard Hylton, Susan Douglas, Canada Lee, Rev. Robert A. Dunn, Grace Coppin, Seth Arnold, Leigh Whipper, Morton Stevens, Royal Beal, Emory Richardson, etc. At the Astor Theatre.

prejudice, he is denied the pride and comfort of being one of his own kind. The world he inhabits is a half-world built on insecurity and filled with fears. Like any Ibsen character, he is condemned to living a lie, though the lie he lives represents society's sin, not his.

The doctor in *Lost Boundaries* has kept his secret from his son and daughter. He is a good man, rightly proud of his Negro ancestry. His original choice was not to pass himself off as white. But economic need and the obstacles lying in the path of a colored man seeking to get on a hospital staff have forced him to do so. Once settled in Keenham, once having proved his worth and having won the confidence of his fellow-townsmen, he has become one of the best liked and most valuable of citizens. His family is as popular as he is.

Yet behind all this outward ease, behind this knowledge of usefulness, and the pleasures of friendship, there is always the secret with which he must dwell. It is the most uncomfortable of companions. It is forever ready to inflict such wounds as those which come when the doctor's son has a young Negro friend as a house guest, and his sister's angry comment is, "Of all the boys in college my brother's got to bring home a coon!"

The doctor's secret might have been kept had not the most ironic of circumstances brought it to light. In the film as in life the doctor is penalized for his patriotism. When the war comes he volunteers and is about to get his commission as a lieutenant commander in the Navy. An investigator, doing his routine duty, digs into his past. The American who was respected and wanted when thought white is spurned and rejected after he is found to be a Negro. The Navy's language in refusing him his commission is a model of double talk and insult. The letter from BuPers speaks of his "inability to meet physical requirements."

Once his secret is out, the good, unprejudiced people of Keenham, who were the doctor's friends, turn on him. His children, in their different ways, are compelled to adjust themselves to the new life which has so painfully become theirs. But at the film's conclusion, because of the sermon of a tolerant though ridiculously persuasive minister (considering the uncountable Sundays on which ministers have had a chance to make their eloquence persuasive), the doctor's neighbors have had a change of heart. They have come to see the error, the meanness, and the foolishness of their ways, and are ready to accept the doctor for the man he is.

Inevitably, any story dealing with a white man who discovers he is part Negro calls to mind *Kingsblood Royal*. The differences, however, between *Lost Boundaries* and Sinclair Lewis's novel are illuminating. For all its good intentions, *Kingsblood Royal* never rang true. It was a phony; well meant, but at best a crude cartoon. There was something cheap about it, something shoddy. Although the product of a benevolent curiosity and a righteous indignation, it seemed planned and planted. Believing in its palpable fabrications was not easy.

It is because *Lost Boundaries* is so much less shrill in its tone that it gains in both persuasion and poignancy. It, too, is propaganda, but it is propaganda scenarioed by actuality. As a film, it lacks the impact of such another honest statement of the indignities to which American Negroes are subjected as *Home of the Brave*. Yet its honesty is unmistakable and irresistible.

As an example of picture making, it is not as imaginative as it could be or as one wishes that it were. Many of its single scenes seem undeveloped. They loiter at the door of fulfillment without quite crossing the threshold. Even so, *Lost Boundaries* must be admired for its courage. It is another welcome proof of Hollywood's new-found willingness to treat adult subjects in an adult way. Its acting is as honest as its writing, and at its most sensitive in Mel Ferrer's reticent performance of the doctor. Although its happy ending may be too pat for credence, it is the kind of film which may open some eyes—and even some hearts.

I speak of opening eyes because it is our sight that is the source of what is at once resolute and unreasoning in the antagonisms between peoples of different colors. "Were the whole world blind, there would be no race prejudice." It is Hector Chevigny who assures us this is true. In *My Eyes Have a Cold Nose,* a title describing his dependence upon a Seeing-Eye dog after his sudden blindness in his middle years, Mr. Chevigny proves his point by an unforgettable story.

One noon, he says, he was walking up 53rd Street in New York on his way to the restaurant at which he usually lunched. Wiz, his dog, was guiding him. A friendly voice called to him. He recognized it as belonging to Billy, his publisher's office boy. The two men walked and talked together for a while. Mr. Chevigny suggested that Billy join him for lunch. There was a pause. "Are you sure they'll serve me?" asked Billy. "Of course," answered Mr. Chevigny. "Why shouldn't they?"

The next few minutes, Mr. Chevigny confesses, were among the most profoundly embarrassing he has ever experienced. Billy had to tell him a fact about himself of which Mr. Chevigny was completely unaware. Billy was a Negro. Mr. Chevigny, being blind, had no way of knowing this. As both his book and *Lost Boundaries* make clear, it is those who are blessed with sight who can be cursed with blindness.

September 10, 1949

SOME WELL-MEANT but mis-guided and dangerous attempts to achieve tolerance by intolerant means, or the folly of pretending that what was wasn't and what is isn't.

Wishful Banning

MR. CHURCHILL'S is the right approach. Explaining in *Their Finest Hour* why epidemics did not sweep London when millions were crowded in air-raid shelters, he says, "Man is a gregarious animal, and apparently the mischievous microbes he exhales fight and neutralize each other. They go out and devour each other, and Man walks off unharmed." Then Mr. Churchill adds, "If this is not scientifically correct, it ought to be."

There are so many things that ought to be, even if they are not. The microbes which assail men's minds are as mischievous as those which attack their bodies. One wishes that they, too, would fight and neutralize each other, allowing Man to walk off unharmed. Unquestionably they should, but they do not, as is proved by the epidemic of odd and sorry suppressions which has swept the world with increasing fury since V-J Day and the coming of the "cold war" or, more accurately, the hot peace.

Freedom was a big and beckoning word in wartime. There were even the Four Freedoms, the first of which was dedicated to "freedom of speech and expression—everywhere in the world." The fourth—who can have forgotten it?—promised freedom from fear. The source of fear it suggested did not go far enough. It was limited to aggressive warfare. It failed to include those other fears which can destroy freedom of speech. I mean those fears to which minorities and special groups appear to be heir; those fears born of insecurity, false pride, hypersensitivity, or a strange, self-deluding surrender to the notion that safety and esteem can be guaranteed by the placing of a ban or the action of a censor.

Take the now notorious case of *Oliver Twist*. This British film has provoked rioting among displaced Polish Jews in Berlin. Protests against it have been lodged by Jews in Vienna and other Old World cities. So far its public release is not planned in the United States. Indeed it has been prohibited in New York because of the action taken by the New York Board of Rabbis under the leadership of Rabbi Theodore N. Lewis, who admits he has not seen the film.

Why this rioting, these protests, and this suppression? Of course because of Fagin; because some Jews there and here have objected to the alleged indignity done their people by showing on the screen a Jew who is such a deep-dyed villain. Their fear is that Fagin will arouse anti-Semitism; that movie audiences will forget Fagin is a caricature of an individual and be persuaded that all Jews are Fagins. Precious few of the millions still free to read Dickens's novel have, I will wager, succumbed to such an error. Yet this is the point of view as stated by Rabbi Lewis. The Rabbi, incidentally, is as adamant on the subject of *The Merchant of Venice* as he is on *Oliver Twist*. He is determined to have it kept off the stage and banned from schoolrooms for the same reasons—because in his eyes Shylock and Fagin are equally insulting, unbearable, and dangerous as characterizations of Jews.

I know this is the Rabbi's attitude because I heard him state it when, some two months back, he appeared on A.B.C.'s television program *Critic-at-Large* with Morris Ernst, Louis Kronenberger, and myself. In combating the Rabbi's stand, the three of us found ourselves as one. All of us abhorred the idea of such censorship. All of us felt that it was contrary to the American tradition. All of us insisted that the film was entitled to be shown before being condemned and that, if it proved offensive, the case could and should be carried to the courts. All of us expressed our conviction that the Rabbi, with the best of good intentions, was doing his people greater harm than good. All of us believed that more anti-Semitism would result from such a banning by a minority pressure group than would ever be created by Fagin.

Mr. Ernst was the only one of us who had seen the film, a fact which did not subtract from his right to an opinion. Instead of being offended by *Oliver Twist*, he had found it commendable as a transference of a classic to the screen. Mr. Kronenberger's judgment was that literature could not get along without its villains, and that a villain role in *Oliver Twist* on or off the screen just happened to be Fagin's, precisely as it was Bill Sikes's or the Artful Dodger's.

When I asked the Rabbi if, on the basis of his logic, the Danes would not be justified in picketing *Hamlet*, since it shows that a Danish prince can be indecisive, Mr. Kronenberger pointed out that the Danes had an even more valid reason for suppressing the play—i.e., it specifically states that there is something rotten in the state of Denmark.

The Jews who have protested against *Oliver Twist* and sought to have it, *The Merchant of Venice*, and now it seems

Ivanhoe, banned are not the only persons who have reached for censorship as a weapon with which to combat the horrors of racial or religious discrimination. Some Negro groups appear to be equally touchy, just as humorless, and no less given to trying to change what is past, or pretending that classics, written long ago and still available, can be unwritten and erased from men's minds by the edict of a censor.

There was, for example, the case of *Uncle Tom's Cabin* —of all things. Three years ago in Bridgeport a new musical version of it was temporarily banned because of the protests sent in by CIO Negro groups, the Bridgeport Pastors' Association, and the Communist Party. Their incredible objection was that *Uncle Tom's Cabin* "refreshed memories that tend to portray only the weaknesses of a racial minority," and held up to ridicule "peoples who in the early days of our country were unfortunately subjected to exposures that today would be considered atrocious." In other words, the desire of these protesting Negroes was to forget, and have others forget, that their people had ever been slaves.

What they forgot, however, was that it was the slave owner, not the slave, who came out badly in Mrs. Stowe's pages. They also seemed willing to overlook entirely how much *Uncle Tom's Cabin* had done for their people. Yes, and to deny the encouragement it offers today by making clear how far both the whites and the Negroes in this country have advanced since the novel first needed to be written. Booker T. Washington did not attempt to dodge history when he wrote his autobiography. He called his volume *Up from Slavery.* The significant word in his title is not the "Slavery." It is the "Up."

There are, too, some well-meaning Negroes, working for

that true realization of democracy which should be every American's preoccupation, who object even to *The Green Pastures,* I am told, because they find its naïveté offensive and because the young people in Mr. Deshee's Sunday School class have not a sufficiently enlightened conception of the Bible. There are other Negroes, just as well-meaning and just as falsely sensitive, whose hope is said to be to have *Little Black Sambo* suppressed. Their reason, I gather, is that Little Black Sambo, so endearing as a figure of all childhood, has a rather wholesale appetite for pancakes and is afraid of tigers!

The pressures of Catholic groups are no less evident. The suppression of *The Nation* in the public schools of New York City, because it ran a series of articles critical of the Catholic Church, is a case in point. So, of course, are the operations of the Legion of Decency in the realm of filmdom. The Legion does not have to ban to make itself felt. Fear of its disapproval exerts a constant influence upon motion-picture producers. Perhaps it was dread of this disapproval which resulted in the unfrocking of Cardinal Richelieu in the latest filming of *The Three Musketeers.* In the picture the Cardinal, a gifted and not unworldly cleric, though allowed to be as worldly as Dumas and history demand, is denied his robes, apparently in order to give no offense. Such pressures from other religious groups are, no doubt, continuous even if they are not so well organized.

In Chicago recently Jean-Paul Sartre's *The Respectful Prostitute* was banned. A police captain in charge of the Crime Prevention Bureau reported to his superior that the play was likely to provoke interracial troubles. This, in spite of the fact that it had run in New York for many months without having done so. One explanation which I read, and certainly an odd one, was that Sartre's script was "unfair to the Negro." Perhaps the final word about *The Respectful Prostitute* in Chicago came from Mayor Martin Kennelly. His enlightened statement was, "The title alone would ban it."

As further proof of the growing tendency to believe that abuses can be corrected by running away from the facts, let me cite two other examples. The first of these is the campaign which, out of the highest of motives, Walter Winchell conducted some time back against any comedians who dared to tell stories in dialect. As if all of us did not speak with dialects; as if dialects were not part of the truth as well as the vigor of our speech! It is not the dialect—Jewish, Yankee, Southern, Western, Italian, Irish, or Scotch—which is offensive. It is the story told, the uses to which dialect can be put.

For my second illustration I must come a little nearer home. In fact, to the *SRL* itself and an editor's note which appeared on the letters page. A well-intentioned reader from Charleston, S.C., had written in to ask when the magazine was going to stop "Jim Crowing" Negro writers. "If you always say a book is by a Negro, etc., you should, to be consistent, say another is by a white, etc.," wrote this correspondent. This was followed by one of those thunderous generalities, seemingly so fine in their liberalism, which unfortunately are apt to be as fuzzy-minded as they are untrue. "Only where literature has no race or religion will it be completely free."

Although I cannot speak for anyone else, I know I was saddened and distressed to read the editor's answer. It said, "After having applauded various publishers for omitting racial identification in their promotion of Negro authors, we are ashamed of ourselves. It won't happen again." Rot!

Certainly I would agree that nothing is gained and only harm done by insisting upon cataloguing a writer as a Negro, if his book has nothing to do with the problems which he himself has faced as a Negro. But I do not see how anyone could make an intelligent or just approach to such volumes, say, as Richard Wright's *Black Boy,* Walter White's *A Man Called White,* William Gardner Smith's *The Last of the Conquerors,* or Ann Petry's *The Street,* without mentioning the fact that the Americans who wrote these books are Negroes. The whole point of their writing and the reason for their having been written as they are is that they reflect the handicaps and humiliations to which Americans who are Negroes are heir. The source of their authority is that their authors are what they are.

As I see it, any citizen of the United States is an American. It is as simple as that. Yet it is absurd to pretend that all Americans, just because they live here, are sprung from the same race, are of the same color and the same religion, have the same accents, enjoy identical opportunities, are equally endowed, and have been exposed to the same agonies or privileges. These differences are facts. To ignore them is to surrender to the silliest and most self-deluding form of ostrichism.

We get nowhere by banning books just because they contain characters which do not flatter us. We get nowhere by pretending that there are not heroes and villains of all creeds and colors. We get nowhere by allowing any minorities to enjoy what John Haynes Holmes has admirably described in the *Saturday Review of Literature* as a "literary immunity from the sins that beset the rest of the human family." Our one hope is to face the facts.

· 267 ·

Nowadays we appear to be misled by the best of good intentions. To conquer the horrors of intolerance and racial or religious discrimination, we seem more and more inclined to turn to the book-burning tactics of our enemy in the last war or to the gross suppressions of our opponent in the present peace. Neither literature nor freedom gains anything by such means. Certainly minorities are entitled to the protection of their rights. But in a democracy a majority also has its rights. "Ye shall know the truth, and the truth shall make you free." Apparently there are those today who would reverse this, and have it read: avoid the truth, and such avoidance shall make you free. Thomas Jefferson's "I have sworn on the altar of God eternal hostility to every form of tyranny over the mind of man" is a pledge which nowadays is as important to minorities as it is to majorities. That is, if freedom which is everywhere imperiled is to endure as we have cherished it and enjoyed its benefits.

March 12, 1949

A MOTION-picture version of Oliver
Twist *in which, as in the original, Fagin
is but one villain among many and the
real villain is a society that ignored its
poor and did nothing about its slums.*

≈≈≈≈≈≈≈≈≈≈≈≈≈≈≈≈≈≈≈≈≈≈≈≈≈≈≈≈≈≈≈≈≈

Curiouser and Curiouser

"IT APPEARED to me," explained Dickens, "that to draw
a knot of such associates in crime as really do exist; to
paint them in all their deformity, in all their wretchedness,
in all the squalid poverty of their lives; to show them as they
really are, forever skulking uneasily through the dirtiest
paths of life, with the great, black, ghastly gallows closing
up their prospects, turn them where they may; it appeared
to me that to do this, would be to attempt a something which
was greatly needed, and which would be a service to society.
And therefore I did it as I best could."

The result, and a memorable best it remains, was *Oliver
Twist*. It seems important to stress "the service to society"
Dickens had in mind, since one would gather from all the
foolish agitation about Fagin, which has kept the British film
of *Oliver Twist* * from being shown in this country, that the

* *Oliver Twist*, a screen play by David Lean and Stanley Haynes, based
on Charles Dickens's novel. Photographed by Guy Green. Sets by John Bryan.
Costumes by Margaret Furse. Music by Sir Arnold Bax. Directed by Mr.
Lean. Produced by Ronald Neame. Presented by J. Arthur Rank. With a
cast including John Howard Davies, Robert Newton, Alec Guinness, Kay

sole purpose of the novel, its author, and the movie was to do a great disservice to the Jews.

In the outraged speeches and the suppressive tactics of the protesting Jewish groups (most of whose members have not seen the movie and are determined that no other Americans shall see it), Fagin has emerged as if he were the only character in *Oliver Twist*. Some prominent Jews, such as Rabbi Theodore N. Lewis and Henry Epstein, have found him objectionable, not because he is a villain, but because he is a Jewish villain. They have argued, therefore, that he is at once a danger and an insult; a gross libel on a proud and fine people and a possible contributor to the spread of anti-Semitism in a world which, of late, has suffered hideously from the horrors of racial persecution. The claim has been made that moviegoers, still free to read the book, would, if they were permitted to see the film, mistake all Jews for Fagins and Fagin for all Jews.

No decent person in these constantly indecent times would think of adding one twig to the smoldering fires of intolerance. But the tolerant attitude of the many will never be achieved by the intolerant actions of the few. In a land dedicated to freedom, it still seems advisable to consider the specific case before springing to the generality. When I first wrote about *Oliver Twist*, I did so without having seen it. Then I was concerned with a principle; a principle of democratic rights and freedom which seemed to me imperiled by the increasing tendency of hypersensitive minority groups to seek to censor whatever happens to be unfavorable to one of their members.

Walsh, Francis L. Sullivan, Henry Stephenson, Josephine Stuart, Ralph Truman, Anthony Newley, Gibb McLaughlin, etc. No theatre.

Since then, however, at a small private showing, I have seen the new screen version of *Oliver Twist*. For the life of me, I cannot understand how any gentile American who is not a moron or any Jewish American who is not suffering from hallucinations or a persecution mania could discover a provocation for anti-Semitism in either Fagin as a character or *Oliver Twist* as a picture.

That Fagin, as brilliantly played by Alec Guinness, remains a villain in the film, I cannot deny. That in spite of never being referred to as a Jew on the screen, though he is so identified in the novel, he continues to be the bearded, beak-nosed, and gabardined figure of Dickens's descriptions and Cruikshank's drawings, I will admit. But Fagin, Jewish villain that he is, is only one rogue in a crowded rogues' gallery; a single culprit in a long police line-up.

Wicked and merciless as Fagin is, he seems almost kindly compared to the villainous gentiles who are his confederates, or have been his predecessors, in maltreating Oliver. At least he smiles occasionally at Oliver. And feeds him, when the others have starved him. And makes him laugh. And does not spend his whole time beating or abusing him.

As a master of thieves and a receiver of stolen goods, Fagin must be an arch-conniver. Even so, his brutality is as nothing compared to the brutality of that total and terrible brute Bill Sikes. Fagin is, of course, unburdened by morals. But at any rate he does not pretend to intrude into the moral world to which Monks has the appearance, and only the appearance, of belonging. Certainly, Fagin's share is passive, compared to Nancy's active part, in the kidnaping of Oliver.

All of these characters, the Jew no less than the gentiles, are the products of "the cold, wet, shelterless midnight streets

Freedom's Battle

of London; the foul and frowsy dens where vice is closely packed and lacks the room to turn; the haunts of hunger and disease, the shabby rags that scarcely hold together." In the film, as in the book, these creatures are professional criminals. They are at once the victims and the expressions of the filth and the slums of early nineteenth-century London. One of the film's many merits is that the festering streets and hovels in which these people hide away are as graphically realized in John Bryan's settings as they are in Dickens's pages.

The criminals, however, in *Oliver Twist* are not limited to Londoners or to those who have thieving as their avowed profession. This was clear in the novel, and is even clearer on the screen, where the emphasis on the workhouse chapters is far greater than it is in the book. Indeed, this very shift in emphasis, and this long dwelling upon and exploring of the tortures to which Oliver is exposed in his pre-London days, may seem to some loyal Dickensians a distortion. But since good movies are bound to be equivalents rather than the duplications of good books, and *Oliver Twist* is an exceptionally fine film, these changes more than justify themselves even if they entail the sacrifice of such well-known and expected incidents as the burglary chapter.

These other, these provincial criminals, so vividly realized on the screen, live in a town which Dickens, for understandable reasons, thought it "prudent to refrain from mentioning." They are a shocking crew of hypocrites, cheats, sadists, and liars. If anything, they are more terrible and less forgivable than Bill Sikes, Fagin, the Artful Dodger, and the rest, because either charity is their business or grief their stock in trade. Christians though they suppose themselves to be, they have made a travesty of Christianity. They are drawn deliberately—and clearly—as disgraces not only to the Church of England but to the human race. As paid servitors of the parish, they have sinned against the ill and the dying, the old and the young, the trusting and the helpless. They have grown fat in the fashion of Mr. Bumble, the beadle, by starving orphans. Or inhuman in the Matron's manner. They are as flinthearted as the comfortable members of the workhouse board; as violent as Mrs. Sowerberry, the undertaker's wife; or as mean as Noah Claypole, the undertaker's assistant. They live by doing those things they ought not to do, and there is no good in them.

Yet all these other characters, though they out-Sikes Sikes, are not the real villains of *Oliver Twist*. The real, the final, the appalling villain of the film, as of the book, is poverty. It is the poverty tolerated by a society which has no conscience, which leaves its slums uncleared, degrades its unfortunates, and shuts its eyes, as Dickens could not shut his, to the conditions which breed precisely such wretches.

In other words, the major impact of *Oliver Twist* as a movie continues to be what it was as a novel. In spite of the absorption of its storytelling, the overwhelming power of its individual scenes, and its unforgettable characters (or aren't they caricatures?), it is the challenging and unsparing work of a social reformer. Its low-life figures shocked Thackeray. Other Englishmen when it first appeared, though they did not think of stooping to suppress the book, were made no less uncomfortable by it. As Hesketh Pearson indicates in the immensely readable pages of his *Dickens*, there were even those who objected to its "sort of Radicalish tone."

The people from whom you might expect to hear resounding protests because of this new film of *Oliver Twist* are the

British. It is the uglier aspects of their past which this English-made movie ruthlessly exposes. It is English institutions in the late 1830's which it pillories. It is English women and English men from whom it draws all but one of its numerous villains. Yet contemporary Britishers, instead of being outraged by the film, instead of seeking to ban it, instead of resorting to censorship and claiming that they must all be shown as heroes or not be shown at all, have said nothing. They have accepted it for what it is—an uncommonly exciting and skillful movie made from a long-established and long-cherished classic.

The British attempts to show *Oliver Twist* in Germany and Austria were unwise. But the attempts of some of the Jewish minority groups to suppress it in this country seem equally unwise. Ignoring for the moment the all-important principles threatened by such pressure-group tactics, I can only say that, having seen the film, I am the more surprised at the hurt feelings and indignation the mere thought (though not the sight) of Fagin has provoked. These seem to me not only unfounded but curiouser and curiouser.

May 28, 1949

Fact and Fiction

*RUINS CREATED by our own times,
and a film which vividly reminds us
that ours is, among other things, the
age of rubble.*

᠅᠅᠅᠅᠅᠅᠅᠅᠅᠅᠅᠅᠅᠅᠅᠅᠅᠅᠅᠅᠅᠅᠅᠅᠅᠅᠅᠅

Living Death

RUINED CITIES, when most of us were young, belonged to antiquity. Troy, Carthage, Mitla, Mycenae —such names as these came to our minds. They stood for the victims of Time, not the product of our own times. They were remote instead of near. But things are different now. We have lived through years which have created their own ruins. Wherever the war was actually fought they are to be found. As Roberto Rossellini's new film *Germany Year Zero* * vividly reminds us (if we need reminding), ours, among other things, is an age of rubble. The charred buildings, the blasted homes, the chipped and broken monuments, the ugly stumps of what was once Berlin provide this picture with its melancholy background.

There was a period when Berlin seemed impregnable. Goering's boast was that no Allied planes would ever reach it. That boast was as hollow as other Nazi claims. They did arrive—first the British, then the British and the American

* *Germany Year Zero.* Written, directed, and produced by Roberto Rossellini. Released by Superfilm Distributing Corporation. With a cast including Edmund Meschke, Ingetraude Hinze, Franz Cruger, Ernst Pischau, Erich Guhne, etc. At the Ambassador, New York City.

—in frightening numbers and with devastating results. No one was more surprised than Goebbels. His *Diaries*, found in the wreckage, their pages scattered, singed, and smelling of smoke, indicate that he must have been taken in by his own propaganda.

On November 22, 1943, he was writing: "To compensate for vanishing hopes of victory the London press now supplies its readers with tall stories about the damage alleged to have been done to Berlin during the last air raid. It is claimed, for instance, that even at this hour communications in Berlin are completely interrupted. As a matter of fact not a single tram, subway, or elevated has failed to run because of the raid. Nevertheless I shall refrain from denying these English reports. It is a good thing for the English to imagine that their new tactics achieved great successes; they will cling all the longer to these tactics, much to our advantage."

Two days later, however, Goebbels had changed his tune. "I just can't understand how the English are able to do so much damage to the Reich's capital during one air raid. . . . The picture that greeted my eye on the Wilhelmplatz was one of utter desolation. Blazing fires everywhere. . . . Transportation conditions are still quite hopeless. . . . Large English formations are once more on their way, headed straight for the capital. It means we must stand a second blow."

This time the havoc he recorded was far worse. Everything around Potsdamer Platz was destroyed. The damage done to the Government section as well as to the Western and Northern suburbs was appalling. The workers' area in the Wedding and the region along Wolgast Street were especially hard hit. Countless incendiary bombs were dropped on the Kaiserhof Hotel. The State Theatre and the Reichstag were aflame. One after another the most important buildings began to burn, including Goebbels's own Propaganda Ministry. A fire started in the Reich Chancellery. As Goebbels put it, "Hell itself seems to have broken loose over us. . . . The Government quarter is nothing short of an inferno. One can hardly recognize the Wilhelmplatz."

More, infinitely more, destruction was to come. These British raids were just the beginning. The final shambles of the proud Berlin many of us once knew supply the settings for *Germany Year Zero*. They are shown as monuments to an evil and ill-starred plan for world domination. As Rossellini makes clear, living in this long, long mileage of rubble are people who have been reduced to rubble, too.

Perhaps this explains why *Germany Year Zero*, in spite of its excellences, is not as moving as such of Rossellini's fine earlier films as *Open City* and *Paisan*. The varied characters in those pictures were individuals who, although hideously tried, had lost neither their spirit nor their humanity. The adversities they faced did not prevent life from still running strong in them. The Berliners in *Germany Year Zero* are of another breed. Rossellini shows them during the first months of their release from war when peace has brought them only further humiliation and discomfort. They are numbed and broken, made subhuman by their misery and their hopelessness. They not only live like rats, they act like rats. They are a cornered lot; sad proofs of the sadder fact that the wreckage of our time is flesh and blood no less than sticks and stones.

If Rossellini's story were stronger, *Germany Year Zero* might command the same interest as a drama that it does as a documentary. But his plot, as he develops it, is weak. It tells how a young boy, a starving member of a starving family, gets into bad company, determines to kill his sick father in order to gain more rations for his sister and brother, and finally commits suicide by throwing himself off a building when his remorse has become unbearable.

Such a narrative acted against such a background would, you might think, tug irresistibly at the emotions. This, however, is exactly what it fails to do. Notwithstanding its admirable moments and its ghoulish interest as a travelogue, it appears as contrived as Berlin's ruins are real. The tale it tells, though possible beyond question, never seems quite plausible.

Few directors can approach, much less equal, Rossellini when it comes to giving fiction the urgency of a newsreel. His genius for employing reality to underwrite make-believe has not deserted him in *Germany Year Zero*. His camera gives us a more vivid sense than anything else has of what life is like for Berliners in the blasted sections of their city. Its pictures of gutted houses in a capital turned into a ghost town; its vistas of demolished avenues; its shot of a famished crowd pouncing, knives out, to cut flesh from the body of a horse that has died in the street; and its usage of nonprofessionals, picked up here and there to serve as actors—all these are in the familiar and welcome Rossellini tradition. But this time, although his story is focused on so pathetic a subject as blighted and twisted youth, Rossellini's details prove more moving than his film as a whole. Its action is jumpy; its characters are left sketchy. Especially when it hints at perversion among the young, it appears to suffer, and suffer seriously, from censor trouble.

Edmund Meschke, the boy found by Rossellini in Berlin to play the central figure, is a thin, long-legged child, with a face upon which the privations and barbarisms of war have left their cruel marks. At all times his acting has a truth to it which makes it uncomfortably clear that he may not be acting at all. Yet even he, tragic as are his situation and his fate, is not as touching as he should be.

Just why one can sit detached before a film compounded of so much misery is hard to say. Perhaps the simplest, assuredly the most shocking, reason is that the characters in *Germany Year Zero* are, as I have hinted, people who have been made subhuman by their suffering. Although they have our sympathy, Rossellini fails to ferret out the qualities which would individualize them or make them endearing. They are only parts of the rubble. This may be Rossellini's point. Certainly it is a disquieting truth in many areas of the modern world. But *Germany Year Zero* does not succeed in fully communicating the emotions inherent in its theme.

October 15, 1949

*THE DIFFERENCES between Amer-
ican and European sidewalks, and what
a universal story gains by having the
Eternal City for a background.*

˜˜˜˜˜˜˜˜˜˜˜˜˜˜˜˜˜˜˜˜˜˜˜˜˜˜

Struggle for Survival

THE BICYCLE THIEF * could not tell a simpler story.
Its story is as simple as the needs and the anguishes of
the hungry. This is a source of the extraordinary power of
Vittorio De Sica's new Italian film. It is also a measure of the
desperation with which it deals.

Although postwar Rome supplies the background, *The
Bicycle Thief's* real scene is the human heart anywhere, at any
time, when a family, eager to work but unemployed, faces the
fears and agonies of poverty. The picture reduces this family's
whole hope of economic survival to one object—a bicycle. Perhaps the very straightness of the story's line explains why it
can claim a fluency missing even in such an earlier and notable
example of De Sica's work as *Shoe Shine.*

An unemployed husband at last gets a job as a billposter.
To hold the job he must have a bicycle. His bicycle has been
pawned long ago. His wife is able to redeem it only by selling

---

* *The Bicycle Thief*, screen play by Cesare Zavattini, based on the novel of
the same name, by Luigi Bartolini. Directed by Vittorio De Sica. Produced
in Rome by De Sica Production Company and released here by Mayer-
Burstyn. With a cast including Lamberto Maggiorani, Lianella Carrell, Enzo
Staiola, Elena Altieri, Vittorio Antonucci, Gino Saltamerenda, etc. At the
World Theatre, New York City.

all six of the family's sheets. Full of hope, the husband goes
to work on a Saturday. During the day, however, his bicycle is
stolen while he is up on a ladder. Although he sees the thief
and runs after him, he fails to catch him. This is the beginning
of a heartbreaking search.

The police offer him no help. They tell him he will have to
look for the bicycle himself. Accordingly, he, his little son, and
some friends start out on a hunt which the father and the boy
ultimately continue alone. A rainy Sunday at least provides
the father with a day of grace before he must report for work.
At one moment he is confident he has located the actual thief,
but he has no real evidence. He cannot bring himself, therefore, to prefer charges against this young man, an epileptic
who is as hard driven as he is.

The father's hopelessness increases. His knowledge of what
is at stake finally drives him into becoming a thief himself. He
sees a bicycle left against a wall. He cannot resist it. He jumps
on it and peddles away furiously, only to be overtaken by a
street crowd. The owner of the bicycle, sensing the father's
difficulties, refuses to turn him over to the police. Thereafter
the father and the little boy start off again, hand in hand, to
begin their long walk home. It is getting late. Not only night
but Monday is overtaking them. The needed job is lost. So is
the family.

It is on this desperate note that De Sica's distinguished study
of despair ends. Yet part of *The Bicycle Thief's* truth is that
in the midst of its desolation and tension it finds time for
humor. This humor is not of that obvious, palliative kind
known as comic relief. It is as human, as quiet and real as are
those sufferings which are the picture's uncompromising concern.

The impatience of some night-club entertainers to get on with their rehearsal. The volcanic explosiveness of the Italian temperament. A church service disturbed by the father's whispered but insistent questioning of an evil old man, a confederate of the real thief. The naïve and trusting pathos of a group of people who, because of their ignorance and misery, have implicit faith in the Delphic pronouncements of a medium. A rich boy guzzling heavy food in a restaurant at a table next to the one where the father and the son, because they have reached the breaking point, have been driven to eat a meal which they can ill afford. The son's unwillingness, in a moment of anger, to walk on the same side of the street with his father. All of these are instances of De Sica's refusal to overplay the sentimentalities of a story which in other hands could easily have been sentimentalized.

They are not funny for the sake of being funny, these lighter touches of De Sica's. They are not extraneous either. Although they win a smile here or a quiet laugh there, most of them bear an unmistakable relevance to the film's theme. They are born of its agony; proofs of mortal frailty, hence of humanity.

De Sica's approach, realistic as it is, is not tough. It is more bruising than that. It is matter-of-fact to the point of casualness. Like so many of the outstanding foreign films which have reached us since the war, *The Bicycle Thief* can claim a documentary's validity. Brilliant as is its planning and emphasis, it creates the illusion of being a "Neediest Case," unposed and uncontrived, which just happens to have been overtaken by a camera. This increases its power by making everything exceptional in it appear to be average.

De Sica, for example, takes magnificent advantage of the

tenements, the courtyards, the bridges, and the streets of Rome. That an eternal tragedy of poverty is played against the setting of the Eternal City does more than add to the picture's photographic interest. Such a background heightens the story's poignancy. The same tragedy could be laid in any of the world's younger cities. But in them its sense of historic melancholy would be lacking. A comment, unmade yet implicit in so ancient a setting, would be lost. For *The Bicycle Thief* takes place in a capital, great in both pagan and Christian times, which in spite of its antiquity has failed to learn how to meet the needs of all of its citizens.

There is a difference between the sidewalks of the Old World and the New. All of us sense it when we arrive in Europe or return to America. In *You Can't Go Home Again* Thomas Wolfe described the American pavement, our universal city sidewalk, as "a wide, hard stripe of gray-white cement, blocked accurately with dividing lines." He insisted it is "the hardest, coldest, cruellest, most impersonal pavement in the world." In Europe's cities, he noted, we tread on "worn stone, all hollowed out and rubbed to rounded edges." We realize that "for centuries the unknown lives of men now buried touched and wore this stone, and when we see it something stirs within our hearts."

There is more, however, to the cleavage than newness or age. A second world war has made this distressingly clear. There is a matter of confidence opposed to resignation, of the individual's belief or lack of belief in his own importance, of energy set against fatigue, and hope contrasted with hopelessness. Then, too, there is the difference between living with the weight of too much made history and the buoyancy which comes from the conviction that history is still in the making.

This tired and trapped feeling—this awareness of human erosion—this consciousness of struggling to survive rather than striving to succeed has found deliberate or unintentional expression in all the significant European films shown in this country since the coming of what we choose to identify as peace. It is unmistakable in every sequence of *The Bicycle Thief*.

Hollywood, even in its most courageous moments, continues to approach our very real, though dissimilar, problems in terms of make-believe. Instead of showing things as they are, it puts on a show. Its professionals do not allow us to forget that they are professionals. They do not make a film from life; they lose life in a movie. Poverty is one of the facts of life which they seldom admit. The things which are all around them—and us—they do not, as a rule, choose to see. In spite of encouraging signs of growth, the erroneous assumption of most Hollywood producers seems to be that American moviegoers do not care how empty the mind may be in a film so long as the sweaters are full. All too often these same producers devote their energies and gifts to documenting an unreal world and let the real world go hang.

The reality of *The Bicycle Thief* is doubtless due in part to the professional use De Sica makes of nonprofessionals. They have no tricks to unlearn, these actors of his. They have only their own lives to remember. Most of us have long since realized that acting on the screen seldom is, and does not need to be, acting in the stage sense. More often than not it is a matter of obedience and patience; the product of editing rather than endowment. The all-important role is played by the director.

De Sica must have looked far, and could not have done better, in selecting his principals. Lamberto Maggiorani is a gaunt, harried man; modest and determined as the father. In happier times, under more agreeable circumstances, he would have been called handsome. But he has more than good looks to offer. The misery of present-day Europe thins his mouth, narrows his eyes, and lines his face. By this I do not mean to suggest he is incapable of a wide and appropriate variety of moods. He rises to these changes. No doubt he is helped in doing this by his complete immersion as an individual in what his own experiences have taught him to be the script's truth.

Enzo Staiola, as his little son, is equally impressive, indeed unforgettable. He is a child uncursed by any of the regrettable qualities of the average child actor. He is older, tragically older, than his years. His childhood is shown as having none of the natural childish diversions. Although there is iron in his character, something indestructibly young and vital shines in his performance and his face. As his mother, Lianella Carrell manages to be both tough and tender. She is the kind of woman to be seen in any Italian city today.

All of De Sica's actors, whether playing the larger parts or participating only in the street scenes, are blessed with this same authenticity. He has welded them into a picture, high and bleak in its beauty, and irresistible in its force.

January 7, 1950

SOME ENCOURAGING advances
we have made since Bedlam was a tour-
ist mecca, and a fine, brave film about
the anguishes of unhinged minds.

Buried Alive

"A CONSCIENTIOUS visitor would no more have missed seeing it than he would have missed seeing the Abbey or the Tower." Thus Louis Kronenberger in *Kings & Desperate Men*, his admirable study of English life in the eighteenth century. It was Bedlam that Mr. Kronenberger had in mind; Bedlam, that hospital for the raving mad which has become the synonym for all derangement and confusion; Bedlam, which, as a four-starred item on the tourist's lists of those days, was so popular that tea was served there for the crowds who on a free afternoon would gather just for fun— for good clean sport—to watch the maniacs rave and yell, beat on the walls, and rattle their chains.

It would be nice, at this point, to be smug about the present and insist such cruelty belongs to the past. It would be reassuring, particularly just now when we are hungry for proofs of progress, to maintain that at least in our attitude toward the mentally ill we have grown more merciful. I had thought we had, and still think we have. Yet after hearing the howls of laughter which greeted several of the most anguishing scenes in *The Snake Pit*,* I cannot be as confident as I once was. There were moments during the course of an unusually brave and fine film when the behavior of some people in the audience persuaded me that they had mistaken what they were seeing at the Rivoli for a lark at Bedlam.

No one who read Mary Jane Ward's *The Snake Pit* is apt to have forgotten it. Her novel lingers like a nightmare in the memory. Nor is it likely that anyone who sees the picture which has been made from it will ever forget the film. It is not a film for everyone. It was not meant to be. Count that among its many virtues. Certainly, it is not a movie to be *enjoyed* in any ordinary understanding of the word. There is far too much pain in it for that, too much grief, too much tragedy. It is, however, an exceptional film. It is fascinating, adult, and uncompromising. Moreover it is possessed of a quality almost nonexistent, hence unexpected, in Hollywood's products. This is integrity.

All too often the worthiest books become unworthy when the West Coast studios get through with them. Although the California moguls pay fabulous sums for what they purchase, frequently it seems as if they buy merely to spoil what they have paid for. Someone with whom I recently talked had the perfect image to describe what occurs. "The good books bought," said he, "arrive in Hollywood with their stories clear and their pages clean. But then, somewhere, somehow, in the

---

* *The Snake Pit*, screen play by Frank Partos and Millen Brand, based on the novel by Mary Jane Ward. Directed by Anatole Litvak. Produced by Mr. Litvak and Robert Bassler for Twentieth Century–Fox Pictures. With a cast including Olivia de Havilland, Leo Genn, Mark Stevens, Celeste Holm, Glenn Langan, Helen Craig, Leif Erickson, Beulah Bondi, Lee Patrick, Howard Freeman, Natalie Schafer, Katherine Locke, June Storey, Lora Lee Michel, Betsy Blair, etc. At the Rivoli. Opened November 4, 1948.

process of converting these volumes into movies, someone with dirty hands lays hold of them. The unsoiled pages get smudged. So does the story. And this smudge becomes an abiding part of the movie." My friend dubbed this smudging "the Hollywood touch."

By this he meant something heavy-handed, wounding, vulgar. He was not talking about what is morally censorable. He was thinking of a misplaced honesty. He was describing figuratively what we have all seen happen. He had in mind the sudden lapses in taste, the deliberate untruths, the false opulence, the specious glamor, the intrusive immaturities, and the pathetic compromises which again and again undo what was on the point of being well done in American films.

All moviegoers, much as they must admire the technical excellence of our pictures, have their own notions of what can be regrettable in "the Hollywood touch." They can cite instance after instance of interesting and self-respecting books which have lost both their self-respect and their interest in the act of being screened. In the presence of *The Snake Pit*, however, they will look in vain for that particular touch. No cowardly or coarse hands have soiled Mrs. Ward's novel in the hope of making it "box office."

It comes through with its anguish undiminished, as uncomfortable yet grimly fascinating as it was in its printed form. It comes through so honestly acted, directed, and dramatized that it creates in us outfront—almost unbearably—the sense of being inmates in an institution. It makes us feel as if the doors to freedom and normal living had been locked upon us. It gives us the illusion of being citizens who have lived day after day, night after night, when the visitors have left, in that other world, that tragic half-world where minds are on vacation, hopes are grounded, and clouds hang heavy.

It persuades us that we have inhaled the very smell of the wards, that we have eaten in the dining rooms under the watchful eyes of nurses, met patients of all classes in all stages of madness, or faced the ordeal of a cross-examination by the staff. It even exposes us to electrical shock treatments, and shows us how the overwrought are quieted by being dunked in sheeted tubs. Indeed, as it follows the case of a young wife, the victim of a severe nervous breakdown, who is restored to sanity and her husband after being psychoanalyzed, it comes near to putting strait jackets on us all.

When turned into a film, Mrs. Ward's novel could so easily have gone wrong in two ways. It could either have dodged the truth by avoiding the unpleasant or overdramatized it for the sake of horror. It does neither. The courage Twentieth Century–Fox has shown in electing to make such a picture at all is matched only by the skill and the taste with which Anatole Litvak has directed it.

Mr. Litvak's eye is alert both to the details which document the appalling institutional aspects of an asylum and the individual tragedy represented by each of its inmates. He shows us the sweep of the large rooms, the overcrowding of the wards, the confinement of the single cells. Without overemphasizing them, he never lets us lose sight of the bars at the windows or the doors that must be locked on these luckless prisoners whose only crime is illness. He makes us feel the full and terrible pathos of the dances held in pleasure's name in the great hall and the heartbreak of an audience of the insane who, by way of entertainment, listen to a patient sing, of all things, "Goin' Home." Yet, in spite of his wealth of detail and incident, Mr. Litvak manages to keep the line of his main story clear.

This story is, of course, the case of the psychotic young wife whose tottering mind finally regains its stability. Perhaps, from a psychiatric point of view, the case is oversimplified as its causes are traced and cured in flashback indications of its origins. For screen purposes, however, the treatment proves more than satisfactory. We have Olivia de Havilland not only to thank but to congratulate for this. Miss de Havilland gives one of those wonderfully unglamorized and true performances generally associated with only the more distinguished foreign films. She is a woman—any nice young woman—trapped by misfortune, and never the actress at work. Above all, she is brilliant in suggesting the torments of a mind not mad but wavering, and uncertain in its knowledge of when the darkness is settling upon it or the interludes of clarity have come again.

Leo Genn is admirable as a soft-spoken psychiatrist whose gentleness under rushed and cruelly standardized conditions effects a cure. Indeed, the whole of the large cast is so contributive that it is at once difficult and unfair to particularize. Even so, some mention must be made of Betsy Blair's sullen and shiny-eyed maniac, who ultimately speaks; of Beulah Bondi as the ornate patient who fancies herself a great lady; and of Helen Craig as a stony-hearted but jealous nurse.

You may ask why such a disturbing film, however absorbing, on so unpleasant a subject. There are several answers. First of all, if the motion pictures are to function as an adult medium, they must be as free as the novel and the stage to deal truthfully and unflinchingly with adult subjects. Secondly, there is the matter of treatment; of the challenge, in this instance finely met, of doing justice to such themes. Also there is the purpose served. *The Snake Pit* serves such a purpose. It forces audiences to become aware of the terrible conditions in understaffed and overcrowded public and private asylums up and down the land.

The amusement seekers at Bedlam in their callous approach to human suffering were guilty of a cruelty which today we find shocking. Ours, in the name of mercy, is a different guilt. They may not have spared the insane; we spare ourselves. We know too little about what happens on the far side of those iron curtains behind which so terrifying a percentage of our citizens lives. Knowing little, we do less. Among the many virtues of *The Snake Pit* is that, by opening our eyes and hearts, it should also open our pocketbooks.

November 27, 1948

SIR JAMES BARRIE'S share in a famous expedition to the South Pole, and the similar dangers which confronted Scott as faced by the American Navy.

❛❛❛❛❛❛❛❛❛❛❛❛❛❛❛❛❛❛❛❛❛❛❛❛❛❛

Man against Nature

"COURAGE," said Barrie, in that still-remembered Rectorial Address he delivered at St. Andrews, "is the lovely virtue—the rib of Himself that God sent down to His children." "Unless a man has that virtue," insisted Dr. Johnson, "he has no security for preserving any other."

I quote Barrie, who quoted Dr. Johnson, because recently I have seen *The Secret Land,** that stirring documentary about our Navy's latest Antarctic expedition. It set me thinking inescapably of Captain Robert Scott, the site of whose camp in these same frozen wastes is shown in the film. Thinking of Captain Scott, I had no other choice than to think of Barrie.

Why the two of them together, these men so different and so unlike in their kinds of courage? Because they were great friends. Because Scott had invited Barrie, the least likely of

---

* *The Secret Land.* A Technicolor documentary of Operation Highjump, the Navy's expedition to Antarctica in 1946–47, under Admiral Richard E. Byrd and Admiral Richard H. Cruzen. Photographed by United States Navy, Marine Corps, Coast Guard, and Army cameramen. Commentary written by Harvey Haiflit and William C. Park. Narrated by Robert Montgomery, Robert Taylor, and Van Heflin. Produced by Orville O. Dull. Released by Metro-Goldwyn-Mayer.

polar explorers, to sail southward with him on the *Terra Nova*, and Barrie had been tempted to go along, anxious as he was "to know what it is really like to be alive." Because Barrie contributed generously to financing the expedition. But most of all, of course, because in that tent in Antarctica, where the bodies of Scott and his two comrades were found, a penciled letter from Scott to Barrie was also discovered. The writing was still quite clear, though, as Barrie put it, toward the end some of the words trailed away as into the great silence that was waiting for these men.

"We are pegging out in a very comfortless spot," Scott wrote. "Hoping this letter may be found and sent to you, I write you a word of farewell. I want you to think well of me and my end. As a dying man, my dear friend, be good to my wife and child. Give the boy a chance in life if the State won't do it. He ought to have good stuff in him. I never met a man in my life whom I admired and loved more than you, but I could never show you how much your friendship meant to me, for you had much to give and I nothing. Goodbye—I am not at all afraid of the end, but sad to miss many a simple pleasure which I had planned for the future in our long marches. . . . We are in a desperate state—feet frozen, etc., no fuel, and a long way from food, but it would do your heart good to be in our tent, to hear our songs and our cheery conversation. . . . Later—(*here the words became indistinct*)—We are very near the end. . . . We did intend to finish ourselves when things proved like this, but we have decided to die naturally without."

When Scott wrote this letter, he and four companions had pushed their way to the Pole only to discover that Amundsen had been there ahead of them. On their way back to their camp illness, inadequate supplies, and the cruel coldness of the

Fact and Fiction

weather had compelled them to move slowly. On February 17, 1912, one of the men, Edgar Evans, a petty officer, had broken under the strain and died. A month later Captain Oates, too ill to go on, had wandered out into a blizzard alone, trusting by his death to lighten the burden of his companions. The weather, however, continued bad, and Scott, Dr. E. A. Wilson, and Lt. H. R. Burrows became prisoners in the tent in which they perished.

When word of their deaths reached England, Barrie sent Lady Scott a draft for a public statement describing the manner of their dying. It read, "Wilson and Burrows died first and Captain Scott enclosed them in their sleeping bags. At some unknown time thereafter he removed the fur coat from his shoulders, bared his chest, and, seated against the centre pole with his head flung back and his eyes wide open, awaited death. We know this because it was thus that the three were found when the search-party looked into the tent six months afterwards." *

The perils faced by Scott and his companions are those faced by each and all of the four thousand officers and men whose expedition to the Antarctic is recorded in *The Secret Land*. Such dangers are the common lot of those who have it in their blood to do war with nature.

They are dangers that Admiral Byrd has invited again and again. They are dangers familiar to Nansen, Peary, Stefansson, Wilkins, Amundsen, MacMillan, Shackleton, and others of that dauntless company of moderns whose spirits have been magnetized by the pull of polar exploration. They are dangers which create a fellowship between the men we see in *The Secret*

* *Letters of J. M. Barrie.* Edited by Viola Meynell. New York: Charles Scribner's Sons. 1947. 311 pp. $3.50.

· 296 ·

Land and Balboa, Magellan, Drake, Leif Ericson, the Greek
and Roman settlers, and those first Phoenicians who elected to
leave the comfortable security of their homes to head their
ships across unknown waters to unknown lands. That is one
reason why this film, featuring men and ships of the United
States Navy in peacetime action, fills us not only with wonder
at machines as machines or at the intricacies of highly complicated planning, but with pride at what men are as men.

The virtues of *The Secret Land* as a chronicle of exploration
are much the same as those which that fine Navy film *The
Fighting Lady* possessed as a record of combat. There is the
identical sense of turning participant; of being ship- or air-borne
by the camera; of becoming acquainted with the crew, the problem, and the enemy. No doubt, the "log" has been subjected to
a good deal of dramatic polishing. Unquestionably, certain sequences are the result of "retakes" cannily contrived to create a
unity or a suspense that in actuality may have been different or
lacking.

Why not? To make an interesting film of interesting events
is in itself a problem. Wagner's contention that "art begins
where reality ends" is beyond denial. It is applicable even to a
documentary. It, too, must have been edited, selected, and arranged into an arbitrary pattern. It, too, requires a certain
falsification in order to do justice to the truth which is its concern. The makers of *The Secret Land*, for example, have been
both wise and right in avoiding the monotony of a single nar-
rator by relying on the varied voices of Robert Montgomery,
Robert Taylor, and Van Heflin. They have been no less wise in
their chaperonage of the camera and the details of the heroic
saga which is theirs to photograph. Yet, in spite of their necessary nudgings and omissions and the heightened form their

· 297 ·

narrative takes, the feeling of actuality is there. It is excitingly, unmistakably there, giving the most timid of stay-at-homes the illusion of having ventured forth to share in the rugged challenges and hardships of men, eager and equipped to open new and hazardous frontiers.

The sources of the film's fascination are many. It has, for example, its definite revelations to make about the thoroughness with which our armed forces are preparing for arctic warfare. It indicates how ardent is the world's search for those new resources imperative to the atomic age and those old ones of which our plundered planet will soon stand in need. As a most spectacular of *National Geographic* travelogues, as a demonstration of infinite foresight and masterly synchronization, and as a proof of the progress of science, it is equally absorbing. It shows us men winging their way at three hundred miles an hour over plateaus of ice on which Scott, and even Byrd, in dogsleds considered themselves lucky to make three.

It permits us to see with a camera's eye, and with emotions not unknown to "stout Cortez [*sic*] . . . upon a peak in Darien," thousands of square miles, including unguessed lakes and dark mountain ranges rich in coal, which no man has looked upon before. It has penguins and seals as its comic relief. It has the unbounded sky as its cyclorama; an untouched continent, vivid in its colors, as its setting; and the icebreaker *Northwind* as a rescuer, arriving, Marine-wise, always in the nick of time. If as its villain it can claim nature with her sudden storms, her murderous indifference, and limitless obstacles, it offers man— the gob and the ground-crewman no less than the brass hat—as its hero. For suspense it provides the ever-present threat of death.

The nearness of the threat of death invariably sharpens the

values of living. This is one of the ironies of that security which is everyone's hope. The menaced moment causes the blood to tingle and the perceptions to increase if for no other reason than that in it nothing is taken for granted. There are many moments of such open peril in *The Secret Land,* even as almost every mile of the expedition was an invitation to danger. An officer dropped fifty feet by the snapped line of a breeches buoy into icy Antarctic waters, in which no mortal can live for more than eight minutes; the jet-propelled take-off of outsized planes from a carrier; the first landing in the snow of these same planes equipped with skis instead of wheels; the engine that conks out on a return flight to the base; the three young fliers who perish in a crack-up; the saving of their companions who survived; the moments when the bulkheads of giant ships seem on the verge of being crushed like paper by the pressure of an unstoppable ice floe—these are but samples of the risks which chart the action of *The Secret Land.*

Much as we admire the machines, greatly as we are impressed by the organizational skill shown, rightly proud as we are made of our Navy, in the presence of such a quiet and constant display of courage we are forced to give our final respect to men. This kind of boldness is not, of course, the only manifestation of courage. Charles Lamb showed great courage of a totally different sort. So do thousands of physically timid mortals faced with the challenge of living unhappy lives with gallantry. But, however commendable and necessary the fortitude may be that can meet and accept the testings of humdrum living, it is not the same sort of bravery which rushes out by its own choice to seek adventure.

Fairly or unfairly, the latter always exerts the greater tug on our imaginations. Instead of meeting life on its own stern daily terms, it escapes from routine to defy death in ways both exceptional and melodramatic. It is this living with the "great de-fy" which lends a special exhilaration to *The Secret Land* and fills us, in the safety of motion-picture theatres, with admiration for those who made its filming possible.

February 5, 1949

*AN ENTHRALLING biography of
Michelangelo in which no actors appear
and the masterpieces of an artist tell his
life story.*

ᴬ̃

The Camera Creative

THERE WAS a person, his name is not known, who on
an undated day of the highest excitement and importance,
looked upon a block of marble and suddenly realized that in
that cold stone the spirit and body of a man or woman existed,
if only (this was the tantalizing "if"), if only he could employ
his chisel so as to set them free. In some such fashion stones
long used for buildings were put to a new and unsuspected
use, and sculpture began.

Of course, it may have begun earlier with man's urge to
represent life, or personify his deities, first expressing itself in
a more malleable substance such as clay or even in that design-
ful whittling of wood called carving. But the marble guaranteed, or seemed to guarantee, permanence, and artists being
human are not exempt from vanity. What people had lived in
as homes or flocked to as temples and public edifices, they now
started to inhabit in a novel and undreamed-of fashion. They
were not housed in stone; they were caught in it. Denied their
flesh, when so portrayed they were not what they once were.
Yet their loss was a gain. They were not such men and women
as they themselves had seen or as we see. They were such men
and women as an artist had seen and wanted us to see. Al-

though their motions were arrested, their bodies were alive with motion. That their hearts were of stone did not mean that they could not feel and express great emotion.

All of us had thought that by now we knew what the camera could do. All of us were certain of our familiarity with its proved wonders. All of us were aware that, due to it, within our lifetimes another new medium, thrilling in its possibilities, had raced from the crudest of infancies to incredible technical maturity. With the advent, first of radio, then of television, we had come to regard the motion pictures as almost venerable. We were conscious that in them, as in a play, a novel, a poem, a painting, or a sculpture, things could be done and said as they could be nowhere else.

Like many another, I had thought, until I saw the story of Michelangelo as told in *The Titan,** that I knew what these things were. But this extraordinary film, the first of its kind ever to be shown in this country, has opened my eyes to a world of the camera hitherto unexplored and superb in its resources. *The Titan* is an old picture, as pictures go. Yet it is newer in its technique than the latest picture to be produced. It was made in 1938–1940, chiefly in Florence and Rome, by the Swiss producer Curt Oertel. In its original form it lasted ninety-five minutes, whereas in the reassembled and re-edited American version, equipped as it is with a new script, an excellent score, and a fine running narrative finely spoken by Fredric March, it runs for only seventy minutes. During the

* *The Titan—Story of Michelangelo,* an adaptation of the Curt Oertel film. Produced by Robert Snyder. Directed and edited by Richard Lyford. Written by Norman Borisoff. Art interpretation by Michael Sonnabend. Music by Alois Melichar. Narration spoken by Fredric March. Presented by Robert J. Flaherty, Robert Snyder, and Ralph Alswang. A United Artists Release. At the Little Carnegie Theatre, New York City.

war it is said to have been seized by the Germans, distributed proudly as a proof of Nazi culture, and was afterward discovered in France by the American Army.

When seen by Robert J. Flaherty, one of the screen's true artists, it won his immediate interest. As a director responsible for welcome innovations in such sensitive and unhackneyed films as *Nanook of the North, Moana, Man of Aran,* and *Louisiana Story,* Mr. Flaherty was quick to appreciate the innovational virtues of *The Titan.* It was he who acquired its American rights. And it is he who, with Robert Snyder and Ralph Alswang, has brought together such a talented group of craftsmen as Richard Lyford, Norman Borisoff, and Alois Melichar, to direct and edit and supply the script and music for the picture as it is now shown in the United States.

The novelties, the fascinations, and the excitements of *The Titan* are many and irresistible. Although in procedure no less than in purpose it is a documentary in a stricter sense than those pictures usually so described, it is like none of the documentaries to which we are accustomed. We have had documentaries which have dramatized geography and elevated the travelogue into the realm of art. We have had documentaries which, because of the eloquent use to which they have put newsreel clips, have presented us with history in the making. We have had documentaries which in their animated maps and diagrams have demonstrated the unrivaled role they can play as swift elucidators of complicated problems. We have seen them do their stirring part as propagandists, watched them breathlessly as they had recorded battle exploits or true sagas of adventure. We have grown increasingly grateful for the sense of truth their methods have created in fictional scenarios. Until *The Titan,* however, we had never sat before a documentary in which the chief concern was beauty and an artist's biography was told in terms of his art.

The screen, of course, has offered us biographies galore— some good, some bad, some tasteful, and more tasteless. But all these previous re-creations of the past have depended upon living actors; actors dressed up and bewigged; actors pretending to be Pasteur, Queen Christina, Henry VIII, Madame Curie, Woodrow Wilson, Thomas A. Edison, Zola, or George M. Cohan. *The Titan* is different; wonderfully, stirringly different. It dispenses with flesh-and-blood players as completely as if it had taken to heart Duse's famous hyperbole: "To save the Theatre, the Theatre must be destroyed, the actors and actresses must all die of the plague. They poison the air, they make art impossible."

In *The Titan*, although no one impersonates Michelangelo, Lorenzo, Savonarola, or Pope Julius II, each of these great Renaissance figures seems to be present. Their struggles, their hopes, their plots, their cruelties, and, above all, the works of art which they either created or commissioned are present, too. Florence, Bologna, and Rome in all their glory supply the settings. Portraits, prints, paintings, architectural details, and statues emerge as players. The dialogue is written not with a scenarist's pen but by Michelangelo's chisel and brush.

The tragic tenderness of his first "Pietà," the vigor of his "David," the pagan abandon of his "Bacchus," the power of his "Moses," the agony of his "Slave," the richness of the Sistine ceiling, the brooding profundity of his "Dawn" and "Night," the soaring greatness of the dome of St. Peter's, the fury of his "Last Judgment," and the final sorrow of his "Deposition"—all these speak both for themselves and for

Michelangelo. Without seeing him we see what he was. With the aid of the narrative and especially due to the camera's chaperonage, we follow his life and sense the grandeur of his genius. The result is a masterpiece composed of masterpieces. In it a period writes its own history even as the art of an artist writes his biography.

All of us who have made our pilgrimages to admire Michelangelo's works may have felt that we were well acquainted with their marvels. But most of us would, I suspect, now have to confess we had never really *seen* them until we saw *The Titan*. As highlighted by Klieg lights, as surveyed through the camera's eye, as approached from unexpected angles, or viewed in dramatic close-ups, they leap and lunge into a life even more amazing than that which we had prized as theirs.

One can only hope that what *The Titan* does so magnificently for the work of one magnificent artist will be done again and again with the same brilliance and integrity for other artists and their works.

March 25, 1950

By Way of Explanation

IN WHICH some of the problems,
agreeable and irksome, both of conduct-
ing a column and writing in general are
touched upon in personal terms.

༺༺༺༺༺༺༺༺༺༺༺༺༺༺༺༺༺༺༺༺༺༺༺༺༺༺

Pleasant Agony

FOR SEVERAL years now, mine has been the privilege, hence the pleasant agony, of filling a page each week, or almost every week, in the *Saturday Review of Literature*. I say pleasant agony because I know of no other words with which to describe what writing is to me.

I claim no singularity in this. There may be, there must be, writers to whom writing comes as effortlessly as breathing. There may even be (though I doubt it) writers whose happiness is complete while they are actually writing. But most of us who live by putting words together are not so fortunate. We are tortured while we write and would be tortured were we not allowed to do so. Although when we are done we feel "delivered," as Sainte-Beuve put it, this delirium of delivery is not accomplished without labor pains for which medicine has, as yet, provided no soothing drugs. If all attempts to coerce words into doing what we would have them do are at best painful pleasures, the pains and pleasures of summoning the right words to meet a weekly deadline are of a special kind.

A cook faced with getting dinner when lunch is over knows something of the routine, if not all the anguishes, of a columnist. No mortals, however, have appetites as insatiable as a column's. A column is an omnivorous beast. Its hunger is never appeased. Feed it, and almost at once it demands to be fed again.

Though he used a different image to express this same idea, even Shaw, seemingly the most easeful of writers, knew this. When he abandoned the job of drama critic on London's *Saturday Review,* he protested against the weekly deadlines which had confronted him for nearly four years. He likened himself to a man fighting a windmill. "I have hardly time," wrote he, "to stagger to my feet from the knock-down blow of one sail, when the next strikes me down."

His successor in the same job on that same fortunate magazine shared an identical dislike of deadlines. For twelve years, Max Beerbohm admitted in his valedictory article, Thursdays had been for him the least pleasant day of the week. Why Thursday? Because that was the day, the latest possible one, he set aside each week to get his writing done. On every Wednesday, therefore, he would be engulfed by "a certain sense of oppression, of misgiving, even of dread." It was only on Friday, when once the danger was passed, that the sun would shine again. Then he would move on dancing feet.

I quote my betters to console myself by the reminder that they, too, knew the pangs of weekly columnizing. Yet the consolation I seek is denied me when I discover, for example, that it took Beerbohm one, and only one, short day of pain to turn out the delectable copy which he could write. Shaw, I am certain, was also a one-day man. I wish I were. I wish even more ardently that I could claim any of the merits which glorify their reviews for what it takes me two, three, or sometimes five days of ceaseless sweating to produce as fodder for my columns.

Beerbohm ascribed his disrelish for the act of writing to "the acute literary conscience" with which he had been cursed. It was this conscience, he maintained, which kept his pen from ever running away with him. I know what he means. Unblessed with any of his gifts, I am nonetheless cursed with something of his conscience. Beerbohm insisted that "to seem to write with ease and delight is one of the duties which a writer owes to his readers." If he worked hard at his sentences, it was because Beerbohm hoped they would read easily. In other words, he was in complete agreement with Sheridan's "easy writing's vile hard reading." One statement of Beerbohm's I could truthfully apply to my own efforts for the SRL. It runs, "I may often have failed in my articles here, to disguise labor. But the effort to disguise it has always been loyally made."

There is a passage in The Goncourt Journals which has haunted me since I read it. Envy has kept it green for me, and wonder (or is it disbelief?) has kept it alive. I have in mind Gautier's boast that he never thought about what he was going to write. "I take up my pen," he explained, "and write. I am a man of letters and am presumed to know my job. . . . I throw my sentences into the air and I can be sure that they will come down on their feet, like cats. . . . Look here: here's my script: not a word blotted."

When I think of the one-legged kittens that land on my pages; when I remember the false starts, illegible scribblings, unfinished sentences, discarded drafts, changed constructions, and altered words which mark my beginnings, my continuings, and my endings, I blush with shame and, like the voyagers in Dante's realm, abandon all hope.

In these journalistic days the first word that pops into an author's mind is held to be the acceptable, if not the best, word. We are supposed to smile because Wordsworth, at a day's end, was wearied from his quest for the exact word. But where Wordsworth the man may win a smile, Wordsworth the writer, fatiguing himself by doing what is a writer's duty, is far from laughable. The *mot juste* is not just any word. Even if it eludes its pursuer, the search for it seems to me to remain among the obligations of authorship. Indeed, the true hope of anyone who loves the language and respects it is to stumble upon, not the correct word or phrase, but the word or phrase which is so right that it seems inevitable.

The word and the phrase are not the only hurdles—and joys—of authorship. The sentence and the paragraph, by means of which points are made, thoughts communicated, emotions transferred, pictures painted, personalities caught, rhythms established, and cadences varied, offer other challenges and should supply their own sources of delight and pride. When so much hurried writing is done for hurried reading, I find it comforting to have Shaw, a veritable geyser with words and ideas, admit in his *Sixteen Self Sketches* how depleting he found his labors as a weekly feuilletonist for ten years. Why? Because, says he, of "taking all the pains I was capable of to get to the bottom of every sentence I wrote."

One of the modern world's luckier occurrences was what happened at Harrow when a boy named Winston Churchill was being "menaced with Education." Three times, he tells us in *A Roving Commission*, his backwardness as a classical scholar forced him to remain in the same form and hence repeat the same elementary course in English. "Thus," writes he (and who can question him?), "I got into my bones the essential structure of the ordinary British sentence—which is a noble thing. . . . Naturally I am biased in favor of boys learning English. I would make them all learn English: and then I would let the clever ones learn Latin as an honor, and Greek as a treat. But the only thing I would whip them for would be for not knowing English. I would whip them hard for that." One trembles to think how many of us whose profession is writing would be flogged today if lapses in English, or American, were whippable offenses.

Later on in that same grand book, Churchill has his more precise say on the subtleties, intricacies, and possibilities of the writer's craft. It is his opinion, and one worth heeding, that, "just as the sentence contains one idea in all its fulness, so the paragraph should embrace a distinct episode; and as sentences should follow one another in harmonious sequence, so the paragraphs must fit on to one another like the automatic couplings of railway carriages."

I quote Churchill and these others belonging to the peerage of prose writers because, for any author with a memory, one of the disheartening and humbling aspects of writing is the recollection, as his own pen moves, of how those whom he admires have faced and solved identical problems. This recollection of what has been done, this sensing of what could and should be done, this awareness of what one hopes to do regardless of whether one can or cannot do it—these are parts of that literary conscience, mentioned by Beerbohm, which keeps a writer's pen from running away with him. I know they are factors in retarding my own pen (meaning my typewriter, pencil, or dictation) even on those happy days when a subject seems to write itself, when sentences come easily, and one paragraph gives way to another.

Style is a strange and mysterious thing. Some contemporary writers appear to get along without it and to want to do so, and most of us rightly disparage it when it shows the effort that has gone into it. Few of us, for example, can read Pater today without being irritated and put off by the labyrinthian intricacies of his sentences. His style, once held to be a model, remains a model, although as we see it it is one to be avoided rather than followed. Pater could not bring himself to say a simple thing simply. His orchestration is so elaborate that the melody of his thought is lost.

Hazlitt comes closer to present-day tastes. More than being the enemy of the gaudy and "Occult" schools of writing, Hazlitt was not only a champion but at his best a matchless practitioner of "The Familiar Style." Although he had the art to make a long sentence seem short, he knew the value of short sentences. "I hate anything," wrote he, "that occupies more space than it is worth. I hate to see a load of band-boxes go along the street, and I hate to see a parcel of big words without any meaning in them."

The perpetual challenge of writing, the challenge presented by each new sentence is to say exactly what one wants to say exactly as one wants to say it. This is where the anguish of composition mixes with the delights. This is where, too, style, as I see it, comes into the picture. Style is merely the means, chosen or instinctive (doubtless both), by which a writer has his precise and personal say.

Certainly, style is not affectation. Conscious though it may be, when self-conscious it is an obstruction. Its purpose, to my way of thinking, is to give the reader pleasure by sparing him the work which the writer is duty-bound to have done for him. Writers, notwithstanding their hopes or ambitions, may or may not be artists. But there is no excuse for their not being artisans. Although in the final and spiritual sense the style is the man, it is more than that. It is the writing man *in print*. It is, so to speak, his written voice and, if it is truly his voice, even in print it should be his and his alone. The closer it comes to the illusion of speech, perhaps the better. Yet the closeness of the written word to the spoken can, and in fact should, never be more than an illusion. For the point of the written word is planning, as surely as the charm of the spoken word can be its lack of planning.

Without shame I confess that, regardless of how unsatis-factory the results may be, I have labored when writing my weekly pieces to lighten the labor of those who may read them. That I have failed again and again I know to my own chagrin, but I can honestly say I have tried. I not only rewrite; I often rewrite and rewrite again. I do this though I am well aware that the result is sentences and paragraphs which do not bear rereading. I rewrite partly in longhand, partly by dicta-tion, occasionally sitting down, sometimes walking, but most often snaking my way across the floor on my stomach. My desk, a migratory one, is the small piece of beaverboard I push before me. On it are sheets of typewriter paper darkened with hiero-glyphics which must be deciphered immediately to be read at all.

Endeavoring to square my writing with my writing con-science, and having to live with the difference between what I would like to have done and am able to do, is one of the rea-sons why writing is to me an agony, however pleasant.

There are other contributors to the pleasures and the agonies of trying to keep these columns fed. Time is one of these; time in the sense that it confronts a writer for a magazine with a special problem.

Newspapermen, accustomed to meeting daily deadlines, must think it absurd for a fellow on a weekly to mention time at all. Compared to the one frantic hour, or even two or three hours, of enforced fluency at their disposal, the seven long days I have, if need be, in which to do my stint must seem to the daily boys the life span of a Methuselah. No wonder they might be inclined to sneer at me for daring to speak of pressure, or mutter, "How much time does he want? What does he think he's writing anyway?"

Once I would have shared their astonishment, had anyone told me it could take the better (or is it the worse?) part of a week to get a review done. Once I would have laughed at a schedule so leisurely and a pace so snaillike. But that would have been during those thirteen hard-driven years before the war when, in ways at present mysterious to me, I also managed to meet daily deadlines, first on the *New York Evening Post* and later on the *New York World-Telegram*. Now, however, I know that, as surely as the daily journalist fights against the clock, the weekly journalist must contend with the calendar. Both are the victims of time, the one because of having too little, the other because of having too much (though never enough).

In my newspaper days—and nights—I used to read, and reread, with envy the sentence with which Matthew Arnold introduced his essay on Amiel and his *Journal*. It ran, "It is somewhat late to speak of Amiel, but I was late in reading him." As a man who was the thrall of what had happened last night; as a person whose job naturally did not permit him to be "somewhat late" in seeing, reading, or writing anything; as someone then laboring furiously under the tyranny of news, this lead by Matthew Arnold seemed to me an expression of the finest and most desirable kind of journalistic freedom. It still does. But, now that the *SRL* (bless it!) has granted me something of this same freedom, I have come to realize such freedom imposes its own responsibilities.

Newspaper reviewing and columnizing, especially when the theatre was the only subject allowed me, was quite different. It was bound to be so. It was at once far more arduous and much simpler and, if I may say so, not nearly so much fun. It had its agreeable aspects, however. One of these was the Western Union messenger boys, oldish men most of them with a G.A.R. look. Since I worked with evening papers with offices far downtown, these messengers were merciful enough to stop by my apartment every night to pick up the copy.

They would jab the front doorbell with an energy at once frightening and insistent, and were always in a hurry. Their coming meant there was no chance to rewrite, to alter, to discard, or to add. What I had written before their arrival was hurriedly marked for the printer and no less speadily folded into an envelope. Off it would go beyond recall; off until the next noon when I would be confronted with it on the newsstands.

Time after time, this confrontation left me sick of heart, mind, and hope, and feeling slightly ill. My one desire was to stay in hiding all that day. Yet, even while in hiding, I would console myself by saying, "It's not really my fault. It's the messenger's. If only he had come half an hour or an hour later, my stuff might have been what it ought to have been and what I wanted it to be." The truth is I miss those nightly messengers. By appearing no longer they have robbed me of a soothing alibi. Now I have no one to blame for the inadequacies of a week's work except myself. This means my periods of hiding are not as brief as they once were.

There were other consolations in a daily deadline. For instance, there was the mere phrase, "Last night at such-and-such a theatre," which, because of the hocus-pocus of journalistic ritual, had to be incorporated somehow or other in the introductory paragraph of almost every play review I wrote. This used to irritate me mightily. My conviction was that the subhead or the box giving the cast covered such a temporal fact. But the fact, even the phrase, was not without its simplifying advantages.

News interest, as well I know, supplies copy with water wings of undeniable buoyancy. Although a real news story does not write itself, it does not have to be written carefully to possess interest. A daily review, regardless of what else it may be and frequently is, is bound to be news, good or bad. In itself this helps the writer on many a tired night. This I also know well, because in moments of fatigue, inanition, apathy, confusion, or mental paralysis I often used to take advantage of it.

The more a first-night review sticks to the point, the better. Its job is to cover a specific opening, not go beyond it. It is written hot, not cold; written as a reflex to an experience just had rather than from a re-created or treasured emotion. (Count this another aid.) Once a satisfactory lead has been found that will establish the tone and mood of the opinion stated, its outline is almost provided for it by these inevitable topics which in turn must be touched upon—the play, the acting, the direction, the settings, the costumes, and the music, if there is any. The sooner a first-night review has its direct say, and hence proves its serviceability to the reader, the better. Unlike articles appearing in a national magazine such as the *SRL*, newspaper notices are chiefly written for the use of those living in the towns where they are printed. However agreeable they may be as reading, they are meant to do a definite, practical, and immediate service for the reader.

New Yorkers, for example, may or may not be devotees of criticism. But they are prospective ticket-buyers. Understandably, they want to know if what has just opened is something which they would be wise to see or avoid. Their first concern (and often their last except, perhaps, on Saturdays or Sundays) is whether the critical light is green or red. Reading quickly and not without self-interest, they are the more apt to forgive the worn-out phrases upon which the writer who writes quickly is sometimes forced to rely.

All these props, which once I knew and leaned on, have been snatched away from me by the very freedom I now relish on the *SRL*. The sustaining interest of spot news; a single assignment written from the heat, indifference, or indignation of the moment; the reader's curiosity about a first-night verdict; yes, and even those messengers who by snatching away my copy used to provide me with a solacing alibi—all these, as I say, are now denied me. But from my own point of view there are compensations, and these are as large as the challenges which go with them.

Poverty might but horses could not drag me back to daily reviewing or newspaper work. Or, for that matter, to writing only about the theatre. My debt to the *SRL* is a genuine one. The *SRL* has relieved me from the constabulary duties which must be done, night after night, for the theatre's sake

as well as the public's, and which my confreres perform with
incredible patience and skill. It has spared me from having
to sit before those dreary ineptitudes, those costly and dispiriting barbiturates, those utter time-wasters and monumental
bores which seem bound to form so large a percentage of every
season's offerings. It has permitted me to put away the flit-
gun which has to be used on so many of Broadway's fly-by-
night productions and which once upon a time I enjoyed using myself.

It has allowed me to pick and choose, to write about only
the better plays or those which, though failures, were interesting in their faults. Above all, it has not limited me to the
theatre. Each week it has left the choice of subject up to me,
and given me full latitude in everything I have written.
Parental experiences, the more significant films, the Nurem-
berg trials, Ernie Pyle, the U.N., Mayor La Guardia as a
broadcaster, London revisited after the war, the plight of
Negroes in Detroit or in a little town in Iowa, the comics,
good conversation, a schoolteacher seen many years later,
Addison and Steele, Woollcott, Edith Hamilton, Robert
Sherwood, and Charles Lamb, even one of the Little Rollo
books which I came upon more tardily by far than Matthew Arnold stumbled upon Amiel—the *SRL* has tolerated
these and many other subjects from me under the heading
of "Seeing Things."

If it were not that each week the writing of these pieces
had to be done, I would have to thank the *SRL* for providing me with the ideal set-up. But the writing must be done,
and trying to get it done in a manner that in any way justifies
such freedom is where both the pleasure and the agony come
in.

There was a time when the theatre as theatre seemed to me all-absorbing. That, however, was before the war. Though I still dote upon it at its best, even at its best it no longer interests me merely as theatre. For me, as for many another, the world has forced open the windows that once seemed securely shut, and it is for drafts from this outer world that I now look even in a playhouse. The point of a weekly article, regardless of its subject, is, as I see it, to keep these windows open.

As impatient readers may have observed to their annoyance, I no longer try or want to write a review which is a notice and only that. If I lack the inclination to do so, I think I also lack the excuse. The cream of the news has been skimmed off long before I come to my desk and even longer before the *SRL* appears. Sometimes, I admit, what emerges is a straight notice. But when this happens, it is contrary to my intentions. Endeavoring, no matter how unsuccessfully, to do something more than that involves an effort, an approach, and a method which are very different from daily reviewing, as my happy and unfettered years on the *SRL* have taught me.

My hope each week, even when "covering" a play, a movie, or a book, is to be led by the specific instance from the particular to the general. This means attempting (please note that I say *attempting*) to reflect as well as to react, to apply no less than to report, and to use a topic not as an end in itself but as a springboard to something larger. It means searching for the overtones, parallels, and implications suggested by a subject, and not limiting myself to the subject itself.

The real work of weekly columnizing lies, I find, not in the actual writing, hard as that is for me, but in the getting ready to write. In other words, it lies in the quest for a point of view, hence a point of departure, which is not dependent upon news as news. My deadline being what it is, I do not come to my typewriter hot from the thing seen, though naturally I struggle to retain or recapture something of that first heat. I have the time to live with my reactions for two or three days and nights, to let them simmer in my thoughts, to rummage in my mind and memory for experiences or illustrations which have a bearing on the subject discussed.

If I dare to be discursive, my digressions are deliberate and, to me, relevant. Their aim is to widen the ripple of application, to extend the subject by following up the hints it has given. For what I struggle to write each week is an article which, though it may not manage to become an essay, is in intention at least nearer to the essay-review than to the review.

The *SRL* has made it possible for me to write of what I want to write about and to avoid having to have my say on plays, pictures, or books which have said nothing to me. The fact that I do not swat flies as jubilantly as once I did does not mean I have grown benevolent (or is the word mellow?). It means merely that fly-swatting is no longer one of my chores.

Shaw in his reviewing days once insisted that the artist who accounted for his personal disparagement by alleging personal animosity on his part was quite right. "When people do less than their best, and do that less at once badly and self-complacently," he fumed with that delectable immoderation which can be his, "I hate them, I loathe them, detest them, long to tear them limb from limb and strew them in gobbets about the stage or platform." Shaw's point was that the man with a genuine critical spirit "becomes your personal enemy on the sole provocation of a bad performance, and will only be appeased by a good [one]."

Although I share his fierce point of view fiercely, and trust I remain the implacable foe of the bogus, the pretentious, the empty, and the mediocre, the longer I live the more convinced I am that the most challenging function of criticism is rising to appreciation rather than excelling at denunciation. It is easier by far to hold the attention while damning than when praising. If this were not true, so many conversationalists would not be considered witty whose sole equipment is malice. The bludgeon, the nightstick, the ax, the bazooka, and the flame-thrower are weapons every critic should have in his armory. But criticism of the arts, which as I see it is bound to be a criticism of life, would be a dull and sorry business were it prepared only to stalk, attack, and extinguish.

Although the heat of proper indignation or contempt is a heat both necessary and healthy, it is not by any means the only heat with which I, for one, would choose to have my copy warmed. There are the juices, the joys, the pains, the dilemmas of living, and something of these I wish I could capture. This is why the jargon of the so-called "new critics" repels me. It has no compassion, little humanity, and less gaiety. It is arid, bloodless, and absurdly, cloyingly overspecialized. It does not flow from the heart but trickles from the head, and only a small part of that. It is written from books rather than life; written, and most successfully written, to be unreadable.

I deplore this other approach to writing because I belong to a different, more conciliatory school. Without shame I confess I am a writer who would like to be readable and read. I do not ask or expect to be agreed with. The only truth I can state (and it takes struggling to get it half stated) is a personal one. Accordingly, I have no other choice than to write personally. What a man is is the basis of what he dreams and thinks, accepts and rejects, feels and perceives. It is, too, the stuff from which he writes. If he can speak with any accuracy for himself, he may speak with some accuracy for others. But only if he interests them. It is in the hard, hard rockpile labor of seeking to win, hold, or deserve a reader's interest that the pleasant agony of writing again comes in.

June 25 and July 9, 1949

Index

Index

Index

Index

Index

Index